GOLD AT FORTYMILE CREEK

MICHAEL GATES

GOLD AT FORTYMILE CREEK: *EARLY DAYS IN THE YUKON*

UBC PRESS / VANCOUVER

Printed in Canada on acid-free paper ∞

ISBN 0-7748-0468-8 (hardcover)
ISBN 0-7748-0492-0 (paperback)

Canadian Cataloguing in Publication Data

Gates, Michael.
   Gold at Fortymile Creek.

Includes bibliographical references and index.
ISBN 0-7748-0468-8 (bound). – ISBN 0-7748-0492-0 (pbk.)

1. Yukon River Valley (Yukon and Alaska) – Gold discoveries. 2. Gold mines and mining – Yukon River Valley (Yukon and Alaska). 3. Gold mines and mining – Yukon Territory. 4. Yukon River Valley (Yukon and Alaska) – History. 5. Frontier and pioneer life – Yukon River Valley (Yukon and Alaska). 6. Frontier and pioneer life – Yukon Territory.

FC4045.Y8G37 1994   971.9'1'02   C94-910199-0
F1095.Y9G37 1994

Publication of this book was made possible, in part, with financial assistance from Chris Sorg (Maximillian's, Dawson), Elaine Smart (Mac's Fireweed Books, Whitehorse), Earl Bennett (Whitehorse), Dave 'Buffalo' Taylor (Gold City Tours, Dawson), Loki Gold Corporation (Vancouver), Bill and Jeri Weigand (Whitehorse), Bill and Nella Berry (California), Lowry and Barbara Toombs (Yukon Gallery, Whitehorse), and Jim Robb (Whitehorse).

UBC Press gratefully acknowledges the ongoing support to its publishing program from the Canada Council, the Province of British Columbia Cultural Services Branch, and the Department of Communications of the Government of Canada.

UBC Press
University of British Columbia
6344 Memorial Road
Vancouver, BC V6T 1Z2
(604) 822-3259
Fax: (604) 822-6083

F
1095
Y9
D37
1994

To the memory of my father, John Stewart Gates

The history of the prospectors in any new country, especially in Alaska, would be a record of intensely interesting pioneering. Unfortunately, these men have no record, and their hardships, lonely exploring tours and daring deeds, performed with a heroism so simple that it seems almost comical, have no chronicler. They penetrate the deserts, they climb the mountains, ascend the streams, they dare with the crudest preparation the severest danger of nature. Some of them die, others return to civilization and become sailors or car-conductors or janitors; but they are of the stuff that keeps the nation alive. By that I do not mean the false or imitation prospector, who has no courage or patience, but only the greed of gold. Thousands of such poured into Alaska after the Klondike boom, and many of them turned back at the first sight of the Chilkat Pass ... But before the Klondike Rush nearly all the Alaskans were of the hardy pioneer style that I write about.

— Josiah Edward Spurr, *Through the Yukon Gold Diggings*

CONTENTS

ILLUSTRATIONS AND MAPS

PREFACE AND

ACKNOWLEDGMENTS

People who live in the Yukon often ask other Yukoners they meet how they came to the Yukon in the first place. It is part of the ritual by which they assess the merits of the person they are getting to know. In the same manner, people might ask me why I decided to write this book. In the twenty years that I have been involved with the Yukon, I have been fascinated by the decaying remains of old cabins and rusting mining equipment which litter the countryside. It is from this historical debris that I began to assemble an image of the way things used to be in the Yukon.

In the early 1980s, with funding from a Canada Council grant, I conducted a recording project in the Dawson area. It was apparent that some of the artefacts I was examining predated the gold rush of 1898. When I asked questions about the early pioneers I could not get precise answers, because very little had been written about the time or the people. Consequently, I decided that I would assemble as much information as I could.

I took this interest further when I enrolled in a graduate program of museum studies in 1984 in Cooperstown, New York. I must credit the faculty there for their encouragement and forbearance with regard to this project. After my studies were complete, I continued to track down documents from remote sources and proceeded to reorganize my earlier work so that it would appeal to a broader readership.

This book tells the story of those who sought gold in the Yukon valley before the Klondike gold rush. By using the words and observations of the early pioneers, I try to portray the era as accurately as possible. The view presented is primarily that of White men, because it was they who championed the search for gold.

There are many misconceptions about the discovery of gold in the Yukon, one of these being that it happened more or less overnight. In fact, the search for the big strike went on for nearly a quarter of a century. This book attempts to chronicle the events that led to the Klondike discovery and to show that it was actually the result of two decades of concerted effort.

Another misconception harboured by many of those unacquainted with the early history of the Yukon has to do with the image of the miners. Many people think of the grizzled miner who comes into town with a gold poke and goes on a spree, indulging in wine, women, and song. Actually, as I hope this book will demonstrate, the life of the miners was very difficult indeed.

I sometimes mention the Native people who lived in the Yukon valley, but I do not give any details of their lives. For the most part, Native people do not appear in the writings of the participants in the Klondike gold rush. Hidden behind a veil of cultural differences, their story is hard to pull from the writings of the early pioneers. There were relatively few White women in the Yukon during this time, and their story, too, remains to be told.

Much of what has been written may be viewed as an opening chapter to the story of the Klondike gold rush. Pierre Berton, for example, does a decent job in *Klondike: The Last Great Gold Rush, 1896-97*. Yet neither his nor any other work has fully examined the life and times of the early pioneers. Al Wright's book, *Prelude to Bonanza*, is another commendable work covering the early White history in the Yukon, but it is derived from the works of the early explorers/geographers. These men documented their brief trips through the Yukon – trips during which they charted the rivers and mountains. Yet while these people came and went, there was a growing company of men who came and stayed, and, consequently, who knew the country much more intimately than did the explorers/geographers. It is time that their story be told.

During the course of my research, I encountered a wide variety of documents, some more informative and reliable than others. Quite by accident, I discovered that L.A. Coolidge, who wrote *Klondike and the Yukon Country*, had cribbed lengthy passages from A.E. Sola's book, *Klondyke: Truth and Facts of the New Eldorado*. Hence, Coolidge's book does not appear in my bibliography, while Sola's, being the primary source, does. Even William Ogilvie, who is one of the most highly respected chroniclers of early Yukon history, was prone to confuse some of the events and names, mainly because he was getting some of his stories by word of mouth rather than from first-hand observation. George T. Snow, whose unpublished collected papers were a major source of both information and inspiration for me, tended to colour events with passages of purple prose. He describes many events as though he had directly witnessed them, when, in fact, he did not. I used his information with caution, trying, to the best of my ability, to establish the accuracy of his work.

My list of names of Yukon pioneers in Appendix B came about by accident rather than by intent. As I proceeded with my research, I came to realize that, for the benefit of their descendants, this was an excellent opportunity to compile a list of early visitors to the North. (Indeed, if anyone who reads this recognizes a family name, I would like to help you fill out your family tree. My address is Box 245, Dawson, Yukon, Y0B 1G0.) I have attempted to provide the names of these pioneers as much as possible, given the circumstances. Many of the chroniclers of this early period were vague on names – spellings are often wrong, and first names frequently omitted. In Appendix B, I have listed all the variations of a name which could possibly be attributed to a single pioneer. With respect to women, I have given their complete names where I have been able to find them. Often, women were simply listed by their husband's name, preceded by 'Mrs.' By today's standards, this kind of reference is unacceptable. However, by the standards of the 1890s, it was not considered unusual. Consequently, the personal names of many women pioneers are often missing in the text and in Appendix B. I hope that some readers will be able to help me fill in the missing names.

It should be noted that, throughout this book, I use the old British units of measure (feet, inches, pounds, ounces, and degrees Fahrenheit) because that is the system with which the pioneers lived.

I assume all responsibility for any errors in this book, and I hope that, in producing it, I have stimulated others to take a closer look at this period in history. Perhaps they will be able to add to the picture which I have tried to paint. For all readers, I hope I have been able to provide a glimpse into the past – a glimpse which both entertains and informs.

I would like to thank the following people for all the assistance they offered. Professors Gilbert T. Vincent and Langdon Wright of the Cooperstown Graduate Program provided insightful comments on my earlier work, as did Pauline Scott, Teresa Sheward, and Paula Hassard, all of Klondike National Historic Sites. Linda Johnson (Yukon Territorial archivist), David Neufeld (Yukon historian with Parks Canada), and David Ross (also with Parks Canada) offered information, comments, and advice on particular aspects of my work. Ed McCann (RCMP Museum in Regina), Don Chase (superintendent, Yukon Charlie National Park, Eagle, Alaska), and Stan Hutchinson (regional surveyor, Yukon Territory, Energy, Mines and Resources Canada) provided me with helpful maps and photographs. Angela Wheelock of Ross River and Whitehorse exchanged useful bits of historical information with me. Both David Neufeld of Parks Canada and Bruce Barrett of the Heritage Branch of the Yukon government provided useful comments regarding portions of the final draft of the manuscript which I submitted to UBC Press. Steven Robertson, owner of the *Yukon News*, kindly converted my entire manuscript into a computer-readable form.

Various institutions facilitated my research, including the Anglican Church Archives in Toronto, the Metropolitan Toronto Reference Library, the RCMP Museum in Regina, the Dawson City Museum, the National Archives of Canada in Ottawa, the Elmer Rasmussen Library in Fairbanks, and the British Columbia Archives and Records Service. In particular, the interlibrary loan service of the Yukon Library Branch was of considerable help to me in obtaining books and articles pertinent to my research. Without them, I could not have done what I did. The staff of the Dawson Mining Recorder's Office, particularly Marion DeJean, allowed me access to old documents and the microfilmed records for the Klondike. The Yukon Archives and all their staff have been exceptionally supportive and helpful over the years. I give them special praise, and my thanks for treating me seriously.

I would like to thank the Canada Council for the financial support it provided me and my colleague, Richard Hartmier, for a project that we conducted many years ago in the gold fields surrounding Dawson. It was that work which sparked my interest in writing this account. The Yukon Foundation provided me with support to search for additional images in numerous photo collections in archives in both Canada and the United States, as well as with support for the publication of the manuscript. The Yukon government's Department of Education also helped with publication costs.

I am particularly grateful to the following for their support: Chris Sorg (Maximillian's, Dawson), Elaine Smart (Mac's Fireweed Books, Whitehorse), Earl Bennett (Whitehorse), Dave 'Buffalo' Taylor (Gold City Tours,

Dawson), Loki Gold Corporation (Vancouver), Bill and Jeri Weigand (Whitehorse), Bill and Nella Berry (California), Lowry and Barbara Toombs (Yukon Gallery, Whitehorse), and Jim Robb (Whitehorse).

The biggest thank you of all goes to my wife Kathy and my family. Kathy provided me with incredible support and encouragement while working on this project, particularly in the early stages. My family had to go without my presence in the home for many weekends and evenings while I prepared this manuscript. I hope that they, above all, believe that it has been worth it.

If I have missed acknowledging anyone, to them I apologize. So many people have helped me with the production of this work that I fear some oversights may have been inevitable.

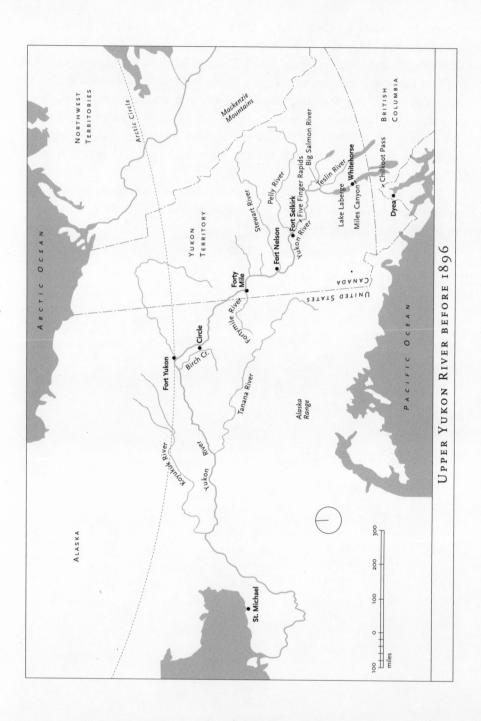

UPPER YUKON RIVER BEFORE 1896

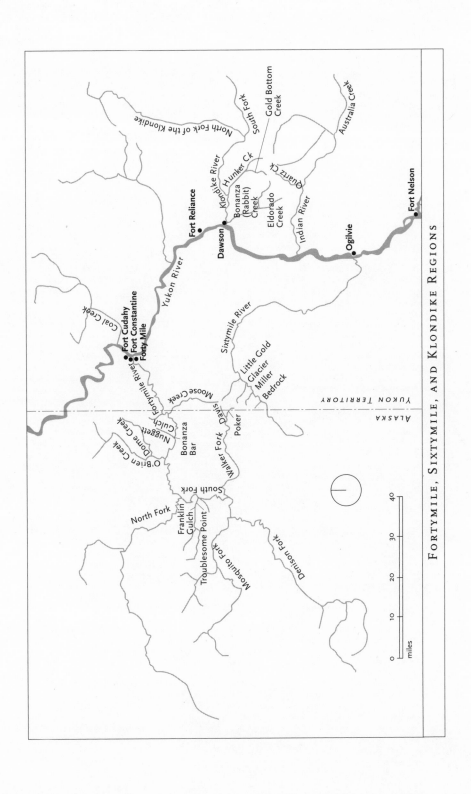

FORTYMILE, SIXTYMILE, AND KLONDIKE REGIONS

North Fork of the Klondike

North Fork of the Klondike

Klondike River

South Fork

Hunter Ck

Gold Bottom Creek

Australia Creek

Fort Reliance

Dawson

Bonanza (Rabbit) Creek

Eldorado Creek

Quartz Ck

Indian River

Fort Nelson

Ogilvie

Yukon River

Coal Creek

Fort Cudahy

Fort Constantine

Forty Mile

Fortymile River

Sixtymile River

Little Gold

Glacier

Miller

Bedrock

Moose Creek

Nugget Gulch

Davis

Walker Fork

Poker

YUKON TERRITORY

ALASKA

Bonanza Bar

O'Brien Creek

Dome Creek

North Fork

Franklin Gulch

South Fork

Troublesome Point

Mosquito Fork

Denison Fork

0   10   20   30   40

miles

GOLD AT FORTYMILE CREEK

1

EARLY DAYS: THE FIRST GOLD-SEEKERS ARRIVE

The Land

Starting as a trickle at its headwaters in the coastal range of the Rocky Mountains, just a few miles from the Pacific Ocean, the Yukon River winds its way through the heart of the Yukon and Alaska. In its route to the sea, it forms a gigantic arc, almost grazing the Arctic Circle at its most northerly point. From the interior of the continent, it grows in size as it moves downstream and finally disgorges its voluminous, silty load into the Bering Sea, over 2,000 miles from its source. Draining an area of some 327,000 square miles of rugged northern terrain, it is the second largest river in North America and one of the largest rivers in the world.

The Russians called it the 'Kwikhpak,' which, in Aleut, means 'great river.' The Tanana called it the 'Niga-to,' which, in their language, meant the same thing. The name which stuck was given to it by the Hudson's Bay Company (HBC) trader, John Bell, when, in 1846, he descended the Porcupine River to its junction with the Yukon River. The name stems from a White corruption of the Loucheux word for 'big river.' In 1848, Robert Campbell proved that Bell's river was the same great watercourse which passed Fort Selkirk, the newly established trading post at the Yukon River's confluence with the Pelly River, deep in the heart of uncharted territory.

The Yukon basin is a region of extremes: of endless summer daylight and sunless winter twilight; of temperatures which peak near one hundred degrees Fahrenheit and plummet to eighty degrees below zero. Here, over a thousand miles above the mouth of the Yukon River, is some of the harshest and most challenging wilderness in the world. It is a land where you strip down in comfort to bare skin in the summer heat, while only a few inches below your feet, the ground is perpetually frozen. The differences between the seasons are equally extreme. There are two major seasons, summer and winter, and compressed between them are two dramatically rapid transition periods. The condition of the Yukon River forewarns of these seasonal transitions, with winter freeze-up in October and spring break-up early in May. The temperature stays below the freezing mark for seven months of the year.

The vegetation is less diverse than that found in more temperate and southerly regions, and consists of forests of birch, black and white spruce, mountain alder, and willow. Spread at the foot of the trees is a thick blanket of insulating moss and organic matter, beneath which is permafrost (which turns quickly to quaking bog when the ground cover is removed). Interspersed throughout this region are wet, boggy zones of muskeg, which make overland transportation a nightmare. At higher elevations, and in latitudes north of the Yukon, there are broad stretches of tundra. Even the largest trees in the Yukon basin are stunted and easily dwarfed by the massive fir trees in the coastal rain forests of Alaska.

Prominent species of Yukon animals include bear, wolf, lynx, moose, caribou, and several varieties of northern fish. The mainstay of the northern diet, these resources are subject to the area's dramatic climatic cycles – cycles which may lead to either feast or famine. Interestingly, the most formidable creature of the North is not the largest but, rather, one of the smallest – the mosquito. The accounts of the early pioneers are filled with complaints about these diminutive tyrants. Said one northern visitor: 'I do not think that any description or adjective can exaggerate the discomfort and even torture produced by these pests, at their worst, for they stand peerless among their kind ... for wickedness unalloyed.'[1] They drove men to exhaustion, tears, madness, and suicide.[2]

And there is the gold. Embedded in massive rock formations which are the result of geological movements going back hundreds of millions of years, the gold was locked up in quartz found throughout the region. Over eons of weathering and erosion, this material was slowly freed from the stony matrix and washed into the valleys, concentrated in the stream beds, covered over, and trapped in the frozen ground where it stayed undisturbed for millions of years, waiting to be discovered by a corps of ambitious, optimistic, peripatetic men called prospectors.

The Dreamers

The term pioneer is a misnomer when applied to early White visitors, for they entered a region which had, in truth, been pioneered millennia before by various groups of Native people. More completely self-sufficient than the European/American newcomers (who did not arrive until the middle of the nineteenth century), Native people were displaced, ignored, and abused by the intruding White culture. The Native population consisted of several thousand people, thinly scattered over hundreds of thousands of square miles, from the Chilkat on the coast, to the Tagish and the Tutchone inland, to the Han and the Kutchin, who occupied the regions to the north. In the early accounts of the development of placer mining, Native people are always there, but they are hidden in the back pages.

The first White intruders into the Yukon basin were not looking for gold; they were seeking to trade with the Native people for furs and to offer them 'Christian salvation.' Robert Campbell, trader for the HBC at Fort Selkirk, found traces of gold during his stay from 1848 to 1852. A decade later, a second report of gold came from another HBC trader, and, in 1864, Reverend Robert MacDonald, a missionary for the Church of England, found gold in the vicinity of Birch Creek, Alaska. However, the discovery of gold remained unexploited for another thirty years.

Both the early traders and the missionaries shared one sentiment: neither wanted the area invaded by prospectors and miners.[3] As a consequence, it was another decade before the first gold-seekers arrived and another decade after that before they started to make an impact on the region.

Gold was discovered in California in the late 1840s. Subsequently, a succession of gold discoveries sparked stampedes to new regions, each one farther to the north. Gold was found in Oregon, then on the Fraser River in British Columbia, then in the Cariboo and on the Stikine River in the central and northern part of the province. One of the results of this series of gold finds was the evolution of a new breed, the prospector. Ever seeking gold, impatient, moving on as new finds turned into productive mining areas, always on the outer fringe of the mining frontier, the prospector was always ahead of 'civilization.' It was not difficult for these men to eye the unfilled spaces on the maps of the northwest and conclude that the gold outcrops which had already been found would extend into those voids.

Arthur Harper   *Frederick Hart*

Arthur Harper was one of the visionaries who dreamed that the uncharted areas on the maps of North America were filled with gold. Born in county Antrim in Ireland in 1835, Harper, an Ulsterman, emigrated to New York as a boy and, at the age of twenty, moved west to California. By the 1860s, he had become a full-fledged prospector. In the fall of 1872, he departed from the headwaters of the Peace River in northeastern British Columbia with four other men, most notable among them a fellow Irishman from the same county by the name of Frederick Hart. The country before them was not well charted, so they were travelling into essentially unknown territory.

Instead of following the Peace River, which would have taken them into the MacKenzie River, they travelled up the Halfway River, and, after winter set in, they built sleds and drew their supplies overland to the Liard River watershed. They camped for the winter in canvas tents at the head of navigable water on the Sikanni Chief River, and, while waiting for spring, they constructed dugouts from the large cottonwood trees common to that region. In the spring, the party started downriver until they reached the mouth of the Nelson River, where they met another party of prospectors, which included Leroy Napoleon (Jack) McQuesten, Alfred H. Mayo, and James McKnipp.

Jack McQuesten was born in Litchfield, New Hampshire, in 1836. He, too, was drawn west by the California gold rush and eventually went to British Columbia. He prospected and mined on the Fraser River in 1863 and then joined a stampede to the placer field of the Finlay River. Over the next decade, he was involved in the fur trade, part of this time being in the employ of the HBC. During the winter of 1871, he encountered an HBC trader by the name of Sibistone, who had been into the Yukon a number of times as far as Fort Yukon. Sibistone told McQuesten and his partners of the spoonful of gold which had been found in one of the creeks in the region. Although this was enough to convince McQuesten to investigate, he never felt the lure of gold to the same extent as did, for example, Arthur Harper, and he always had a proclivity for the mercantile trade. Upon learning of the sale of Alaska to the United States, he decided to go into the Yukon River basin.

While McQuesten wintered at the HBC post at the mouth of the Nelson River, the trader there convinced him and his travelling partners that, rather than ascending the Liard River to Frances Lake and portaging to the Pelly River, they should try the more well-travelled trade route down the MacKenzie River and over to the Porcupine River. As it happened, both McQuesten's and Harper's parties decided to travel over the HBC route via the Porcupine River. This route follows the MacKenzie River to Fort MacPherson, then goes up the Rat River, over an eight-mile portage to the Bell River, and, once this stream reaches the Porcupine River, on into the Yukon River. The Rat River provides rough travel; for about twenty-five miles it is continuous rapids and, during low water, the passengers have to manoeuvre their boats by walking in the icy water beside their craft.

Harper arrived at Fort Yukon on 15 July 1873; McQuesten arrived one month later. That the trekkers had not had any flour for two years, and that it was at Fort Yukon that they saw their first repeating rifle, gives some indication of the isolation and hardship they endured in their travels. Harper commenced his prospecting activities immediately upon his arrival in the Yukon. Finding that some of the Native people at Fort Yukon carried samples of indigenous copper, he determined to investigate the region from which they came – the White River. Prospecting as they went, they made their way up the White River and camped for the winter.

Over the next decade, Harper continued his determined effort to find and to promote the gold deposits of the Yukon. During that time, he dipped his pan into the waters of every significant tributary of the Yukon

River between the White and the Tanana rivers. On none of them did he find the deposit that would make him rich, but, within twenty years, most of those creeks would yield discoveries which would attract more and more prospectors until, eventually, the biggest discovery of all would be made. As the years progressed, Harper continued to augment his prospecting income by trading. Eventually, he married a Native woman, and, as his family grew, his commitment to trading became stronger than his commitment to prospecting. Throughout this period he wrote letters to friends in other gold camps, expressing his optimism at the prospects for the Yukon. It is largely due to his letters, and to those of Jack McQuesten, that interest in the Yukon's potential was stimulated.

The year after his arrival in the Yukon basin, Jack McQuesten established a trading post, which he named Fort Reliance, at a point six miles below the present site of Dawson. This became the main trading centre in the region until its closure in 1886. In fact, other places along the Yukon River were named in relation to their distance from this post, and, to this day, names such as Forty Mile, Sixtymile, and Seventy Mile give testimony to this practice. McQuesten was a more dedicated trader than was Harper, and, from the beginning, his wanderings in search of gold were much less frequent than were those of the latter. Both men, however, can be credited in large part for opening up the Yukon for further exploration, and it is because of their policy of grubstake that the creeks were explored and prospected as quickly and as extensively as they were.

To begin with, progress in the exploration for placer deposits was extremely slow because the cost and effort required to get into the Yukon were great; the only two routes of access were over the HBC trail, which was arduous and slow, and by steamer from St. Michael at the mouth of the Yukon River, which was both slow and unpredictable. The net effect was that, until 1880, there were only a small handful of White men in the entire Yukon basin, and these were looking for gold in a primitive, part-time fashion. The first hint that this was about to change came as a result of the efforts of a man named George W. Holt. Sometime in the mid-1870s, Holt crossed the Chilkoot Pass, prospected in the tributaries of the Yukon River, and succeeded in bringing out a small quantity of gold.[4] The letters being sent out by Harper and McQuesten, plus the accounts of George Holt, stimulated prospectors from Juneau, enterprising individuals in any case, to cross the Chilkoot Pass in their search for gold.

2

THE CHILKOOT PASS AND

EARLY TRANSPORTATION

Eighteen hundred and eighty was the first year in which prospectors crossed the Chilkoot Pass to reach the headwaters of the Yukon River (before then, with the exception of George Holt, the Chilkat people effectively prevented White men from using the pass). For the first time, there was easy access to the interior of the Yukon. Despite the precipitous climb over the treacherous coastal mountains, this new route had two important advantages over the upriver route from St. Michael: first, it was accessible from Juneau, a growing mining town to the south; second, the headwaters of the Yukon River were just a few miles from tidewater, and, once on the river, prospectors and miners could travel downstream to their destination. Their incursion started as a trickle, then became a stream, and, finally, a torrent as they poured through the tiny notch in the mountain barricade.

The first party to enter the interior by way of the Chilkoot Pass was made up of twenty-five men under the leadership of Edmund Bean, who, with the assistance of the American navy, had reached an accord with the Chilkat people.[1] The Chilkat served as guides and packers for the prospectors and assisted them over the pass, reaching Lake Lindeman on 17 June 1880. Here they began building boats to carry them into the interior to search for gold. These men were followed shortly afterwards by two more prospectors, 'Slim Jim' Wynn and Johnny McKenzie. The two dozen prospectors worked their way down the Yukon River as far as the mouth of the Teslin River and up the latter for about two hundred miles. Their explorations were cut short by the approach of winter, and all of them retreated back over the Chilkoot Pass before it became utterly snowbound. For their efforts, these men found only a trace of gold along the Teslin River.

Far more important than the expedition itself was the implication that more men would continue to enter the Yukon in the future. For McQuesten, Harper, Mayo, and others, this meant new customers and, eventually, the discovery of rich deposits of the 'yellow metal.' However, even though they had breached the palisade, making the trip both simpler and cheaper, prospectors still did not have an easy task. What would later become familiar landmarks for the Klondike stampeders were, at this time, unfamiliar and dangerous obstacles.

To enter the Yukon, prospectors shipped their supplies from Juneau to Dyea (at the head of the Lynn Canal) by boat. From there, they transported them, by physical labour, up the Dyea Valley, making a number of crossings of the rushing, glacier-fed Dyea River, and over the 3,600-foot high Chilkoot Pass. From there, the goods had to be hauled down from the snowy summit of the pass to the head of navigation on Lake Lindeman.

If they had the money, the prospectors could afford to hire Chilkat packers to make the job easier. The Chilkat were traditional traders with the Native groups of the interior. Raised from early childhood for the arduousness of trading and transporting goods to and from the interior, they were capable of carrying a hundred pounds or more of supplies up the trail and over the Chilkoot Pass, day after day. Charging twelve to thirteen dollars for carrying one hundred pounds of supplies over the summit, these people were superbly adapted to the labour demanded by the Chilkoot Pass. Although maligned by some of the new prospectors as being dangerous and charging exorbitant rates for their work, the peaceful Chilkat in fact supplied an essential service at a reasonable price. They realized, perhaps, that the prospects of maintaining their monopoly over the Chilkoot Pass were dim, but they were pragmatic businesspeople and took advantage of the opportunity immediately before them.[2]

If the prospectors could not afford the price charged by the Chilkat packers, they faced, instead, the back-breaking task of carrying all of their essentials over the summit of the Chilkoot Pass themselves, making numerous trips back and forth, carrying their outfit to Lake Lindeman bit by bit, until the job was complete. By the time they were ready to build their boats, these men had trekked hundreds of exhausting miles over the same trail. Of course, crossing the Chilkoot Pass was never a pleasant experience. Frequently wrapped in cloud and bad weather, it received hundreds of inches of snow every winter. Blizzard-like conditions often closed in for days at a time, trapping travellers in an area lacking both trees and sustenance. Bill Stewart, an old Caribou miner, was caught in one of these storms. He crawled into his sleeping robe and existed there for nine days by eating raw oatmeal and tallow candles. Two other men, Sid Wilson and John Reid, were trapped at the summit of the pass where, for ten days, they survived on a diet of raw corn meal and dried dog salmon. They cut their dog team loose and never saw the animals again. Whiskey Thompson, another miner, was forced to kill his dogs and eat them raw in order to survive.[3]

At the summit of the Chilkoot Pass, travellers always faced the threat of avalanche, as thousands of tons of snow hung precariously from the peaks overhead. At the best of times, the snow itself proved an insufferable obstacle. In both winter and spring, men struggled through snow many feet deep, sinking to their shoulders as they pulled their belongings to their destination at Lake Lindeman. If the weather warmed up, a crust of icy snow formed, through which a man could fall at any time, further frustrating him and draining his energy. There was also the risk of succumbing to snow blindness and/or exhaustion. Nonetheless, most of the prospectors persisted and eventually reached their destination.

Once they arrived at the headwaters of the Yukon River, they had to haul their supplies along a series of frozen lakes that dotted the route like pearls on a necklace. Some raised a simple sail on their sleds, so that the coastal winds would push them along on their journey. On the lakes travel was fraught with danger, for large airholes – voids in the ice surface – lay hidden beneath a thin covering of snow or ice.

After taking three weeks or more to get their supplies the twenty-three miles from tidewater to Lake Lindeman, the prospectors set to building a boat or raft to carry them down the Yukon River. Starting by cutting down the necessary timber and whipsawing it into lumber, they completed their craft in five to ten days. An ideal prospecting party consisted of three to five men; enough to divide up and lessen the work but not too many to make transporting supplies by boat difficult. If they launched a boat at Lake Lindeman, they had to portage to reach Bennett Lake. If they arrived early enough in the season, they could haul their equipment farther down the chain of icy lakes to Tagish Lake or beyond before launching their boats after spring break-up.

Between Tagish and Marsh lakes, the prospectors passed a small cluster of Native buildings and a cemetery. The Native people cremated their dead and interred the remains in small boxes, which, in turn, were placed in small wooden structures on top of posts. 'I remember a man,' said Arthur Walden,

> who found one of these boxes in the woods. Not knowing what it was, he took it to use for a grub-chest, and did not discover his mistake until some days later, when the widow and some other Indians called at his camp for something to eat and recognised it. After scaring the poor prospector almost to death, they allowed him to keep it on payment of most of his outfit. He did not want it by this time, and neither did the widow: but he paid well for his mistake and was the laughing stock of the River.[4]

The Yukon River originates in Marsh Lake and meanders through a broad valley for a few miles before reaching what is now a tranquil stretch of water held back by a hydro dam, but was then the most formidable obstacle on the river: Miles Canyon and the Whitehorse Rapids. At the canyon, the water from the river is, at some points, squeezed between sheer basalt cliffs no more than thirty yards apart. The water which boiled through this constriction was terrifying. Walden described Miles Canyon as winding 'between sheer blank walls of rock that tower far up into the air, the water sucking down into this natural sluice box at about 18 miles an hour. The current is ridged up in the middle five or six feet high, and on top are tremendous rollers, so that a boat is always standing on one end or the other.'[5] Part way through this canyon there was a sharp turn in the channel, which created a whirlpool capable of trapping hapless prospectors and whirling them in circles before they could escape.

If they managed to escape this whirlpool, it was only a short distance before they entered the narrow, rocky passage known as the Whitehorse Rapids and found themselves descending a chute several hundred yards long, their boats crashing into huge, standing whitecaps all the while. It is small wonder that by the middle of the decade the prospectors had constructed a substantial portage road along the west side of the canyon and had built roll-ways of logs over which they could push their boats. They also constructed some windlasses with which they could haul their boats up the hills, the most notable one lying at the foot of the canyon.[6] After this, the only other rapids that had to be prepared for were the Five

Early view of Miles Canyon

Finger Rapids, so named in 1882 by one of the early prospectors because the current was split into five separate channels by four prominent rock masses spread out across the river.[7] If they remembered to keep to the extreme right-hand channel as they descended, most travellers managed to get through with only a small amount of water in their supplies.

Beyond the Whitehorse Rapids, travel was once again slower and safer. Lake Laberge, the largest open body of water over which the gold-seekers would travel, represented some days of exertion with a paddle, although if there were a healthy breeze many of them would raise a make-shift sail to speed up their fifty-mile journey. If the wind picked up, however, the lake quickly became a frenzied, white-capped hazard, at which time it was wiser to take to the shore than to try to navigate the rough waters.

Below the lake, the pilgrims entered the transparent, emerald green waters of the 'thirty mile' portion of the Yukon River, below which it joined with the murky Teslin River and widened substantially. From here, it followed a sinuous course for many miles. Along this length of the river, among the hazards that confronted unsuspecting navigators were the deadfalls hanging precariously from its undercut banks. If swept into one of these by the current, a raft could easily be overturned or the passengers dumped into the water. Another hazard to river travellers came from slumping of the banks. As the permanently frozen ground was thawed by river erosion, large chunks would slump unexpectedly into the river, swamping passing boats. At least one group of prospectors lost their entire outfit in this fashion.[8] The force of the river current could not be underestimated, for it pushed its guests along with incredible force. According to Arthur Walden:

> One of the most unpleasant nights of my life was ... when a strong wind and current swept us almost under one of the[se] overhanging banks, where the water had melted the silt and the stream was rushing under the banks for goodness knows how far. To avoid going under, we threw out a home-made anchor which, luckily for ourselves, held us a few yards from this swirling water-made cavern. But having little faith in either the anchor, or the strength of the rope, we lay awake all night speculating as to whether we were getting any nearer to these caves or not. When the wind dropped in the morning, we cut the rope and by hard rowing were just able to get by.[9]

Over the years, many outfits (and a few lives) were lost by prospectors caught unprepared in one of these traps laid by nature. But it was by this means – the various river bars along the Yukon River and its tributaries – that the seekers of gold were able to reach their destinations. If they were lucky, the prospectors might enjoy good weather during the months of June and July, during which time they could search in earnest for rich outcrops of gold.

Summer in the Yukon basin is lamentably short. By the beginning to middle of August, prospectors, aware of the coming winter, started to leave the interior. The journey out was far more difficult than the journey in; leaving the Yukon, travel was against the current, and the journey lasted for several weeks, depending upon river conditions, weather, and the size of the load being transported.

The men usually travelled by poling, for the current was too fast to paddle or row against for any distance. Israel C. Russell provides a firsthand description of poling:

> Each of my companions was provided with a strong pole, about ten feet long, furnished with a spike at one end. Armed with one of these, two of the men took their stations in the prow of the boat and two in the stern, and by pushing

with the poles on the bottom or against the river bank, the boat was forced along. In this mode of navigation the most experienced polemen occupy the ends of the boat and guide its course. To handle a boat in this manner requires even more skill than when oars are used. Especially is this true, when rounding headlands about which the current is swift. Sometimes when with greater labour we had succeeded in nearly passing a butting bluff, the rear poleman would be unable to turn the prow towards the bank by forcing his end of the boat out from the shore, and the strong current would immediately sweep us out into mid-stream, where the water was too deep for the poles to reach the bottom, and we would be carried far down the river before the rude oars could be brought into play. When swept away from the bank in this manner, we would row across to the opposite shore; usually the concave side of a sharp curve, where eddies tending upstream were to be expected and in the next projecting headland regain the space that had been lost.

When the character of the shore would permit, a towing line would be fastened to the side of the boat and the four men would track along the bank, while I remained in the boat and guided her course with one of the poles. In this manner, we could frequently make better progress than by poling, but, unfortunately, the vegetation overhanging the banks was usually too dense to admit of tracking for any considerable distance.[10]

By various accounts, from seven or eight up to twenty or thirty miles could be travelled per day, depending upon the load and the conditions of travel.[11] Considering that most of the men who went upstream had several hundred miles of river to traverse, one can quickly calculate that such a journey was going to take many weeks of numbing, back-breaking effort in order to reach the Chilkoot Pass before winter set in.

Since there were no roads or even trails into this new frontier, travel by river was by far the easiest part of the journey. Once ashore, the prospectors faced even tougher going. The bush was thick and unending. Below the surface lay ground frozen for millennia. Once disturbed, this solid footing would turn into a quaking bog. Feared by all were the 'nigger-head' swamps, mushy terrains interspersed with matted clumps of tall grass and sod. They were avoided like the plague. Said one traveller: 'When you want to walk through one of these flats, you must step over these mounds and place your foot between them, and if you have far to go, you become very tired, and if a foot slips or you stagger from any cause, down you go. Sometimes you think you can walk on the tops of

Two men pulling supplies through Fortymile Canyon, 1894

the mounds, but you cannot. They sway under you and down you go on
your knees in the mud between them.'[12]

Whenever possible, the men would take to high ground on the hill-
tops, where the terrain was rocky but firm and dry. However, this mode
of travel led to complaints such as the following: 'My feet had become
raw at the start from hard boots, and every step was torture; yet the boots
could not be taken off, for the trail was covered with small sharp stones,
and the packs on our backs pressed heavily downward.'[13] There was no
relief from toiling under heavy loads and fighting swarms of mosquitoes
over unfamiliar terrain. Every man carried his own load; there were no
teamsters or dog teams. Winter was the best time to travel, for then the
ground was firm and the snow made it possible to drag heavy loads.

During the early period of development on the Yukon River, there was
limited steam-powered transportation. From 1869 onwards, the tiny
sternwheeler *Yukon* plied the lower reaches of the great river, carrying
supplies to the trading posts thinly scattered along its banks. It was
replaced by the *Yukon II* in 1879. The *St. Michael*, a second vessel, was
added to the river fleet in 1871. The *New Racket* was added in 1882. These
vessels laboured heroically under adverse conditions to provision the
posts along the Yukon River, but they became increasingly inadequate as

Steamers, such as the Arctic, *plied the Yukon River carrying supplies to remote posts.*

the years passed and the river wore them down. In some years, conditions on the river would not allow passage beyond the Yukon flats. When that occurred, everyone upstream faced a winter of deprivation. It was many years before river steam transportation became common and reliable.

3

EARLY DEVELOPMENTS ON

THE YUKON RIVER

Over the next half decade, the number of prospectors entering the Yukon slowly but steadily increased, fired partly by word-of-mouth reports and augmented by occasional letters to the Alaskan newspapers from those who had visited the new territory. However, it was not yet catching the interest of the outside world.

In the summer of 1881, a party of four prospected the Big Salmon River and became the first producing miners in the Yukon. That summer, farther down the Yukon River, Arthur Harper, a man named Bates, and two Native people left David's Village, near the present-day location of Eagle, Alaska, and crossed the highlands to reach the Tanana River. Crossing the North Fork of the Fortymile River, Bates nearly drowned. While Bates was drying out from his brush with death, Harper prospected and collected a sample of sand from along the banks of the river. Bates left the Yukon and took the sample of sand to an assayer in San Francisco. When Harper learned that it assayed out at $20,000 to the ton he tried, but failed, to relocate the deposit.[1] Probably that same year, a party of prospectors entered the Yukon and travelled as far down the Yukon River as the Stewart River, then up the latter for about 200 miles. They carried word of their findings to Edward Schieffelin of Tombstone, Arizona, who subsequently brought a party to the Yukon in 1882 aboard the small steamer, *New Racket.*[2]

In 1882, fifty men came over the Chilkoot Pass to prospect for gold. Twelve of them travelled downriver and wintered at Fort Reliance with Jack McQuesten (this was only the second time McQuesten had someone to talk to during the winter). The party included Joe Ladue, Thomas Boswell, Howard Franklin, Frank Densmore, and George Powers. Densmore had searched up the Pelly River as far as the Hoole Canyon without finding any good prospects. In September Jack McQuesten and these men travelled into the Sixtymile region, to a point about fifteen miles below Miller Creek, and tried their luck. They lit fires to thaw the frozen ground (the first time this method is recorded as being used in the Yukon) and sank a prospect hole ten feet deep, but they abandoned it before getting to bedrock when it filled with water. The following year, in 1883, the party prospected on both the Fortymile and the Sixtymile, but did not strike anything of note. All of the men who wintered at Fort Reliance with McQuesten left the Yukon during the summer except Ladue and one other.

The methods of prospecting and mining employed at this time were primitive, superficial, and highly inefficient, yet they were the only means by which poorly capitalized prospectors could proceed. The earliest intrusions were seasonal, being restricted to the summer months, during which much time was spent in moving from one place to another (particularly in poling out of the region in the fall). Being restricted in what they could carry, the prospectors' mining equipment consisted of a limited number of tools.

The primary device required by every prospector was the gold pan. Once a promising prospect was located, the prospector would quickly assemble a rocker, a small device resembling a child's cradle. This had a handle protruding from the top which allowed the prospector to move it from side to side while passing the 'paydirt' through a screen on the top of the device and pouring water from a dipper over the material to wash it through a series of inclined riffles. The tailings escaped through the lower end of this device, while the gold, one hoped, was trapped in the riffles.

The material trapped in the riffles would then be panned out in a gold pan. Gold, which was mixed in with black sand, was extracted by adding mercury to the mixture. The gold would form an amalgam with the mercury and, thus trapped, could be removed from the magnetic black sand. The amalgam was then poured into a soft buckskin bag and the mercury squeezed out through the pores in the bag, leaving the gold behind. The remaining mixture would be placed in a frying pan and any remaining mercury would be driven off by heating it over a fire.

Early prospecting was restricted primarily to the bars along the Yukon River and its main tributaries. These were the most accessible and the easiest to work, as their proximity to water allowed them to thaw more quickly than other areas. Furthermore, water is essential to the extraction of gold and, of course, here it was in abundance. Yet even on the banks of the Yukon River the ground was frozen just below the surface. The prospectors would surface skim over a fairly wide area, working over the ground day after day, skimming away newly thawed layers of dirt and shovelling it through their rockers. Soon the miners started using fire to speed this process along.[3]

Prospecting demanded that men be constantly searching for a productive body of ore. Consequently, throughout the early years, miners led a peripatetic existence, frequently moving on to new prospects, forming new partnerships, and dissolving them just as quickly. Of necessity, the small society of miners on the Yukon River was highly fluid in both structure and composition.

After wintering at Nuklukayet the previous winter, the Schieffelin party (the first well subsidized gold-seeking expedition to search the Yukon River) returned to San Francisco late in 1883, having found prospects along the lower Yukon River but nothing rich enough to offset the high cost of mining in the region. The *New Racket*, the little steamer they had travelled on, was sold to Harper, McQuesten, and Mayo and, in subsequent years, became one of the regular transport steamers.[4]

In 1883, another fifty men entered the Yukon via the Chilkoot watershed. Some of these, including Boswell, mined and prospected the bars of the Yukon River above Fort Selkirk. Richard Poplin, Charles McConkey, Benjamin Beach, and C. Marks prospected on the Stewart River as far as the McQuesten River. They went down to Fort Reliance for supplies, but since the steamer was broken down on the lower river, they continued down the river to Tanana, where they spent the winter.[5]

Eighteen eighty-three was also the year the first non-prospecting visitors arrived at Fort Reliance. Frederick Schwatka, of the US Army, stopped briefly at the post while conducting a military reconnaissance along the Yukon River. Reverend Vincent Sims visited the post for about two weeks in the late summer to tend to the religious 'needs' of the Native people quartered there.[6]

In 1884, some seventy-five men came over the Chilkoot Pass into the Yukon. Poplin, McConkey, Beach, and Marks returned to the Stewart

River, where they prospected for three months, then they went up the Yukon River and out over the Chilkoot Pass. On the way, they encountered Thomas Boswell and Howard Franklin on the upper Yukon River. After hearing of the prospects of the out-bound party, Boswell and Franklin went downriver to Fort Reliance for the winter.[7] The following summer Boswell, Franklin, and a third miner, Henry Madison, discovered Cassiar Bar, one of the first major placer bars on the Yukon River. News of finds such as this one stimulated more men from Juneau to try their luck in the Yukon valley.

Among those who wintered at Fort Reliance that year was Joe Ladue. He and some other prospectors went moose hunting upriver from the post on Rabbit Creek, a tributary of the Deer River. Little did they realize that the Deer River would someday be known as the Klondike, and that Rabbit Creek would someday be known as Bonanza Creek. Their camp, which was situated a short distance above what would become known as the Grand Forks, lay on top of a fortune of buried gold![8]

In the spring of 1885, Boswell and J. Fraser went up the Stewart River, hauling their supplies over the ice. They prospected the bars of the river, thawing them with fire in order to free the gravels. When they reached Chapman's Bar ninety miles up the Stewart River, they found the gold they were looking for. Rocking by hand, they each averaged one hundred dollars per day. From this extraordinary deposit, they extracted $6,000 over the summer. Seven miles above Chapman's Bar, Richard Poplin, Pete Wyborg, Francis Morphat,[9] and Jeremiah Bertrand occupied 'Steamboat' Bar. They mined $35,000 worth of gold that summer, and they remained in a camp about twenty-five miles above the mouth of the Stewart River for the winter. More than half of the seventy-five miners who came into the Yukon for the summer worked on the Stewart River.

McQuesten and his partners realized that the influx of miners was going to grow in future years so, for the first time, they brought fifty tons of miners' supplies, which arrived at Fort Reliance on 10 August. From there, McQuesten travelled upriver to Fort Selkirk to trade with the Native people, dropping Boswell off at the Stewart River to prospect, and Franklin and Madison at the mouth of the White River, where they spent the winter. Tom Williams, Joe Ladue, and Mike Hess went on to Fort Selkirk, where they built a boat and went upriver to try some of the bars which had been worked the year before. They then returned to the mouth of the Stewart River to spend the winter. In total, fifteen men endured a bitterly cold winter, planning to strike it rich the next season.

Early in the spring of 1886, the men started up the Stewart River with dogs but found nothing that would pay. Meanwhile, dozens of miners from Juneau were waiting to come into the Yukon in the spring. Two hundred men crossed the Chilkoot Pass that year. One hundred of them were scattered along the bars of the Yukon River, between the Teslin and the Big Salmon rivers, at more than half a dozen favourable locations. Four men on Cassiar Bar recovered $6,000 worth of gold in one month.[10] Encouraged by the successes of the previous year, a hundred men prospected on the Stewart River as far as the falls and for some distance up the McQuesten River. Most of them planned to stay the winter in order to be able to start prospecting early in the spring and to work late into the autumn, thus doubling the time available for their search for gold.

With the growing interest in the prospects of a rich strike, many men were heading out in new directions to find their fortune. That summer, from Fort Reliance, Joe Ladue, Dan Sprague, and John and Pete Nelson struck out overland to the northeast in the hope of finding gold. They eventually found the headwaters of the Thron-Duick, or 'Tron-deg,' River (also called the Deer River) and travelled down it, testing the bars but finding nothing to spark their interest. A decade later, the Thron-Duick River (Thron-Duick was a White corruption of the Native name) would become known as the Klondike River.[11]

Encouraged by the increasing number of prospectors on the Stewart River, McQuesten, Harper, and Mayo abandoned Fort Reliance and established a post just below the mouth of the river, where they could more easily supply the wintering miners. This new post was given the name Fort Nelson, after Edward H. Nelson, an American signal observer who spent several years at the mouth of the Yukon River. Nelson became known in the scientific world for the superb collections he made for the Smithsonian Institution in Washington.[12]

Fort Nelson became the sole outpost of 'civilization' for miners on the Yukon River. Fronting on a half-moon bay facing the Yukon River, Fort Nelson consisted of 'a disconsolate row of low, primitive, dirt-roofed cabins'[13] scattered on a flat beside the river amidst a forest of burnt tree stumps. 'Desolation was the keynote of the whole scene,' reported one observer, with the only service to its citizens being provided by the trading post, which consisted of a large log structure and two cabins.[14] Also known as 'Harper's Place'[15] and 'Mayo's Post,'[16] the settlement was split into three distinct groups of cabins, each given its own name by the miners and each providing its residents with an identity: one group was called 'Blowville,' the second was called 'Crank Flat,' and the third was called 'Sourdough Island.' It was the third group of cabins from which the term sourdough was coined. Little by little, the names of the other two groups were forgotten, while 'sourdough' came to be the general term used to refer to seasoned Yukon veterans.[17]

On 7 September 1886, Jack McQuesten departed for San Francisco,[18] where he planned to obtain a shipment of supplies for the miners for the following season. The Alaska Commercial Company (AC Co.), however, was not favourably disposed to supplying the forty or fifty tons of supplies that McQuesten requested; like the HBC before it, the AC Co. did not like miners. While everyone locked in at Fort Nelson scrambled to keep warm, McQuesten scrambled to find an alternative to the AC Co. He went to Portland, Oregon, to start his own company. When the AC Co. heard about this they had a change of heart and cabled him to return to San Francisco to discuss the matter further. Although they finally did supply goods to the miners, these goods were of poor quality; this would not change until the AC Co. faced competition on the Yukon River.[19]

While the men of the Yukon mucked for gold in the icy banks of the mighty river, another party arrived in search of a different treasure: human souls. On 11 July 1886 a party of four men left Victoria to penetrate the Yukon valley. They were the forty-six-year-old archbishop Charles John Seghers, Jesuit priests Pascal Tosi (a fifty-eight-year-old Italian) and Aloysius Robaut, and Frank Fuller, a lay worker for the church. At Juneau, Antoine Provost, a French-Canadian, agreed to accompany the party as cook and guide in exchange for meals.

On 26 July the missionaries, accompanied by a similarly sized party of miners (and assisted in carrying their supplies by fifty Chilkat packers), arrived at the summit of the Chilkoot Pass. At the headwaters of the Yukon River, a curious event occurred. Provost, who had proved an admirable cook and amiable travelling companion, disappeared. Two days of searching for the man revealed no clue to explain his disappearance. This was the first in a series of circumstances that would doom the expedition. Frank Fuller, the lay companion on the journey, displayed increasingly alarming behaviour. Tosi saw the paranoid and erratic actions of Fuller and implored his spiritual leader to dismiss the man from the party. The archbishop disagreed and, from that point on, the relationship between Seghers and Tosi was strained.

From the beginning of the boat journey, the party was plagued by tension and disharmony. Fuller was an unsuitable travel companion, and his unstable personality was a threat to the party almost from the beginning. Seghers, a man whose spirit and energy were excessive, was physically unable to keep up with the demands of travel. He clung tenaciously to the idea of keeping Fuller in the travelling party, despite the importuning of the more robust and practical Tosi.

Finally, on 7 September 1886 they arrived at the tiny community at the mouth of the Stewart River, where Seghers encountered an old acquaintance, Arthur Harper. The party gathered their strength and discussed their plans. By this time, Robaut joined Tosi in no longer being able to tolerate Fuller's company. Tosi, who continued to appeal to the archbishop to rid them of Fuller, had lost his respect for his superior. The rift between them widened. Tosi became impertinent and took offence at Seghers's every word or action. Despite being a good cook, he refused to prepare meals for the party. A strong man with an immense vitality and a robust constitution, Father Tosi was impatient with his physically weaker superior.

Harper informed the party that Anglican missionaries had had some contact and success with the Native people from Fort Reliance down to Fort Yukon. Fearing that they might be affected by the 'taint of Protestantism,' Harper convinced Seghers that it was not too late to settle amongst the Native people and drive out the Protestant influence. The bishop decided to split the party: he would continue to travel down the Yukon River with Fuller; Tosi and Robaut would remain at the mouth of the Stewart River. Ironically, they spent the winter as part of this tiny community, teaching the traders' children to read and write, giving instruction in French to the miners, but rarely making contact with the Native people.

While Seghers and his dubious companion continued down the river, nearly reaching their destination of Nulato, the latter's behaviour became increasingly demented and menacing. Finally, on 28 November, after becoming more restless and withdrawn, Fuller raised the bishop's own 44 calibre Winchester and killed him with a single shot.[20] Fuller was arrested and taken to Sitka by a revenue officer in 1887. There he stood trial and was found guilty of manslaughter. After serving eight and a half years in prison, he was released and moved to Portland, Oregon, where he was later killed in a violent quarrel with a neighbour.

4

THE MINERS' CODE

The men of the early Yukon were as unique an assemblage of individuals as you could find anywhere. They were, in fact, the product of their environment. 'My companions, [were] rough and uncouth as men could well be,' said Israel Russell of these men.

> Their hair and beards had grown long, and their faces were tanned and weather-beaten by constant exposure. Their garments, then in the last stages of serviceability, had been made by those who wore them, from any material that chanced to be available, from buckskin and fur to flour-sacks, and had been repaired without regard to color or texture ... One not accustomed to the vicissitudes of exploration, coming suddenly on such a scene, would certainly believe he had stumbled on a band of the most desperate outlaws.[1]

These men were hardly outlaws, however. As Russell went on to explain, they were

> a rough, hardy race, made up, it would seem, of representatives of nearly every nation on earth. Some are typical frontiersmen, dressed in buckskin, who are never at home except on the outskirts of civilization. Others were of doubtful character, and it is said are seldom known by their rightful names. The remote gulches of the Yukon country seem to offer safe asylums for men who are 'wanted' in other districts. Despite the varied character of its inhabitants, this remote community is orderly and but few disturbances have been known. Summary punishment would follow any

Group of miners at mouth of Fortymile River, 1895

break of the peace. Morality, as understood in more refined communities, is conspicuous in its absence.[2]

Early Yukoners pressed on ahead of 'civilization.' One of them, an American named Nick Goff, had never seen a railroad, having always moved on before one arrived.[3] They were driven by the hope that they would some day strike it rich. They were 'men with the hearts of vikings and the simple faith of a child, living day after day, bearing hardships indescribable. Trials and dangers they faced without question, trusting all would be well and soon they would be able to get a little place back home and comfortably settle down.'[4] These men were an amalgam, a blend of many cultures, shaped and moulded by isolation and harsh conditions, and tempered with enterprising spirits. They abided by a very simple set of rules. There were, for instance, few if any class distinctions. The divisions in the population were, at this time, very simple: prospectors/miners and traders. Anyone who put himself above his fellows would find himself shunned.[5] They were highly informal and extremely independent. Past histories were never sought and seldom given. Mutual trust was a byword, and honesty was expected in all matters. Cheating was, therefore, an uncommon practice, because a man's reputation would quickly sour if such behaviour became known.

Early Yukoners were suspicious of authority and any of the restraints it placed upon them.[6] They were 'courteous in rough countries, where each must travel on his own merits and fight his own battles.'[7] Yet they would offer their home, food, and a bed to sleep in without even asking the guest his name. If someone was short of supplies no questions were asked; whoever had something would share with those who had nothing, even if it were the last morsel available.[8]

A man's real name was not of much importance amongst the community of prospectors, so many of these men became known by particular personal attributes. For example, those who dealt in liquor often had the prefix 'Whiskey' or 'Hootch' added to their name.[9] Others were nicknamed because of a specific event. Swiftwater Bill (Gates), for instance, gained his moniker because he preferred to walk around the rapids of Miles Canyon while his travelling partners went through them.[10] The names add a touch of colour to the pioneer roll call: Nigger Jim, Happy Jack, Siwash George, Calamity Bill, Crooked-Leg Louie, Jimmy the Pirate, Pete the Pig, Slobbery Tom, and Tin Kettle George.

The eccentricities of these men were accepted without question. Cannibal Ike liked to eat his meat raw, while Howard Hamilton hewed wood from the log walls of his cabin until, in some places, they were only two inches thick. He joked that having thinner walls gave him more light inside.[11] Their rules of conduct were simple: take men at their face value, judge them by their actions, share with all, be honest, trust others, and be tolerant. In sum, the miners' code was reduced to a single, simple rule: do as you would be done by.

The miners lived in a political vacuum within a wilderness devoid of boundaries. Thus they had no formal constitution and no formal body to enforce it if they had. Implementing the rules established in the camps of previous gold rushes, they managed their affairs under anarchistic democracies familiarly called miners' committees. These committees were used sparingly and under a limited number of circumstances, nonetheless they functioned as an informal method of establishing rules of conduct and resolving issues of conflict. At various times, they dealt with civil and criminal matters, and they established mining procedures for each vicinity. The first meeting of such a committee occurred in the winter of 1882-3 at Fort Reliance. At that time rules governing the size of placer claims and water rights were established in case any discoveries were made, and Jack McQuesten was appointed recorder of claims.[12] Miners' committees also dealt with community matters, such as the administering of the estates of the deceased and, later, the registering of land titles in the town of Forty Mile.

The miners' committees were styled after the American principle of democratic conduct. Every member who participated had a vote. If a man had a grievance, a moderator was chosen and a meeting was convened to resolve it. Both prosecutor and defence were chosen, each had an opportunity to question and cross-examine the witnesses and, in the end, summations were given. A motion was put before the committee, and it was passed or defeated. The sentence was carried out immediately. In serious cases, such as theft, the guilty party was banished from the Yukon, which, if the sentence were passed in the winter, meant serious hardship for the person banished, as he was compelled to depart immediately.

Offenders feared miners' committees more than they feared any court of law.[13] Even Judge James Wickersham, the first judge on the American side of the boundary, commented on the speed and efficiency with which justice was dispensed.[14] One decision of a miners' committee, (a not guilty verdict in a case of self defence emanating from the town of Circle) was even sent to Washington, where the decision was confirmed.[15] This system of self-administered justice can attribute its success to the fact that it was applied to a small, homogeneous community. All the miners were well acquainted with each other and, for the most part, the meetings stuck to business.

Conflict did not always require the forum of a meeting in order to be suitably resolved, for the miners were generally committed to peaceable coexistence. One time, there occurred a conflict between a Frenchman and an Englishman over the company of a Native woman. An eyewitness described the resolution:

> There was to be a duel between them, with Winchester rifles, stationed five hundred feet apart, and after each shot, each was to advance one pace, until one or both were killed ... A great big Scotchman [Neal McArthur] was the president of the [miners'] meeting, and ten men with rifles were appointed to see fair play, together with the president ... When everything was arranged, the Englishman saw McArthur had about fifty feet of rope on his arm. Asking what it was for, he was told, to hang by the neck, the winner. There was no fight, but they were each given a few days to get the supplies together and leave town forever.[16]

In the winter of 1886-7, a miners' committee found itself faced with the disposition of a serious crime – attempted murder. Jack Leslie spent some months in Seattle during the winter of 1885-6. There, he met many miners from the Yukon and, after talking to them, he made up a story about a fabulous, rich Yukon gold mine. He was able to sell the story to four miners, who assembled the requisite supplies for an expedition to the Yukon, and they all set off for the rich mine – vowing to share equally the proceeds from their discovery.

After conducting the arduous task of crossing the Chilkoot Pass and travelling down the Yukon River, they arrived at the Stewart River and commenced their quest for the gold mine about which they had heard so much. Their quest was unsuccessful, however, and as autumn descended upon the Yukon, they prepared to go into hibernation for the winter. The tyranny of forced idleness combined with disillusionment weighed upon the party, only one of whom had any practical mining experience. And, as time went on, they began to suspect that they had been misled. One of the members of the party, known as the 'giant,' started to discuss what he thought would be an appropriate punishment to inflict upon Leslie for leading them into this predicament. The giant's proposed punishments became increasingly harsh until, at last, he intimated that hanging would be appropriate. This was not taken seriously by his partners, but it set Leslie's active imagination ablaze, and his fears grew until he became convinced of his imminent demise.

Eventually, Leslie resolved to kill all the members of his party and, to this end, he laced their meal of beans with a liberal dose of arsenic.[17] The men ate this meal, despite the terrible taste the poison imparted to it. They became very ill and, for the next thirty-six hours, they suffered tremendously. Leslie feigned illness so that no suspicions were aroused. The poison, however, did not kill them, so Leslie patiently waited until he was certain that they were all asleep, then he picked up a loaded Winchester rifle and prepared to fire upon one of the men. Fortunately, another member of the party, who had remained both awake and vigilant, leaped up and forced Leslie to fire wide. At that, the rest of the party woke up and took him prisoner.

The captors decided that they would put the resolution of this case before a miners' committee. They transported Leslie sixty miles down the Stewart River to Fort Nelson, where a miners' committee meeting was convened. Both parties presented their testimony. Leslie, for his part, explained that his welfare was in jeopardy because of the threats of violence that had been uttered against him. The majority of the committee tended to agree that his behaviour was justifiable but, nevertheless, decided that he was an undesirable character and should therefore be banished from the community.[18]

Leslie was furnished a sled and a supply of provisions, and he was ordered to move upriver at least one hundred and fifty miles or risk being shot on sight. When he arrived at Chris Sonnickson's camp on 1 April 1887 he told him that he and his comrades had been the victims of an 'Indian massacre,' that the Natives had waited until most of the miners were at Fort Nelson and that they had 'then turned loose on the post, killing Harper's boy, wounding Dick Wells, wounding R. Eagle in the leg and Mat Mayon [in the] shoulder and that he [Leslie] had been sent out to warn the incoming men.'[19]

Leslie's story alarmed some of the men in Sonnickson's camp, and they wanted to depart immediately. He continued on his trek and, farther on, encountered Peter Roblin and his party. The story alarmed them considerably but not enough to turn them back.[20] Leslie carried the story with him to the Haines Mission, where he encountered William Ogilvie, Dominion Land Surveyor, who was preparing for his government-commissioned expedition into the Yukon. At first Ogilvie was alarmed, but he dismissed the story after weighing the testimony. It is not known what happened to Leslie after his encounter with Ogilvie.[21]

That same winter of 1886-7, a miners' committee intervened when Missouri Frank stole a quantity of butter from Arthur Harper's cache. After hearing the case, the committee sentenced Frank to banishment, and he headed upriver. Unlike Leslie, however, when he arrived at Sonnickson's camp exhausted, he confessed the nature of his offence and they allowed him to stay for the remainder of the winter. William Ogilvie saw him rocking for gold on a bar on the upper Yukon River during the summer of 1887, and Frank left the country in the fall of that year.[22]

5

THE FORTYMILE STAMPEDE

As the prospecting season of 1886 drew to a close, two men made a discovery that would change the tempo of prospecting in the Yukon within a few short months. Howard Franklin and Henry Madison tried their luck prospecting on the Stewart River as far as the falls and up the McQuesten River as far as they could navigate. They did not like the species of trees growing on the bars, nor did they think that gold could be found where wild onions or leeks grew, so they abandoned this area and moved on.

Their next choice was to go downriver to the Fortymile River and ascend it to just beyond what was later to become the international boundary. There they found coarse gold in bedrock on what was later to be known as Franklin's Bar. This was the first coarse gold to be found in the Yukon, so the men, with great excitement, made the laborious return trip to the mouth of the Stewart River to report their find.[1]

Tom Williams's Death March

The news of the discovery on the Fortymile River was what everyone had been waiting for. However, locked in by the winter ice and snow, they could do very little but wait patiently for spring. Arthur Harper realized that when news of the strike on the Fortymile River reached the outside there would be a stampede of unknown proportions. Jack McQuesten was out in San Francisco making arrangements for next year's shipment of goods. Not knowing about this new event, he could not possibly order enough supplies to deal with the deluge of humanity that would occur. What to do about it?

Arthur Harper wrote a letter to McQuesten describing the new discovery and advised him to increase his order of supplies. Tom Williams, one of the miners wintering at Fort Nelson, volunteered to carry the message to the head of navigation at Dyea, where it could be conveyed to McQuesten in time to increase the shipment of supplies destined for the Yukon. Leaving for the coast on 1 December 1886, with a dog team and a young Native named 'Bob' to help him, Williams had no idea what hardships were ahead. Even if he had known, so determined was he to reach Dyea that he would not have turned back to the security of the little settlement at the mouth of the Stewart River. The trip he faced was formidable: a journey to the coast in the worst of weather (a distance of several hundred miles) with no trail to follow. No prospector had ever before attempted such an undertaking.

The trip started easily enough. That winter was the mildest in years, and, at first, Tom and Bob made good distance – up to twenty-five miles every day. After a week it rained, and the distances covered each day diminished. Travelling along the Yukon River they encountered heavy pack ice – massive blocks frozen into contorted shapes – creating a grossly irregular surface over which, by heavy physical effort, they could force the dogs and the packed sled. At the end of the second week, after passing Rink Rapids, the sled broke, and they had to stop to repair it. The following day, they travelled on ice covered with water. This was hard on the dogs' feet, and it slowed them down even more.

The warm weather weakened the ice. On 17 December, Bob went through into water over his head. The same thing happened the next day and the day after that. On 19 December the floe ice in the open leads in the Yukon River jammed, causing the water to rise and giving them yet another dunking. Travelling became even more difficult. Encountering more open river, the two men, now pushing an exhausted team, had to portage two miles through river-bank brush to reach more solid river ice. On 22 December they travelled only nine miles. It was in this section of the Yukon River that the two determined men encountered some of the bar miners, who were wintering along the river. They were able to replenish their supplies while passing on the word of the new discovery and collecting more letters to take outside.

They pressed on, encountering open water and more warm weather, which slowed them down and forced them to travel along the shelf of ice which shouldered the watercourse. The weather turned bitterly cold as they forged ahead to the coastal mountain barrier. They arrived at Lake Laberge on New Year's Eve, without celebration. Over the smooth lake ice, they made better time, but so obsessed were they with their goal that they refused to rest. By this time, they were feeding their dogs from their rapidly dwindling supply of flour. Both men and dogs were reaching total exhaustion as they moved up the Whitehorse Rapids (now ringed with fairy frost from the spray of the swiftly moving water), past Miles Canyon, and along the string of lakes at the headwaters of the Yukon River.

They advanced on the smooth lake ice, making excellent mileage every day until they reached Bennett Lake, where they encountered a band of wandering Natives, whom they could not persuade to accompany them over the summit of the Chilkoot Pass. Ignoring the Natives' warnings about the treacherous coastal pass, Williams and his young companion continued west and encountered a violent blizzard. Fighting a strong headwind, they struggled for another twenty miles, but by then the weather was so bad that they could not move at all. Eventually they made another ten miles through heavy snow and camped in the middle of Lake Lindeman, without fuel or shelter from the storm.

The hardship continued. They abandoned their sled and began packing supplies on their backs. One dog was too exhausted to continue, so they abandoned it. They made five miles in two days and then camped in the seemingly endless mountain storm. Finally, exhausted and out of food, they reached Stone House, below the summit of the Chilkoot Pass. Somewhere along the trail, they had lost the last of their dogs, along with the precious mail they were taking to the coast.

For five days they were trapped in a snow shelter at the foot of the coastal palisade, without fire or food (other than a little dry flour.)[2] Williams was sick and feverish with pneumonia when they emerged from their shelter on the sixth day. Leaving everything behind them, they struck out through the snow for Dyea. After only a short distance, Williams collapsed, and young Bob struggled on heroically through two feet of snow into a blinding blizzard with Williams on his back. They made only twelve miles in five days, when they encountered a wandering band of Chilkat, who took them directly to Healy and Wilson's post on the shores of salt water.

The trip was too difficult an ordeal for Williams. He died within two hours but not before he told the astonished party in the store of the new discovery of gold. The details were contained in the letters that he had carried with him from the Yukon River. Wilson, the trader, sent out a party to find the pouch of mail, but they were driven back by the raging storm. A few days later, J.J. Healy, Wilson's partner, returned from Juneau. Young Bob and the electrifying news of the new strike were quickly transported to Juneau.

Everyone in the coastal outpost was curious about news that would cause a man to undertake such a dangerous journey. Young Bob, picking up a handful of beans, remarked: 'Gold all same like this.'³ That was all that was needed to send hundreds of men into the Yukon that spring in search of treasure. Healy led an expedition into the pass to find the bundle of letters, which, along with news of the strike, contained a map. Beneath the snowy peaks, they found the mail bag, still being faithfully guarded by the last of Williams's dogs, dead and frozen.⁴

Wintering on the Fortymile River

While Williams was playing out his tragedy on a snow-bound stage, another small group of men followed their script at the mouth of the Fortymile River. The discoverers of gold on this river had already staked their ground on bars about forty miles from its mouth. The miners named them Franklin's Bar and Madden's Bar, after their discoverers. Each man took a claim 1,500 feet in length. This was late in the fall, so there was no time to recover any gold. The men who chose to stay at Fortymile faced a winter of deprivation, far from Harper's post; yet they would also have the advantage of a head start on the mining in the spring.

One of the men who came to the Fortymile River to winter over was Frank Buteau, a wiry, short Quebecker, thirty years of age, with a swarthy complexion, thick, dark eyebrows, and a mustache. Buteau had slowly worked his way west through the United States, starting first in Maine then spending some time in Wisconsin and Oregon before moving back into Canada. Buteau left Victoria in the winter of 1886 to try his luck in Juneau. From there, he left with twenty-one others for the Yukon, crossing the Chilkoot Pass and coming down the Yukon River in the fall. It was as much by luck as by design, therefore, that he and a small party of comrades found themselves at the mouth of the Fortymile River in the middle of October.

Buteau and two other French Canadians immediately built a cabin for the winter. They were located on an island about a mile above the mouth of the Fortymile River, part of a group of sixteen men huddled in three small cabins. The island was named Sixteen Liars Island, because of their alleged storytelling abilities. Below them, in another small cabin at the mouth of the Fortymile River, were five more men. These twenty-one men became the first citizens of the newborn community of Forty Mile. They lived their first winter there in total isolation, without material comfort and short of food.

The home that Buteau and his two partners built was nothing more than a small log shack, barely ten feet to a side, with a simple shed roof; it lacked even the most basic essentials. They had no stove or stovepipe, so they first built a chimney out of wood in the centre of the cabin, with an open fire beneath it – but this was too cold. Their second attempt, a 'Russian' furnace made out of mud and stones, was much more successful. They had no glass for a window, so they resorted to a block of clear river ice. Their shack provided them with little comfort; so cold was it that the same block of ice remained in the window, without melting, for the entire winter! Nor was their winter well illuminated, for they had only half a dozen candles.[5]

The men spent the winter preoccupied with the search for firewood and game. They set out to get some fresh meat for Christmas. Travelling in temperatures below minus forty degrees Fahrenheit, they camped out, got lost, and had to bivouac one night before they found their way home, exhausted and without any prize. They went out again, after resting briefly, and returned a few days later, loaded down with caribou. They spent Christmas, not celebrating, but hauling the last of the meat to their camp.

The only excitement that winter was the fall of a meteor, which was visible for hundreds of miles, the evening of 18 December 1886.[6] The men spent a lot of time telling stories and waiting for spring.

The Stampede to the Fortymile River

There were three stampedes to the Fortymile River in 1887: the first was the return of the men from the mouth of the Fortymile River to their diggings, which occurred early in the spring; the second was the rush of men from up the Stewart River or farther up on the Yukon bars; the third, and largest, was made up of those men on the Alaskan Panhandle, who, acting on newspaper accounts or letters from the Yukon, made their way in over the Chilkoot Pass.

The Fortymile men started upriver to prospect and mine in March, when the weather was suitable for work and travel. During the winter, the 'Sixteen Liars' had discussed the rules of conduct for their mining, and they agreed between themselves that 1500 feet was too large a claim, in view of all the others who would soon arrive. Instead, they reduced their claims to 300 feet.[7] They all departed, each certain in his own mind that he would be the winner in the gigantic lottery which he was entering.

While the Fortymilers were already mining on the Fortymile River, the men at Stewart River were eagerly awaiting the opportunity to leave for the new discovery. Twenty-five men abandoned the post and travelled on foot over the ice to reach the diggings before the flood of outsiders. Al Mayo was left behind, Fort Nelson's only occupant, to mind the post. The men farther up the Yukon River found it more difficult to make their way to Fortymile. Chris Sonnickson, who was among this group, had known about the new discovery since before Christmas, but could do little about it until break-up, which came on 16 May 1887. Along with the open water would come the vanguard of the stampede from outside. Sonnickson sold his bar claim to Missouri Frank, the exile from Fort Nelson, and headed downriver to the Fortymile district. The danger of running the Yukon River during break-up was recklessly disregarded by the stampeders, who were eager to find their fortune in the newly discovered gold fields. The massive blocks of broken ice were subject to the fickle currents of the Yukon River; constantly colliding and grinding against each other, these blocks could crush a canoe in an instant, drowning all passengers. Despite this, Sonnickson and others braved the river and arrived safely at the Stewart River.

The stampeders found Fort Nelson abandoned and short of supplies. The Stewart River broke up on 25 May, and Al Mayo got the tiny steamer, *New Racket*, ready for the trip downriver to St. Michael. On 31 May, he towed Sonnickson and a number of others to the Fortymile River behind the steamer. On 18 June, having formed a new partnership with Henry Davis, Sonnickson started upriver.[8] The stampede of outsiders came close on their heels.

The Fortymile River
The Fortymile River is not a major tributary of the Yukon River. It flows out of the rounded hills south of the 'great river,' most of its headwaters originating on American soil, and winds its way through the ranges of hills across the international border until, a few miles later, it enters the Yukon. Its main characteristics are its fast-flowing current and the

canyon at its lower end. Though not comparable to the Grand Canyon, the constriction of the river between the Canadian hills was not to be underestimated, particularly during high water. At least half a dozen men lost their lives here in 1887.

Tracking upstream through the canyon was brutal, cold, wet work, but it was the downstream passage that took lives. The first fatality that year was Tom Jones. One of a party of three, Jones had come out of the hills from the Sixtymile River. Arriving at the Fortymile River for the first time, Jones and his partner, known as 'Frenchy,' rafted downstream to get flour at Forty Mile. They did not see the canyon until it was too late; they were capsized and stranded on a rock in midstream. After two hours of being stuck in the middle of the river by a mere twenty feet of seemingly calm water, Jones finally decided to swim. He was drawn underwater by the current, and his body was recovered two miles downstream. He was buried in the frozen ground along the shore of the Fortymile River.

The death toll mounted over the course of the summer. The list included the names of Neal Lamont (who drowned a few days after Jones), Saffron, Johnson, Holmes, Wells, an unnamed miner, and a Native man, whose name is also unknown, and who, after capsizing in the canyon and mistakenly thinking that his entire family had drowned, cut his own throat.[9]

Travel down the Fortymile River in the fall, when it was low, did not make the journey any safer. A man known as Gus the Greek died tragically when his party tried to make its way through the ice-swollen channel. Travelling through near darkness, they found themselves stuck midstream, jammed into the river ice. Gus put a rope around his body and tried to crawl to shore on the ice, but he broke through. The others could not pull him out of the water, and he was dead from exposure by morning.[10]

Lady Luck's Lottery
In the summer of 1887, the extent and location of the gold on the Fortymile River were still unknown; the two hundred and fifty men on the river that summer were in turmoil. Constantly changing partners, and trying different locations, the miners kept searching for paying ground. There were three parties of miners working the bars below the canyon, near the US-Canadian border. The first one, about two miles up, was making ten to twelve dollars per day. The others, closer to the

canyon, were making even less.[11] Above the canyon, men were working on Franklin's Bar, Bonanza Bar, and Madden's Bar. Farther up, the river forked into a north and a south tributary, and the men were exploring these, too. Some tested the ground at Troublesome Point, and others went beyond, looking for the elusive streak of gold lying on the bedrock.

One group of miners caused a stampede when they went back down the Fortymile River for supplies and seemed to be in too much of a hurry to stop and talk to others. Suspicious, the other miners along the river stampeded upstream hoping to be the first to reach the new ground. When they caught up with the prospectors at Mosquito Forks, there was nothing. Meanwhile, new arrivals had taken their places on the bars downstream, which were now paying.[12]

Other miners, not satisfied with the results they were getting from their bar workings, sold out. Jack Raynor sold his bar claim forty miles up the Fortymile River to Richard Poplin for three hundred dollars. Poplin took twenty-six and a half ounces of gold in just two hours' worth of work – the largest nugget weighed half an ounce. Another miner, Hughes, took out two hundred and fifty dollars in one day's work.[13] Frank Buteau gained the name 'King of the Fortymile' for taking out $3,000 in gold from his claim on Bonanza Bar.[14] Not everyone was that lucky, and it was certainly not always the first one to arrive who made the big find. Recognizing that they could not allow the less fortunate miners to starve, a miners' committee resolved that any miner who did not have the gold to buy a winter's supply of food by 1 August was welcome to bring a rocker onto the paying claims in order to pan out a winter grubstake.

All of the work which had gone on to that point consisted of bar mining with the use of a rocker. In the spring, Skiff Mitchell and Mickey O'Brien, working on Franklin's Bar, used a water wheel for sluicing until the high water took it away. Some miners had built wing dams to divert water to their claims, but these, too, were washed away in the spring run-off.[15]

Up at Troublesome Point, Howard Franklin came to the conclusion that the gold they were getting had to come from somewhere. He went to the gulch above the point and staked a 1500-foot claim, naming it Franklin Gulch. This was where the first creek gold, lying below the surface, was found. The creek was staked, and the men immediately started to sluice to bedrock.

A New Town is Born

By midsummer of 1887, the miners who had been working their claims and prospecting since the early spring were running low on supplies; they returned to the mouth of the Fortymile River to wait for the steamer with its annual supply. At the end of June, the townsite at the confluence of the Fortymile and Yukon rivers was nothing more than a 'bluffy Point,' which had upon it 'a cache, and a notice board with some directions regarding points up the stream [the Fortymile River], and a few letters stuck to a tree, directed to parties outside.'[16]

About two dozen miners gathered at this point, waiting for the steamer and passing their time playing poker. By the third week in July, the steamer had still not arrived and supplies were getting short. A miners' meeting was convened, and the men resolved to break into the cache for provisions. A 'quantity of flour, bacon, coffee, sugar and other things, were removed by those in urgent need, and receipts made out and deposited for the owner.'[17] Three days later, the steamer was welcomed by the men, who were starved for news, goods, and food. 'Someone raised the Stars and Stripes,' said Henry Davis,

> the steamer blew its whistle like the band, and we all got out our guns and started shooting ... There was no sleep that night, for poor Al Mayo was talked blind. Everybody helped unload the boat. There were lots of willing hands. However, it was not a big load, only about ten tons of flour, beans, bacon, butter, sugar, but no fancy stuff ... Everybody got drunk and slept it off the next day.[18]

Harper set up a packing case as a counter right on the deck of the barge, with scales to weigh out the gold and the merchandise, and everything was gone within forty-eight hours.

Ten days later, another steamer arrived with one hundred tons of goods of every description, and word was sent up to Franklin's Bar that the supplies had arrived. Quickly, the stock of supplies was placed under canvas; meanwhile, the new trading post, the first real building in Forty Mile, was built. Harper, with Fred Hart as clerk, did a brisk business dispensing supplies while ensuring that no one got more than he needed. The prices were double or triple those in Juneau; flour sold at the exorbitant rate of $17.50 per hundred pounds, and the prices of other goods were equally high.[19]

They remembered to bring liquor with their shipment but had somehow overlooked gum boots. These were so important to the miners that Joe Wilson and his two partners left Forty Mile in September and headed for Juneau to retrieve the order. Trapped in vicious weather in the Chilkoot Pass, they stayed with the Native people there and did not get to Dyea until February 1888.[20]

The Canadian-Yukon Expedition

While the miners of the Fortymile River were exploring and mining its shores and tributaries, men with a different purpose entered the Yukon. Thomas White, the minister of the interior for the Canadian government, authorized George M. Dawson (of the Geological Survey of Canada) and William Ogilvie (Dominion Land Surveyor) to explore the Yukon Territory and to establish the Canadian-American boundary along the 141st meridian. Ogilvie came in over the Chilkoot Pass, while Dawson came in from the east, via the Liard and Pelly rivers.

Ogilvie arrived at Dyea in the spring of 1887. The first thing that he heard was Leslie's story of the Native uprising on the Stewart River.[21] Undaunted by this tale, he engaged Chilkat packers to carry their substantial supplies over the Chilkoot Pass, using George Carmack as a translator/intermediary. Although better subsidized for their undertaking than were the miners, the survey party followed the same route, building a boat by hand at Lake Bennett to carry their provisions downriver.

The party travelled down the Yukon River, encountering signs of mining activity below the mouth of the Teslin River. On 3 August, Ogilvie passed a party of men working Cassiar Bar, who, having little of the success of the year before, and having nearly worked out the bar, were trying to thaw the river bank with fire.[22]

Ogilvie stopped for three days at Fort Selkirk to confer with Dawson, who had just arrived from the Pelly River. After writing a brief report of his travels as well as letters to family and friends, he headed down the Yukon River, while Dawson headed upriver for the coast. Some miners had tried their luck on the Pelly River, but there was no word on their success.[23] The survey party continued downriver, taking time at the Thron-Duick River to observe that Native people had set its entire mouth with salmon traps, and that half a dozen families were camped on an island to tend them.[24] He reported that a miner had prospected up the Thron-Duick River to the edge of the mountains which fed it, but nothing came of this.

William Ogilvie, government surveyor, later commissioner of the Yukon Territory

Ogilvie arrived at Forty Mile in early September, and, after a brief excursion up the Fortymile River, he and his party set out to the boundary area to establish a camp for the winter. At this camp they hoped that readings could be taken to confirm the position of the 141st meridian. Later, in February 1888, they proceeded to the Fortymile River and marked the border where the line crossed it.

The arrival of a Canadian government official caused some consternation among the free-spirited and mainly American miners, many of whom treated him with suspicion.[25] Yet when Ogilvie was in Forty Mile, they did not hesitate to approach him with questions regarding mining regulations, which he answered to the best of his knowledge.[26] Forty Mile was an American town on Canadian soil, and it would be seven years before another Canadian government official would return. So the men of Forty Mile carried on as if there were no boundary, abiding by their own rules and the miners' code. Ogilvie departed for the outside in the spring of 1888, travelling to the north and, finally, to the east, following the old HBC routes on his way back to 'civilization.' When he reported to the deputy minister of the interior, A.M. Burgess, he advised him not to interfere with the region for, although on Canadian soil, most of the miners were foreigners, and any effort to interfere would drive them back to the American side of the border, thus greatly hindering exploration on the Canadian side.[27]

That winter, 160 men stayed near the Forty Mile post, and another 120 stayed in the Stewart River area. The winter was the mildest in fourteen years; 23 December was the coldest day, at minus fifty-five degrees Fahrenheit.[28] The supply of food that winter was not very diverse, but there was enough for all. Around Christmas, a party of Native people were hungry enough to go hunting. They obtained a good supply of caribou and were able to bring down a ton of fresh meat, which they sold to the miners at ten cents a pound.[29] Despite the availability of supplies, there were three dozen sick miners that winter, most of them suffering from scurvy (although only one man died of this particular scourge).[30]

6

STRANGERS IN A
STRANGE LAND

Poor Eating, Poor Health

'If you could see the food we had to eat from 1886 to 1893,' said Frank Buteau 'you might laugh, but if you found yourself a thousand miles from civilization, without roads, as it were, it might bring tears to your eyes.'[1] In the early period of Yukon development, the supply of food was neither good nor reliable. There were three ways for the miners to supply their food: (1) they could bring their own supplies with them; (2) they could supply themselves from the land; or (3) they could seek provisions from the AC Co. trading post. None of these methods was totally satisfactory. Those who brought their own supplies often lost and/or damaged them on the trip down the Yukon River (the food becoming mouldy from exposure to moisture); hunting for game was hit and miss; and the food provided by the AC Co. was far from satisfactory: 'one could easily see from the brands and quality of goods received that they [the trading companies] did not want any miners in the Yukon River Valley. The bacon was in slabs three feet long, all of which was yellow. We called it "Yard Bacon." The flour was mouldy, the rice was lumpy, the fruit was green and in the beans were plenty of rocks and gravel.'[2] Chris Sonnickson remembered the poor condition of the food:

I – and I can answer for 16 other men – got flour in the fall [of 1889] ...
that had been soaked in salt water for several days then shipped up the
river, where, while aboard the steamer, it had been soaked and heated, so
that we had to chop a sack, or rather split it lengthwise, like cordwood. In
the middle we could get about 15 pounds of hard lumps that were not

green or yellow like the rest. This we had to powder with a hammer and run it through a sieve before we could use it.[3]

As happened in previous years, any interruption in the tenuous water-supply link caused a shortage of supplies and either an exodus from the Yukon or wholesale starvation. Even in later years, when the supply lines were more reliable, so obsessed were many miners with the quest for gold that they suffered as a consequence of neglecting their own well being. Sergeant M.H.E. Hayne of the North-West Mounted Police (NWMP) saw one of these pitiable characters on the Yukon River in 1895:

> A solitary man who was making his way down to Forty Mile in a boat ... had been up at Sixty Mile all winter – it was now the end of July – and they had run out of food up there ... They had not tasted sugar or salt at Sixty Mile all winter, and they were simply 'existing' – how it is impossible to say – until a steamer should come up with provisions ... He had been sent down as a last despairing measure to see if they had been forgotten.[4]

The variety, as well as the supply, of food was limited.[5] Although the traders were growing vegetables in small gardens at their trading posts, and a few individuals had their own supply, many men went for years without fresh vegetables.[6] The main staple in the diet was flour, which was used to make bannock. Men could and did supplement their diet with fresh berries (in season), moose, bear, and caribou as well as several varieties of fish, including what was taken from the annual salmon run. In fact, by 1894, a small commercial salmon-smoking operation at the mouth of the Klondike River was supplying some food to the miners at Forty Mile.[7] They even developed a substitute for butter, known as 'bone butter.' It was produced by boiling bones and horn for an extended period of time, then adding salt to the mixture before allowing it to cool and congeal, forming a white buttery substance.[8]

But the unpredictability of these food sources meant that they were not always able to enjoy the delight of fresh game. Poor diet (combined with hard work and a harsh climate), ignorance of the origin of disease, and a lack of medical practitioners created serious health problems. Diseases such as dyspepsia, anemia, rheumatism, pneumonia, bronchitis, enteritis, and cystitis were common afflictions.[9] Tuberculosis, or consumption (as it was commonly known), took many of the early miners, who were worn out after years of privation.

Of these diseases, the most insidious and poorly understood was scurvy. Caused by a lack of vitamin C, it was commonly thought to be the result of 'improperly cooked food, sameness of diet, overwork, want of fresh vegetables, overheated and badly ventilated houses'[10] and lack of exercise.[11] It invariably set in with the confinement of winter. The patient first developed excruciating pain in his extremities. The parts affected would swell, discolour (sometimes turning black), and the skin would lose its natural resiliency (one could pinch the skin and the impression would remain, as if made in putty). The gums became sore and started to bleed; the teeth loosened and fell out. The illness progressed for weeks or months, the patient suffering incredibly and slowly weakening, while his partners watched helplessly. The condition would usually be made worse by the mistaken notion that abundant exercise would prevent the disease.[12] Ironically, while these victims suffered cruelly, the cure for the disease was already well known. The miners later recognized the curative value of willow, spruce, juniper, sage, and 'Hudson's Bay Tea.'

The long, cold winters took their toll on the careless and foolhardy, while even the most careful veteran could experience great suffering from frostbite due to accidentally stepping into overflow on the trail or falling through thin ice. Excessive exertion in cold weather leads to hypothermia, and the victim may slowly freeze to death.[13] Steve Custer, a miner who severely froze his feet, was forced to travel to St. Michael, a distance of 1,000 miles, to have his toes amputated.[14] There were no doctors or hospitals in the Yukon basin, so the miners resorted to home remedies or nothing at all.

Be It Ever So Humble ...

If a miner stayed in one area for any length of time, he was likely to build some kind of shelter; if he stayed the winter, it was essential that he do so. Shelters were constructed of logs, both because of the availability of wood and because of the ease with which log shacks could be built using only tools such as axes and augers. Some of the early buildings were constructed in the style of the HBC – horizontal, tenoned logs of intermediate length inserted into mortises in vertical posts.[15] This style was quickly supplanted by a style which utilized horizontal logs notched and overlapping at the corners. These came into place in the early 1880s, as the miners who filtered into the territory began to winter over.

These log buildings were very crude shelters which, at first, did a poor

First log cabin at Forty Mile

job of keeping out the cold.[16] While bar mining on the upper Yukon River in the winter of 1886-7, for instance, Chris Sonnickson lived in a small cabin which had a square hole in the roof. A rock hearth on the floor of the cabin held the fire. As soon as the fire went out, it was as cold inside the cabin as it was outside. Furthermore, such cabins were very smoky.[17]

The advent of the warm cabin followed the strike at Fortymile. The 'Russian' furnace, constructed from rocks and clay, was used before the iron stove. These were, in fact, very functional, holding the heat for a long time.[18] The early cabins did not have wooden floors.[19] By 1888, stoves started coming into the country in quantity. The men no longer suffered the incredible cold as they had in the past. As Henry Davis remarked, there was 'no more smoke in the cabin, no more baking bread in gold pans in the wintertime.'[20]

Due to a shortage of window glass, everything from stretched skin to cloth and bottles was used as window coverings. The interiors of cabins were furnished with wooden fittings made from local timber.[21] These buildings were covered with a sod roof, which kept in the heat in the winter but leaked terribly during the summer rains. These cabins were not considered permanent dwellings. Usually in the spring, when the ground being prospected did not live up to expectations, they were abandoned. Only later, when creeks started producing more gold, did the miners build

Interior of an early cabin. A 'Russian' furnace keeps William Ogilvie's survey party warm.

permanent log structures.[22] Log caches, usually raised off the ground on four posts, were constructed near the cabins to store additional supplies.

Another problem with cabins had to do with lighting. Good lighting was provided by kerosene or candles. The former, though better for illumination, was costly and difficult to transport. J.E. McGrath, in charge of an American boundary survey party, reported that his supply of lamp oil was so small that the survey cabin could only be illuminated four hours per day during the long, dark winter months. This was a government party and better supplied than was the average sourdough. The sourdoughs often resorted to the use of a 'Yukon lamp,' a twisted bit of cotton inserted into a container filled with oil rendered from wild game.[23]

As almost everything was in short supply, the miners found themselves stretching their ingenuity to the limit in order to supply their needs. Tin cans were used for everything from gold pokes, tea pots, and lamps to the brewing of hootch.[24] The gold pan served universally as a cooking implement as well as a mining device. Bishop William Bompas once found himself so short of boards that he had to use a cupboard and shelves from his church to make a coffin for a dead parishioner.

Necessity became the mother of invention. During the winter of 1887-8, some of the picks used by the miners had been heavily worn and required resteeling. John Nelson and Frank Buteau set up a crude blacksmith shop at Forty Mile to do this work. According to Buteau, they had to improvise to get the job done:

> We had to fashion tools out of the crude materials on hand as we had no blacksmith equipment of any kind. We made a bellows out of moose skin which had been tanned by the Indians only to find that it was porous and allowed the air to escape through the skin. We then melted moose tallow and coated the inside of the skin with it after which the bellows worked satisfactorily for our purpose. We used a boulder for an anvil and a pole axe for a sledge. We made charcoal and used it for blacksmithing as there was no coal available.[25]

While Nelson and Buteau were constructing the shop, Joe Ladue made the trip up the Yukon River to Fort Nelson to obtain the steel and borax necessary for blacksmithing.

Closed Book

Just as the material comforts of the men were limited, so were the social opportunities. Everyone clustered around the trading posts during the winter to be near a supply source as well as for social contact. The Yukon, in the winter, was so isolated from the outside world that it might as well have been on another planet.[26] For this reason, the men had to create their own forms of entertainment.

Three of the favourite pastimes in the early days were the telling of stories or jokes, singing, and gambling.[27] Storytelling was a particularly favourite activity, especially in the period before liquor was abundant and the miners had taken to winter drift mining. William Ogilvie described the antics of the Fortymilers in the winter of 1887-8:

> A camp of seven or eight miners was formed on an island in the Yukon a mile or two above Fortymile. This group developed such inventive powers in story-telling that the island became known as 'Liars' Island,' and the denizens, the 'Forty Liars,' it being held that though only seven or eight in number, they were equal in talent to the forty liars in story. The miners evidently had in mind liars instead of thieves. This club held regular meetings which as many outsiders attended as room could be found for in the small cabin club-room ... The stories were generally confined for the evening to one subject, and each story might be commented on or reflected on without offence.[28]

The subject matter of the stories included food and camp supplies or the sagacity of animals. In a community lacking in practically every amenity, the hyperbole that was heaped upon the former subject was particularly ironic.

Gambling was almost universal among the miners, poker being a favourite game. One of the inviolable rules was that, although it was acceptable to bluff, no one could cheat. And they would bet on just about anything. They would bet on when the river ice would break up or who could spit closest to a crack on the trading post floor. Once, they even bet half an ounce of gold on whether the next man to enter the room would do so with his right or his left foot.[29]

Chris Sonnickson brought a pair of skates with him in the winter of 1887, using them not for sport but for transportation. The tracks baffled the Native people, who followed them to see what made them. To pass the time in his winter camp, Sonnickson and his companions fashioned boxing gloves and amused themselves as well as the Native people who came to watch them.[30]

The men observed special events, the most important of which was Christmas. In 1882, the party of men who wintered over with Jack McQuesten at Fort Reliance had snow-shovelling contests, foot races, and a special Christmas meal. The Native people joined in the celebration and had a moose-skin toss (an event which remained for years after). In later years, Christmas also meant a lot of drinking and dancing as well as eating, and the men usually had a hangover that lasted for days.[31]

Another event which the men celebrated was the Fourth of July. A group of miners who entered the Yukon in the summer of 1887 celebrated the American holiday on their bar claim at the lower end of the Fortymile River. In preparation for the celebration, they brewed a concoction which was made of sourdough, hops, oatmeal, and a little sugar. This proved quite drinkable. From their supplies, they improvised a meal of baked pork and beans (frontier style) and a boiled plum duff. The latter was embellished with a sauce made from pain killer (such patent medicines were liberally spiked with opiates before the twentieth century), and this, combined with the special home-brew, they enjoyed very much. Typical of the isolation in the North, they once lost track of the actual date, and some late arrivals at their party informed them that the great holiday had actually passed two days before.[32]

7

YEARS OF CHANGE

Beginning with the Fortymile stampede, the pace of life in the Yukon kicked up a gear. The discovery of coarse gold in the bed of the Fortymile River was enough to stimulate the interest of many Juneau men and, from then on, a steady stream of prospectors surged into the Yukon every summer in search of their own mother lode. For the next decade, Forty Mile became the major supply point for miners in the Yukon Valley.

This was also the beginning of many changes for the prospectors who came into the Yukon. The supply of food and other merchandise became both more abundant and more diverse. Small comforts, such as decent stoves, became, for the first time, commonplace. Liquor began to flow into the Yukon valley and the mouths of the men who dotted the countryside. For the first time, there developed a small corps of men who spent their time, not looking for gold, but serving the miners, and saloons began to establish themselves as social centres. The miners who came into the Yukon earlier in the decade, and who later formed the Yukon Order of Pioneers, considered 1888 a turning point, after which, in their eyes, the integrity of the newcomers declined.

Fort Nelson, which only a couple of years before had been the centre of community life on the Yukon River, was an abandoned shell. When George Snow first arrived at the site in the summer of 1888, he found vacant cabins with 'sagging ridgepoles, windowless openings and gaping doorways ... Desolation was the keynote of the whole scene.'[1] Stripped of anything of value, the cabins looked as if they had been abandoned for ten years rather than for one. The trading post was boarded up, and a message from Al Mayo was left on the door, stating that he had gone to St. Michael for grub. Indicating that Mayo expected to be back by the middle of September, the note went on to tell the readers where they might find the key to the food supply and closed with a trusting request to leave a memorandum listing what they took.[2] That same summer, new discoveries were made on Davis Creek in the Fortymile region.

The experience of Chris Sonnickson that summer captures the flavour of the constant quest of the true prospector. Spring found him below the American border, far downriver from the frozen bar on the upper Yukon River, where he spent his first winter. On 1 April 1888 he struck out across country for a two-month prospecting trip, alone and living off the land. Heading for a nearby range of mountains, he hauled three hundred pounds of gear, all of which had to be transported by double tracking. During this trip, he was caught on a glacier in bad weather and froze his foot. In severe pain, and recovering from the injury, he made camp and spent twenty-two sleepless days, immobile and incapable of hunting. Finally, he recovered to the point where he was able to construct a wooden shoe to replace the defective moccasin which had been responsible for all his suffering.

Despite being low on supplies, he waited another eight days before the river level, swollen with the spring run-off, lowered enough to be navigable. Alone, and travelling downriver in a hand-built craft, he encountered a stretch of boulders which broke both his oars and stranded him on a rock in midstream. By careful manoeuvring, he made it to shore and saved his rifle and supplies. The mishap proved fortunate for him, for around the next bend in the river was a waterfall, over which he would most certainly have plummeted had he not already come ashore. Setting his craft adrift above the falls, he was able to catch it farther downstream. After this, he travelled very cautiously downriver, at a much slower, but safer, pace than before. He eventually arrived back at his camp, a week late, but, much to the relief of his partner, alive.[3]

He then prospected with three other men, Tom O'Brien, T. Evans, and 'Old Herman' on the Beaver River. On this excursion they were not alone; word circulated that there was a new discovery on this Yukon River tributary, and a number of men stampeded to it. It was about this time that Sonnickson got word that something was going on downriver; a story reached the miners that a White man had been murdered on the Koyukuk River.[4]

The Bremner Murder

Old John Bremner had been prospecting up the Koyukuk River. Heading out in June 1888, and being short of food, he encountered Jim Bender and a small party of prospectors, who loaned him a boat and a few days' worth of provisions to help him get to the mouth of the Koyukuk River. Bremner carried with him a rifle and a shotgun.

The old man stopped one day at noon at a Native camp along the river to prepare a meal. He invited a young man from the village to share the meal of duck and tea with him. After he was finished, the old man began reloading his supplies in the boat and, while he was bending over attending to this task, the young man, according to later accounts, picked up his shotgun and shot him. The impact threw Bremner into the river and he was never seen again. John Minook and a small party of others had been travelling down the river behind Bremner. Suddenly losing track of him, Minook set about to determine his whereabouts. Alarmed, he sent word to all local communities about the mysterious circumstances of Bremner's disappearance.

On 4 July Bender and his party learned of the disappearance and boated down the Koyukuk River to the Yukon River and, from there, to Nulato. At Nulato, they boarded a steamer that was headed upriver and arrived at Nuklukayet. The news seemed to electrify the men at this small settlement below the mouth of the Tanana River. A miners' meeting was quickly called, and the consensus was that a party would return to the Koyukuk River, set on avenging Bremner's death.

A couple of days later, the steamer *Explorer* arrived at Nuklukayet, pushing two barges. Against the wishes of the skipper, a vigilante committee appropriated the vessel and, leaving the barges in protective custody at Nuklukayet, twenty men (now worked into a passionate frenzy) set out down the Yukon River for the Koyukuk River.[5] Travelling hastily, the party stopped at regular intervals to refuel. At each stop, the men swarmed ashore and, working at a fever pitch, rapidly resupplied the vessel with cordwood. Gordon Bettles, who had been appointed captain of the boat for this expedition, directed the tiny craft up the Koyukuk River. John Minook, a mixed-blood who knew the region well, served as guide and translator as the boat travelled 140 miles up this Yukon River tributary, only stopping at night while the men camped ashore.

The miners were set for a major conflict. As they approached the camp where Bremner was believed to have disappeared, they became very quiet, and lookouts were posted on either side of the pilot house to watch for signs of trouble. The others quietly oiled their guns and checked their ammunition, certain that there was going to be a serious confrontation. When they neared the camp where the crime had been committed, the miners decided that they would burn any caches that they saw in order to teach the 'Indians' a lesson. Inspecting a cache in one camp, they found some of the tools from Bremner's outfit, his name clearly visible on them. They also found his boat, torn to pieces. Yet the confrontation, when it occurred, was anticlimactic.

Upon arriving at the Native camp they sought, they landed the boat, made a flanking manoeuvre, and captured their suspects without any shots being fired. Young Silas, an eighteen-year-old Native, and his elderly uncle were taken back to the mouth of the Koyukuk River, where, according to the participants, they conducted a fair trial before finding the younger man guilty of the crime. Silas did admit his guilt in the case, apparently without remorse. Though the miners wanted to implicate the uncle as well, they could not find the older man guilty.

To carry out their punishment, the miners tied a pole horizontally between two trees, about ten feet off the ground, and tossed a rope over it. Before slipping the noose over Silas's head, they greased the knot with lard to ensure that it slipped quickly and tightly into place. Every man in the committee got into the act, pulling together on the rope, sharing in the execution. After the hanging, all of the miners were satisfied that justice had been done and were in good spirits. They left the lifeless body dangling where it was, clearly visible to all Yukon travellers, as a warning to other Native people not to commit a similar offence.

The miners, having fulfilled their mission, started back up the Yukon River to Nuklukayet, but they stopped at a Native encampment to warn them not to murder any more prospectors. They left Silas's uncle, now a considerable distance from his kin, with the substantial task of walking overland to his camp on the Koyukuk River. Exhausted, and more than a little disappointed at not having had a shoot-out, the party returned to the mouth of the Tanana River.

The night of their return, they had a big meeting, and both Jack McQuesten and Al Mayo gave speeches to congratulate the men on the 'fine thing' they had done for Alaska. Although the missionaries decried their deed as an act of cruelty, the miners defended themselves, saying that, in this case, it was an innocent White man, with his back turned, who had been killed.[6] In fact, the passive response of the Natives to the heavily armed posse who went up the Koyukuk River expecting to avenge the killing with a bloodbath was most disconcerting to these men. Carrying with them visions of the confrontations reminiscent of the American west,[7] the miners expressed disappointment over the quiet resolution of the crime. Yet the history of the Yukon placer miners is, for the most part, peaceful. For those men who expected to live a repeat of the wild west, they discovered that the search for gold and the struggle for survival were paramount.[8]

Nearly three hundred men entered the Yukon basin in 1889 to look for gold. Attracted by the prospects of the Fortymile region, most of the miners had abandoned the Stewart River, with the exception of Al Mayo, who travelled upriver that summer on the *New Racket* and attempted to mine with a steam pump powered by his boat. In addition, three large wheels were constructed on the Stewart River to work low-grade deposits on high banks, but they failed due to the permafrost.[9] New discoveries were made in the Fortymile region on Poker Creek and Walker Fork. This same year, on O'Brien Creek, William Moore and his two partners constructed a ditch one-third of a mile long to provide water for mining. After having been trading partners for many years, Arthur Harper and Jack McQuesten split up, the former moving up the Yukon River to establish a trading post at Fort Selkirk.

Buxton Mission

While most of the men were out searching for gold, a new outpost was being established at Forty Mile. J.W. Ellington, an Anglican deacon, was sent by the Church Missionary Society to serve Bishop William Bompas in the Yukon. In the fall of 1886, Ellington and another missionary, George C. Wallis, set out with Archdeacon Robert MacDonald and his wife for Rampart House. Here, the two young missionaries set about learning their language and preaching to the Loucheux. Bompas, perhaps sensing the immaturity and/or instability of Ellington, preferred assigning him to a post where he was not alone. However, the young deacon finally had to set out by himself. The following summer, he set out to Fort Yukon and, late in the summer of 1887, he proceeded to the mouth of the Fortymile River, where he joined the new community of Forty Mile.

Immediately upon his arrival at Forty Mile (the mission which was built there was called the Buxton Mission after its British benefactor),

Ellington started holding services for the Native people from the area. The following year, Ellington travelled up the Yukon River to Fort Reliance and the mouth of the Stewart River to meet the local Natives. Upon his return to Forty Mile, he found that the Native people were nearing the completion of the mission house, and that a start had been made on a separate school structure.

Ellington's plans for construction, however, were never completed. He found himself amidst a growing population of miners, and he was never able to adapt to their ways. He was soon victimized by the miners' practical jokes, in debt to the local trading post, and having trouble with his Native parishioners. By the summer of 1889, he was clearly unstable. Ellington made an unexpected visit to Reverend Thomas H. Canham at Tanana Station. The Buxton Mission had been disassembled and was being moved to a new location, but he was not able to have it rebuilt. He would return to Forty Mile, he said, if Canham would accompany him. When the upriver steamer arrived at Tanana Station, there was room for Ellington but not for Canham, who vowed to follow him on the next boat, the *Arctic*.

Unfortunately, the *Arctic* was wrecked on its journey upstream and did not appear with the badly needed winter supplies for the miners; and Canham, as a result, could not follow Ellington. Later, the Forty Mile missionary wrote Canham saying he was busy rebuilding the mission house and was determined to stay at Buxton Mission. A year later, however, Canham found him in a state of complete mental breakdown, and he had to be escorted from the country. As a consequence, the Buxton Mission at Forty Mile was left abandoned, and the Native people and miners were unattended by the church for the next two years.[10]

Starvation Winter

The wreck of the *Arctic* had more serious implications than Canham's unfulfilled appointment. The supply of goods, particularly food, had always been tenuous in the early days of the Yukon.[11] When news reached Forty Mile that the supply steamer was not going to reach the town by freeze-up, there was widespread panic. Jack McQuesten sent word up the Fortymile River that there was not enough food to carry the population over the winter and warned the men to leave the region. The word spread like wildfire, and the miners gathered at Forty Mile to discuss what action to take. Although many decided to stay, a hundred men chose to leave. McQuesten put the *New Racket* at their disposal, with Al Mayo as captain and Morris Johnson as engineer. The steamer departed on 10 October 1889 with enough grub to last a few days.

The progress of the party was hampered by a number of calamities. They were delayed in departing the second morning because one of the miners, Lauzon, had become deranged and had wandered off on his own. After he was found, the party continued downriver. They made good progress until the boat was stranded on a sandbar. With the aid of long poles, several men climbed into the frigid waters of the freezing Yukon River and pried the boat free. The progress was stopped again when sixteen of the miners, including Lambert, Lauzon, and Hamilton, decided to winter at Rampart House. The vessel reached the Tanana River in fine, cold weather, with ice running on the river. Three more miners were dropped off at Nuklukayet and two were dropped of at Kokerines. By the time they reached Nulato, the river conditions were too bad to continue; the boat was beached on 18 October.

The miners waited at Nulato for three weeks, while the river froze for the winter, living on supplies they either bought or obtained from the Roman Catholic mission or the Natives. When the river ice was solid enough to support travel, the party departed on foot, accompanied by Natives with dog teams, for St. Michael, 190 miles overland.

Travel was difficult and exhausting. The river ice was rough and there were many ice jams which slowed their progress. In other places, the Yukon River had not frozen, and the men had to go ashore in order to detour the ice jams. In two and a half days, they reached Kaltag, where two men detached themselves from the party and continued downriver for Anvik. The remainder set out across country for Unalakleet. They travelled through two feet of snow, with only a few members of the expedition carrying snowshoes; every step of the way sapped their energy and drained their will. Without snowshoes, the men would constantly break through the hardpack and flail about in the knee-deep drifts. The men with snowshoes broke trail for the dog teams. Bivouacking each night in frigid November conditions, the thirty men plus their dogs managed to travel the eighty miles to Unalakleet in four days.

Both Oscar Carlson, the Swedish missionary, and the Native people at Unalakleet treated their guests with hospitality. The latter entertained the miners with dances and songs, while Carlson provided them with two days' worth of provisions. They then continued on the remaining sixty-mile portion of their journey. Travel along the coast of the Bering Sea was not pleasant; the terrain is unobstructed, and the wind blows with terrible force across the open ice. When the wind picks up in velocity, it causes the coastal ice to fracture and separate from the shore, carrying unfortunate passengers out to sea.

The men reached St. Michael on the third day and met with an apprehensive Henry Newman, the company trader, who feared that the new arrivals were an unsavoury lot. However, the men were able, with one exception, to pay their own way. They slept in two log houses and ate at a mess. They appointed one man to be cook, two others to be his assistants, and one to cut wood. The remainder of the men foraged along the coast for driftwood to keep the fires burning. The AC Co. provided them with books to read, and, with plenty of talking and jokes, they got through the winter in good spirits.[12]

And what of those who stayed behind at Forty Mile? They, too, survived the winter. With the pressure on supplies reduced by the large-scale emigration in October, the prospects for those who remained were substantially improved. When Frank Buteau received the news of impending famine on 7 October, he had just formed a mining partnership with Pete MacDonald, George Matlock, and John Campbell. They decided that they would stay in Forty Mile that winter to whipsaw lumber for the flume they planned to build on the claims they had just purchased. They were low on food but managed to kill forty caribou. Matlock, MacDonald, and their wives survived the winter living on two sacks of mouldy flour, a few mouldy beans, and a few pounds of dry fruit. Buteau and Campbell had nothing but a single sack of flour and a few pounds of beans from 10 October to 1 July the following year.[13] An American boundary survey party survived the winter on an abundance of wild game, a thousand pounds of turnips, and a meagre ration of bread.[14] Everyone had slim rations that winter, but no one starved.

In 1890, three hundred miners were located in the Yukon basin. The *Arctic* was refloated and began to make more regular trips into the interior. Being newer and larger than the previous river vessels, it represented the gradual change which was taking place in the country as the population and gold production increased.

Eighteen ninety was also the first year in which a new route to the interior was opened up. The Chilkat Pass was jealously guarded by the coastal Tlingit, who denied White people access; but in the spring, a party of White men changed all that. Working for an American newspaper, *Frank Leslie's Illustrated Magazine*, E.J. Glave, E. Hazard Wells, and A.B. Schanz crossed the Chilkat Pass under the guidance of Jack Dalton, a seasoned northern veteran. The party arrived at Lake Arkell (which is now called Kusawa Lake) and divided into two groups. The first, consisting of Glave and Dalton, struck out overland to the west; the latter, including Wells and Schanz, continued to the mouth of Lake Arkell and into the Takhini River, from which they entered the Yukon just above Lake Laberge.

Glave and Dalton had an exciting journey overland along the Alsek River (now known as the Tatshenshini River), down which they travelled, stopping at Native encampments and chronicling the countryside as they went. They eventually arrived at the mouth of the Alsek River.

Wells and Schanz travelled down the Yukon River, arriving at Harper's new post at Fort Selkirk on 18 June 1890, and encountering Al Mayo on the *New Racket* (which was carrying a few prospectors to the Pelly River) two days later. They arrived at Forty Mile on 22 June, where, due to Schanz's ill health, Wells continued on alone. Departing Forty Mile on 3 July, Wells started upriver and arrived, a week later, at Franklin Gulch, near the upper limit of the gold-bearing creeks on the Fortymile River. Here he found forty miners, each working placer claims of 150 feet. The miners, usually working in partnerships of two or more men, were mining a zigzag paystreak some six feet below the surface and were making from six to seventeen dollars per day each. Those who were being paid a wage were receiving eight dollars per day; everyone was making money, but few were doing much better than that.

Wells continued his trek overland from the upper reaches of the Fortymile River until he reached the Tanana River, down which he travelled, arriving at St. Michael in September. He spent the winter travelling overland through Alaska and eventually arrived back in Washington state in the spring. This expedition was the first of a succession of journeys made by 'gentleman travellers' through the Yukon over the next few years. These observers left their mark on the history of the region in the written accounts of their travels. Glave and Dalton returned the following year to further explore the southwest Yukon. As a result of their discoveries, a new route into the interior was established. The famed Dalton Trail was used by Jack Dalton to transport horses and cattle north to the Yukon River and then downstream to Forty Mile. The trail became one of the minor routes of access to the Klondike River during the gold rush.

Eighteen ninety-one was significant because gold was discovered in paying quantities on Miller Creek.[15] In the ensuing stampede and the adjustments in claims which followed, the discoverer's original discovery claim was relocated, despite his protests. Ironically, his new claim proved to be the richest on the creek, and the one which he was forced to vacate was one of the poorest. This was also the year that agriculture was first introduced to Forty Mile. Jack McQuesten used a plough, drawn by two moose (named Kate and Susan), to break up the land, but the animals soon broke down and were replaced by Native labourers, six of whom were hooked up to the plough. The work cost McQuesten several hundred dollars,[16] and one of his moose was killed by a miner, who mistook it for a wild member of the species.

In 1892, another turn of events occurred which would affect the growing population of the Yukon. Newspaper reports during the summer detailed the business transactions of John J. Healy, who had secured backing from several Chicago financiers. By mid-July, Healy and his wife were reported preparing to leave Seattle with the components for a sternwheeler, including the timbers, machinery, and boiler, all headed for the mouth of the Yukon River.[17] By fall, the *Portus B. Weare* had been assembled and it steamed as far as Nulato before winter set in. The following spring, after break-up, the party continued upriver to Forty Mile, where the new post of Fort Cudahy was established at the mouth of the Fortymile River, on the opposite side of the river from the rest of the community.

By the fall of 1893, Healy had established a post competitive with that of McQuesten and, consequently, drove prices down. Where one hundred pounds of flour had sold for fifteen dollars in 1891, the price dropped to eight dollars in 1893. Other staples had dropped by similar amounts.[18] Healy's store also carried a larger stock of goods than did McQuesten's operation across the river.[19] Healy may have been responsible for the lowering of prices, but his practice of billing promptly for his services made him very unpopular among the miners.

Meanwhile, in the years since Arthur Harper and his family were dropped off at the mouth of the Pelly River with a large outfit of trading goods, the post at Fort Selkirk had become well established. In the summer of 1892, Reverend T.H. Canham established a mission at the post, while that winter Joe Ladue was busy sawing lumber. Also, a Native village had grown up adjacent to the post.

The following year, Harper and Ladue established a post (which con-

Joe Ladue's trading post at Ogilvie, near the mouth of the Sixtymile River, c. 1894

sisted of a sawmill and a store) on an island at the mouth of the Sixtymile River. This meant that it was accessible to both the miners on the Sixtymile River and those who travelled down the Yukon River. As many as one hundred miners wintered over at this post.[20] From this location, Ladue gave information to prospectors about developments in the region, and he actively encouraged them to try their luck on the tributaries surrounding his post.

By 1893, the mining in Fortymile was starting to stabilize. Mining began on Dome Creek that year, while activity continued in Nugget, Poker, and Franklin gulches, Davis Creek, and Bettles' Mine.[21] Rather than move around from one prospect to another as new 'discoveries' were announced, many of the miners were establishing themselves on one of the reliable, producing creeks. Jack McQuesten reported that almost 250 miners were at work on six main creeks in the vicinity of Fortymile, the most heavily mined and productive of these being Miller Creek, where eighty men were employed, and $100,000 in gold was produced out of a total reported production of $195,000.[22]

The following year, over $400,000 worth of gold was produced in the Fortymile region, with the lion's share coming from Miller Creek. Frank Cormier left the Yukon with $33,000 after his clean-up and the sale of his Miller Creek claim. William Leggett and Pete Wyborg each made $15,000 from the sale of their respective claims, Leggett selling his share so he could move on to greener pastures in the newly discovered gold field of Birch

Creek.[23] The placer deposits on Wade Creek were discovered in 1895, and those on Chicken Creek were found in the spring of 1896.

By this time, mining was no longer restricted to the bars of the main tributaries of the Yukon River; drift mining was coming into its own as a technique of gold production. Until the beginning of the 1890s, mining was largely restricted by the weather. Once it started to freeze in the fall (which could come as soon as early September), mining ceased due to the lack of free running water, an essential requirement for sluicing. The miners could be unproductive for as much as eight months due to the weather.

Drift mining had been practised, occasionally, for many years. The first recorded instance of thawing being employed (which is essential to drift mining) was in 1882, by Jack McQuesten, Joe Ladue, and others on the Sixtymile River. When the thawing method was perfected is unclear, but by the 1890s, on the creeks of the Fortymile River it was in general use. Where the overburden was deep enough, around fifteen to twenty feet, fires would be set on a selected location and, as the ground thawed, it was regularly excavated before it could freeze again. Then another fire would be set, and more ground would be thawed and excavated, so that, day by day, a shaft was slowly sunk into the permanently frozen ground. Since it was as hard as granite, it was not necessary to extensively crib the walls of the excavation.

Eventually, the shaft would reach solid bedrock. From there, horizontal tunnels, or drifts, would be excavated, usually at right angles to the incline of the creek valley, so that, it was hoped, the paystreak would be intercepted. The excavated material, which was dragged along the drifts to the bottom of the shaft, was raised from the bottom by a hand-powered windlass and was piled up nearby. This material was tested regularly for the presence of gold. If a paystreak was found, the material excavated would be stockpiled in a 'dump' near the entrance of the shaft. Underground, a series of galleries would be started which would follow the paystreak, with occasional pillars of frozen ground left in place to support the roof and to prevent cave-ins.

The material in the galleries was thawed using wood fires, and the chamber was evacuated until the fire had subsided. Due to natural convection, in the winter the stale air, smoke, and fumes were displaced by fresh, cold air, and the miners could safely re-enter the drift to excavate the freshly thawed ground. The temperature in the shafts never went above freezing for obvious reasons, but it could be substantially warmer at the bottom of a shaft than above it; it was often more comfortable to labour below than to labour above. Work would proceed in this fashion through the winter, and the drifts would be abandoned in the spring before the warmer temperatures made further work unsafe.

Because of the problems associated with thawing, melt water, and the risk of collapse, it was unsafe to attempt this method of mining in the summer. In addition, the convection ventilation was not as effective at warmer temperatures, and the shafts would remain fouled with smoke, fumes, and carbon monoxide.

In the spring, the next phase of the operation commenced. Flumes and sluice boxes were constructed, and the melt water, as soon as it started to flow, was directed through the latter. The material which had been stored up in the dump over the winter was then shovelled into the sluice, and the gold was recovered during regular clean-ups.

There were some advantages to drift mining. By exploiting the frozen conditions, it was possible to tunnel down to the paystreak without having to remove tons of overlying material. Thus, the richest ground was removed without touching the unproductive material. All mining was performed by hand, so the cost of labour was a major expense. Unfortunately, the use of drift mining was also controlled by the depth of the rocky material which overlay the bedrock. In the Birch Creek diggings, for instance, Arthur Walden stated that the diggings were so shallow that they could not be excavated in the winter, thus limiting the mining season to a short period during the summer.[24]

In the summer, when drift mining was not possible, and where the deposits were not too deep, open pit excavations were undertaken to remove overburden down to the paydirt zone. The main problem to be overcome was water; in order to successfully dig down to bedrock, the miners had to find a way to keep it out of their excavation. At the upper end of their workings, they would typically construct a dam to control the water. From this dam a waste ditch was constructed around the perimeter of the area to be mined. In this way, the excess water could be entirely diverted. If the flow of water in the creek was small enough and could be contained within the dimensions of a typical sluice box, the water could be run from the dam through the excavation at the grade of the surrounding terrain. When this was the case two flumes were necessary, so that one could carry the water being diverted from the other while the latter was having gold removed from its riffles during a clean-up.

Open-pit mining on Miller Creek, summer of 1894

No matter how successfully the miners diverted water through or around an excavation, it was impossible to keep water from accumulating in the pit. In this early period, the use of steam equipment was almost unheard of; the main means by which water was removed from the exposed diggings was with a bedrock drain, that is, a ditch dug from the lower end of the excavation to carry water away from the working area. The length of this drain depended upon the grade in the creek being mined, but it could be several hundred feet in length. As a prospector's claim was typically 500 feet long, some cooperation with the miners on adjacent claims was required, because the bedrock drain, waste ditches, and other activities would encroach on adjacent mining property.

Open pit mining required the labour of several men. The sluice was designed to pass through the centre of the cut, suspended by upright poles above the bottom of the pit at the same grade as the creek (the miners having excavated below the grade in order to reach bedrock where the gold lay) and braced from either side with more poles. Two men would shovel material into the sluice box from either side of it from a depth of as much as ten feet, while a third would stand at the tail race and shovel aside the tailings which were washed out. The hours were long and the work exhausting, but the labourers were paid up to ten dollars a day for their work. The costs of opening up a mine would quickly accumulate. A.E. Sola estimated that the cost of opening up a claim in the Sixtymile region would not be less than $3,500, but that such a cost was well justified, considering the return.[25]

Other techniques for mining were used but were uncommon. Wing dams and water wheels were used to raise water for sluicing.[26] Flumes and ditches were constructed, upon occasion, to transport water considerable distances for mining purposes (for example, a flume was constructed in 1890 from 50,000 feet of timber to carry water from Franklin Gulch to Troublesome Point for hydraulic mining – the first time this was attempted in the Yukon valley).[27]

With few exceptions, the mining throughout this era was done by hand. One of the exceptions occurred in 1886, when the owners of the *New Racket* allowed four miners to use its pumps for sluicing purposes. The miners made $1,000 each and were able to pay the boat owners an equal amount.[28] Sola also encountered a large scow containing a dredging outfit which had been brought over the Chilkoot Pass and down the Yukon River at great expense to its owners, who discovered, after trying it in numerous locations, that it was no good.[29]

The transition to labour-based mining is significant, as it illustrates the gradual changes coming over the mining industry in the Yukon valley. Production was increasing and more expensive methods had to be employed to recover the gold. A larger population could be supported in this way, but no longer were all the men individual claim holders; many now sold their labour to others for a price. Mechanized mining did not play a significant role in the Yukon until 1898.

Discovery at Birch Creek
While prospecting continued to grow on the Yukon River above Forty Mile, some developments occurring downriver proved to be of great significance. During the summer of 1892, two Creole/Native brothers-in-law, Sergei Gologoff Cherosky and Pitka Pavaloff (known as Pitka), were hunting and prospecting for gold on Birch Creek. On an outcrop which became known as Pitka's Bar, they found colours. They floated down Birch Creek to the Yukon River where they picked up their families and took a steamer up to Forty Mile. The men approached Jack McQuesten for a year's grubstake to test the Birch Creek prospect. McQuesten agreed, in exchange for information on what they found.[30]

John McCloud, a prospector, arrived at Nuklukayet with Al Mayo in the summer of 1892 and got the news that Pitka and Cherosky had arrived with $250 worth of gold, which they exchanged for tea, tobacco, and calico. When asked where the gold came from, the two men became as 'quiet as tombstones.' McCloud and two other miners, Williams and Howard, decided that they would follow the two men and their families to see where they went.

When the *Arctic* arrived in early August, Pitka and Cherosky (along with their wives, children, dogs, canoes, salmon, tents, bedding, and other supplies) came on board, with the three prospectors close behind them. The miners grilled them, but received only a stony silence; a game of cat and mouse developed. Williams and Howard disembarked at a Native village where they thought their quarry might stop, but Pitka and Cherosky, wise to the miners' intent, stayed on the *Arctic* to a point sixty or seventy miles above the encampment, where Pitka's wife got off. Pitka and Cherosky remained on board, and McCloud stuck to them like glue until they reached Forty Mile to petition Jack McQuesten for a grubstake.

Forty Mile was Cherosky's undoing for, while he was there, he got blind drunk and, in the process, told several White men of their discovery but would not say where it was. When the *Arctic* headed downriver, Pitka and Cherosky's wife (Cherosky was still drunk and would come down later in a smaller boat) got on board with their not-so-well-kept secret, followed by McCloud and a number of other miners.[31] Pitka disembarked from the *Arctic* along the shore of the Yukon River and he and Cherosky subsequently commenced building cabins for the winter.

They were not wanting for company that winter; one hundred White men had followed them to their new camp and had settled in to wait out the cold season with them. Manny Hill started a trading post there, and the community became known as Old Portage. In the spring, when Pitka and Cherosky departed for Birch Creek, they were followed by the White men. Upon arriving at Birch Creek, everyone started prospecting, but not enough gold was found to justify working the ground. One party crossed over a range of hills to a tributary known as Squaw Creek (where they found coarse gold) and continued down to its confluence with Birch Creek and found another party using rockers and recovering two to three ounces of gold per day.

Another man heard from a Native that Frank Densmore was seen travelling to the northwest in a hurry. With the smell of gold in the air, such behaviour draws others like a magnet, so he followed Densmore and, upon catching up with him on Harrison Creek, learned that there was not much gold to be found there. He proceeded on to Mastodon Creek, where Pat Kineally, Jack Gregor, and Charlie Colombe located a good prospect. Their first pan yielded one dollar's worth of the coarse gold that everyone sought. Densmore arrived soon after that and, in short order, there was a stampede to Mastodon Creek. About the same time, Missouri Bill found gold in Independence Gulch, yielding one to five dollars per pan, so most of the miners stampeded there to stake their claims.[32]

Meanwhile, Henry Lewis, Gus Williams, and John McCloud worked on Pitka's Bar with good results. Word started to trickle back to Forty Mile that something big was happening. In August, the *Arctic* arrived at Forty Mile, carrying a letter from George Cary advising everyone to come to the new discovery near the town now known as Circle. On credit, Jack McQuesten grubstaked half of the miners in Forty Mile to prospect the Birch Creek diggings.[33] That winter, on Mammoth, Mastodon, Hog'em, Greenhorn, and Independence creeks, $9,000 worth of gold was recovered; the following year, production leaped to $400,000 worth of gold, eclipsing the production of the creeks in the Fortymile and Sixtymile regions.[34]

And what of Pitka and Cherosky, the discoverers? Not knowing how to stake claims, they lost their ground to the Whites.

8

FORTY MILE: ANATOMY OF
A GOLD RUSH TOWN

Eighteen ninety-four represents a significant milestone in the development of the Yukon valley. The exploration for gold-bearing gravels by the small army of prospectors was starting to pay off; a number of new discoveries were made and were increasing production yearly. With the growing population of Whites in the Yukon valley, the scattered community was teetering on the brink of some dramatic changes.

Everyone in Forty Mile that spring was holding his/her breath, waiting for confirmation of the rumours they had been hearing from Birch Creek, Alaska. On 29 July 1894, the steamer *Arctic* arrived, and the rumours were confirmed. As soon as the freight was unloaded, fifty miners took their outfits and stampeded for the new gold fields.[1] The previous fall, Jack McQuesten encountered seventy-five miners at the new riverside community of Circle, waiting for his boat. They had laid out a townsite, and thirty log cabins were under construction. Soon the names of such creeks as Deadwood (formerly Mastodon), Eagle, Hog'em, and Independence were a common part of the local vocabulary.

Meanwhile, a new rich discovery on Glacier Creek in the nearby Sixtymile region slowed the exodus from Fortymile. The creek was quickly staked for fifteen miles, and claims were selling for as much as $2,000.[2] A few miles from Glacier Creek was Miller Creek, the richest and most productive creek in the Yukon. Although it was only six miles long, this creek had more than one hundred men furiously working the fifty-four claims along its bottom. Though they drift-mined in the winter, the bulk of the work was hard labour in open pit mines in the short, intense summers.

Miller Creek produced $300,000 worth of gold in 1894. Of this, $35,000 was worked from a one hundred- by thirty-foot portion of one claim. A single clean-up netted 1,100 ounces of gold. The wage paid to labourers on these claims was high, ten dollars per day, but the cost of everything was also high, as it was either carried over the hills from the Fortymile River on the backs of men or, in the winter, hauled in by dog team. Potatoes and onions sold for $1.00 per pound, flour sold for $19.50 per one hundred pounds, butter sold for $1.50 per pound, and whiskey sold for $1.00 per glass. A pair of gum boots cost $18.[3] Miller Creek was the most productive discovery in the Yukon to date. The recovery of gold continued to be high until it was eclipsed by the finds in the Klondike. One claim consistently produced over $50,000 worth of gold yearly between 1894 and 1896. In 1896, Miller Creek produced nearly half a million dollars' worth of gold. From one claim, a Swiss man named Johnnie Muller was able to clean up 286 pounds of gold, which he deposited in San Francisco.[4] The next year, newspaper headlines announcing a shipment eight times as large were enough to trigger the Klondike gold rush.

Law Comes to the Yukon

The growing population and gold production brought new problems which alarmed Bishop William Bompas. On 9 May 1893, he wrote a letter to the Canadian government from Buxton Mission:

> I think it right to inform you of the danger to which the Indians of the neighborhood are now exposed of complete demoralization for want of any police restraint upon the free and open manufacture and sale of intoxicating liquor among them.
>
> About two hundred miners have passed the present winter in this immediate vicinity, in British territory. The Indians have learnt from these to make whiskey for themselves, and there has been drunkenness of whites and Indians together with much danger of the use of firearms.[5]

A second letter was sent from Bompas in December of that year. He painted a much gloomier picture in this letter, describing a shooting and stabbing incident which took place between two miners as well as the effects of liquor on the Native people. He called for customs authority and police to be sent in.[6]

C.H. Hamilton, the assistant manager of the North American Transportation and Trading Company (NAT&T Co.) post at Fort Cudahy also expressed his concerns. On 16 April 1894, he wrote that there was a great amount of whiskey-smuggling and hootch-making at Forty Mile, both by Whites and by Natives. He recommended that a collector of customs, collector of internal revenue, and police protection could be financed from the revenue generated on duties paid on imported goods. He concluded that any delay in sending in police could result in a Native uprising.[7]

The Canadian government reacted swiftly to these solicitations. In May 1894, the Privy Council resolved to send a representative to investigate the conditions at Forty Mile, with the aim of controlling the illicit trade in liquor, administering lands containing mineral deposits, collecting customs duties, and providing law and order. Inspector Charles Constantine and Staff Sergeant Charles Brown of the NWMP were chosen to undertake this reconnaissance and were instructed to exercise their authority with discretion.

The two men left Victoria, BC, for Juneau, Alaska, on 22 June 1894, and arrived at Fort Cudahy on 7 August, having come in over the Chilkoot Pass and down the Yukon River. During his short stay in the Yukon, Constantine collected $3,248.88 in customs duties. He was able to gather interesting and useful information about the region, including the state of the mining activity in the gold fields, the non-existent mail service, the lack of, but desire for, schools, the pathetic (in his view) state of the Native people of the region, and the diverse nationalities of the men working in the mines. He also verified the importation of liquor.[8]

With the approach of the winter freeze-up, Constantine made preparations to depart for his headquarters. He left instructions for Brown, who was at Fort Selkirk, to take the first boat out to St. Michael in the spring. Constantine travelled down the Yukon River to St. Michael, where he obtained passage on the outgoing US revenue cutter.[9]

In the fall, the usual steamer failed to arrive at Forty Mile, so there was a shortage of bacon and beans in camp. On 2 October, the miners threw up a wing dam across the mouth of the Fortymile River, put a twelve-foot sluice in the intake, and set a barrel, bored full of holes, under the tail of the box. This very quickly produced an ample supply of grayling, which the miners froze for the winter. Nearly everyone was able to obtain moose or caribou, so despite the lack of supplies delivered to the camp that summer everyone was well fed. The Yukon River froze solid on 23 October. Reports to the outside told of a population nearing a

A crowd meets the steamer Arctic *at Forty Mile.*

thousand, with rosy prospects for the forthcoming year.[10] Such optimism stimulated the attention of outsiders, who prepared to flock into the Yukon in the spring.

The Northern Metropolis

In 1886, Forty Mile was born on the flat plain at the mouth of the Fortymile River. In the years that followed, it flourished and grew as the supply centre for all the miners in the vicinity.

In 1894, the first thing that anyone saw when arriving from upriver was the Buxton Mission, located on an island four or five acres in size, about one-half mile above the confluence of the Yukon and Fortymile rivers. This was the mission that J.W. Ellington began constructing in 1888,[11] and it now consisted of two large log buildings, the residence and the school, the latter also serving as the church on Sundays. A cache was situated nearby to store supplies and, as previously mentioned, a community of Native people grew up adjacent to the mission.

The main settlement of Forty Mile was situated on the flat on the south-east side of the junction of the two rivers. It was split in two by a twelve-foot deep gully which was spanned by a simple wooden footbridge. It was the worst jumble of buildings that you could imagine.[12] The main businesses, such as saloons and supply stores, ran parallel to

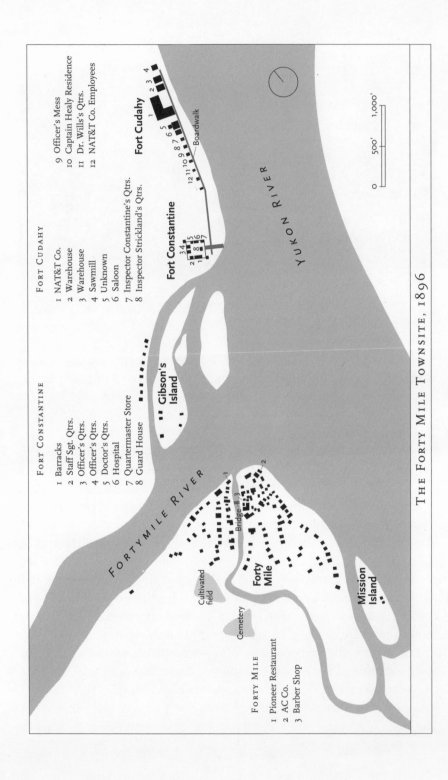

FORT CONSTANTINE

1 Barracks
2 Staff Sgt. Qtrs.
3 Officer's Qtrs.
4 Officer's Qtrs.
5 Doctor's Qtrs.
6 Hospital
7 Quartermaster Store
8 Guard House

FORT CUDAHY

1 NAT&T Co.
2 Warehouse
3 Warehouse
4 Sawmill
5 Unknown
6 Saloon
7 Inspector Constantine's Qtrs.
8 Inspector Strickland's Qtrs.
9 Officer's Mess
10 Captain Healy Residence
11 Dr. Wills's Qtrs.
12 NAT&T Co. Employees

FORT CUDAHY

Fort Cudahy

Boardwalk

Fort Constantine

Gibson's Island

FORTYMILE RIVER

YUKON RIVER

Bridge

Forty Mile

Cultivated field

Cemetery

Mission Island

FORTY MILE

1 Pioneer Restaurant
2 AC Co.
3 Barber Shop

0   500'   1,000'

THE FORTY MILE TOWNSITE, 1896

Forty Mile, c. 1894

Buxton Mission at Forty Mile, showing school and chapel, c. 1985

the bank of the Fortymile River. Behind them stood a collection of other businesses and log cabins huddled together without any order. One man described it as a

collection of eighty or ninety dismal-looking log huts on a mud-bank. The shanties ... scattered without any attempt at regularity, the marshy inter-vening spaces being littered with wood shavings, empty tins, and other rubbish, while numerous tree stumps show the recent origin of this Northern mining-camp ... Huge placards with the words 'Hotel,' 'Saloon,' and even 'Opera House' (the latter a 'dive' of the lowest description) adorn some of the larger dwellings where, though bread is often lacking, whiskey is never scarce.[13]

The miners' log shacks were covered with sod roofs, which were also used as gardens. There were no public services to provide water and sewage needs. If water was required, it was drawn from the river. In the winter, this involved chopping a hole through four or five feet of ice, which froze in immediately after it was abandoned.

The town was dominated, at the very intersection of the Yukon and Fortymile rivers, by the AC Co. trading post, a two-story log structure about thirty feet by sixty feet in size, in front of which the river steamers would land to disgorge their cargoes on the river bars at the mouth of the Fortymile River.[14]

By 1894, Forty Mile could boast an amazing variety of services. There were two bakeries, two restaurants (where one could eat for twelve dol-lars a week), two blacksmiths, and Pat Galvin's tinsmith and hardware

*View of the mouth of the Fortymile River, showing Fort Cudahy in foreground
and the town of Forty Mile in background*

business. If a person was sick, he or she could visit one of two doctors in
town. One could also get a watch repaired, a dress made, or one's hair cut.
The quality of these services was variable. The barber shop, for example,
consisted of 'one broken down chair and an air of general dilapidation.'[15]
Jack Smith, an ex-prize fighter, was the barber. Arriving broke in Forty
Mile, he found the barber shop abandoned. He simply took possession
of the building and became a barber.[16] It is difficult to say what kind of
service passed for medical care.

There was a theatre, operated by George Snow, one or two dance halls,
six saloons,[17] and numerous distilleries. William McPhee and Frank
Densmore were soon to open a billiard parlour and saloon to entertain
the miners, and there were a few prostitutes. There were also three hundred dogs.[18] Later additions to the community for spiritual care included
a Church of England mission for the miners and a smaller Roman
Catholic mission.

Across the mouth of the Fortymile River from the main community,
and half a mile downstream, was Fort Cudahy, the site of Healy's trading
post (owned by NAT&T Co.). It consisted of the trading post and warehouses (which flanked a quadrangle), a sawmill, a free reading room, a
billiard hall, and a row of small log cabins (which were stretched out in a

J.J. Healey's trading post at Fort Cudahy, c. 1895

straight line parallel to the shore of the Yukon River above the trading post). Later, the NWMP would build a detachment in the flat between Fort Cudahy and the town of Forty Mile.[19]

Owing to the wanderings of the miners, their numbers were always in flux. At its peak, Forty Mile serviced a population of around six hundred. This number declined as miners were lured away to Birch Creek and its supply centre, Circle.[20] The men were from all points of the compass, but they were predominantly American, which, as previously mentioned, put Forty Mile in the precarious position of being an American town (which got its supplies from San Francisco and whose post office sold American stamps) located on Canadian soil.[21]

Social Diversion

In a land which was cut off from the rest of the world for most of the year by distance and weather, the social amenities were few and simple. The saloons were the main focus of social activities, and the saloon-keepers were the social leaders. Liquor first started to come into the Yukon before gold was discovered in the Fortymile region.[22] By 1894, Inspector Constantine noted several saloons in operation, selling drinks at fifty cents each. The previous year, 3,000 gallons of liquor came into the Yukon.[23] There was also a burgeoning local industry which produced 'hootch,' the infamous home-brew. This concoction was made from molasses and dried fruit or berries and was fermented with sourdough or hops. It was flavoured with anything that was handy, including old boots and unwashed foot rags. The product was distilled and called 'Forty Rod Whiskey,' that being the distance at which it could reputedly kill.[24] The brew was sold at cut-rate prices.

The miners used any plausible excuse for getting drunk.[25] The fall, when they came in from the creeks to pick up their winter supplies, was a particularly good time for them to have their spree. They arrived in town ready to do business at the trading post but somehow managed to get side-tracked in the saloons. Jack McQuesten was a soft touch, who could always be counted upon to give a miner his grubstake. William Ogilvie once witnessed a strange exchange between McQuesten and a miner:

> A miner who had got an outfit on credit, to be paid for at the next clean-up, came in to see Jack, intending, no doubt, to do the 'square thing'; saw him, and after the usual 'howdy's' and 'ho's,' asked Jack how much he owed. Examination showed the balance to be slightly over seven hundred dollars. The information surprised the debtor into the exclamation
>
> 'Seven hundred! Hell, Jack, I've only got five hundred, how'm I goin' to pay seven hundred with five?'
>
> 'Oh, that's all right, give us your five hundred, and we'll credit you and let the rest stand until next clean-up.'
>
> 'But, Jack, I want more stuff. How'm I goin to get that?'
>
> 'Why, we'll let you have it as we did before.'
>
> 'But, damn it, Jack, I haven't had a spree yet.'
>
> 'Well, go have your little spree, come back with what is left, and we'll credit you with it and go on as before.'
>
> Alas for human frailty, when he came from his spree, nothing was left, and kindly Jack let him have another outfit, increasing the in-debtedness to about twelve hundred, to be paid for next clean-up, and so ad infinitum.[26]

A spree consisted of all sorts of wild living, amply lubricated with alcohol. The celebrant would generally run around town acting crazily, firing his weapon to announce his progress, and spending his money at a hectic rate until it was all gone.[27] One observer remarked: 'Dropping in for a drink is an expensive matter – if you get off with an expenditure of $100 you may consider yourself lucky – for by the unwritten etiquette of the country, you must call in everyone within sight to have a drink at your expense at the same time. To refuse a proffered glass is an unpardonable insult – the only loophole of escape left is to take a cigar instead, and it is a toss-up which is the least deadly.'[28]

Alcohol was not limited to the town. In one instance, at a drunken party on Miller Creek, one man tried to shoot another man's ear off (the latter fled). Another man 'had his head broken by a pick handle, and numerous shots were fired without doing damage.'[29] The sale of whiskey was later banned, but this ban was never totally successful.[30]

When the men were not drinking, and sometimes even when they were, they were gambling. This was the principle pastime for a majority of the miners. Although there were no gambling houses, a card game could develop in someone's cabin or in a saloon. The saloons were kept up in the best style possible, with nicely patterned wall paper, pictures hanging from the walls, mirrors, decorations, and fine, polished hardwood bars. A game would start in the evening and would last late into the night. Some unfortunate souls lost the entire proceeds from their summer's work in a couple of nights. The stakes in a game could be very high. Sometimes the cost to draw a card was as much as fifty dollars, and games with stakes of $2,000 were common. By consensus, violent behaviour was not tolerated, so bloodshed was rare.[31]

Another social event in Forty Mile was dancing. Since there were virtually no White women in Forty Mile, the miners would dance with the Native women. Two leaders in organizing these events were Frank Densmore and Kate McQuesten, herself a Russian/Native woman. As one man described it:

> At twelve o'clock, the dance stopped and the women went home, then after a few hot rums and a song or two, if it happened to be Saturday night, Frank Densmore would call our attention to the fact that the next day was Sunday, telling us that we had better call on the Reverend Bompas and hear what he had to say ... We all followed his advice.
>
> One Sunday ... Mr. Rivers came to church, after being up all Saturday night playing cards and having had a hot drink just before, was overcome by sleep. One of his friends woke him up, and before he realized where he was, Rivers called out: 'Give us a new deck!'[32]

'Squaw dances' were one of the most bizarre social customs practised in the Yukon. One newcomer to Forty Mile witnessed one the first day he arrived:

Interior of saloon in Forty Mile, 1894

We were attracted by ... a row of miners, who were lined up in front of the saloon engaged in watching the door of a large log cabin opposite, rather dilapidated, with the windows broken in. On being questioned, they said there was going to be a dance, but when or how they did not seem to know: all seemed to take only a languid looker-on interest, speaking of the affair lightly and flippantly. Presently more men, however, joined the group and eyed the cabin expectantly. In spite of their disclaimers they evidently expected to take part, but where were the fair partners for the mazy waltz?

The evening wore on until ten o'clock when in the dusk a stolid Indian woman, with a baby in the blanket on her back, came cautiously around the corner, and ... made for the cabin door, looking neither to the right nor to the left. She had no fan, nor yet an opera cloak; she was not even décolleté; she wore large moccasins on her feet ... and she had a bright colored handkerchief on her head. She was followed by a dozen others, one far behind the other, each silent and unconcerned, and each with a baby upon her back. They sidled into the log cabin and sat down on the benches, where they also deposited their babies in a row: the little red people lay there very still, with wide eyes shut or staring, but never crying ... The mothers sat awhile looking at the ground in some one spot and then slowly lifted their heads to look at the miners who had slouched into the cabin after them – men fresh from the diggings, spoiling for excitement of any kind. Then a man with a dilapidated fiddle struck up a swinging sawy melody, and in the intoxication of the moment some of the most reckless of the miners grabbed an Indian woman and began furiously swinging her around in a sort of waltz, while the others crowded around and looked on.

Little by little the dusk grew deeper, but candles were scarce and could not be afforded. The figures of the dancing couples grew more and more indistinct and the faces became lost to view, while the sawing of the fiddle grew more and more rapid, and the dancing more excited. There was no noise, however; scarcely a sound save the fiddle and the shuffling of the feet over the floor of rough hewn logs; for the Indian women were stolid as ever, and the miners could not speak the language of their partners. Even the lookers-on said nothing, so that these silent dancing figures in the dusk made an almost weird effect.

One by one, however, the women dropped out, tired, picked up their babies and slouched off home, and the men slipped over to the saloon to have a drink before going to their cabins. Surely this squaw dance ... was one of the most peculiar balls ever seen. No sound of revelry by night, no lights, no flowers, no introductions, no conversations. Of all the muses, Terpsichore the nimble-footed, alone was represented, for surely the nymph who presides over music would have disowned the fiddle.[33]

The opportunities for entertainment increased in 1894 when George T. Snow, an actor who had prospected in the Yukon in 1888, returned to open a theatre in Forty Mile. This was appreciated by the miners, especially since Snow brought a troupe of 'music-hall girls' from San Francisco. According to one observer,

the entertainment was really excellent, especially the dancing of one or two of the girls. Some of the scenery was really elaborate; one of the favourite turns – a drama in two chapters – in which, by the way, not a soul appeared on the stage from the first to the last, had for its setting a richly furnished and upholstered room with table, Chippendale chairs, heavy curtains and richly carved buffet with pier-glass complete! ... After the performance, the audience and performers could adjourn to the nearest saloon and continue to make things 'a bit lively' in the course of the night. But although they were noisy – often boisterously so – and there was a rough and ready unconventionality about some of the subsequent proceedings, I never saw anything the least bit objectionable take place.[34]

These women had a hard time in the wilds of the Sub-Arctic forest, but they were also amply rewarded by the miners for the 'display of their talents.'[35] They were certainly a change from the Native women, to whom most of the miners were accustomed. One of these women boasted of receiving a gold nugget from a miner for agreeing to have a date with him. To her embarrassment, the nugget weighed out at a value of eighty-five cents, and she was forever after known as 'Six Bits.'[36] Another, the youngest of the troupe, was lovingly known as 'The Virgin' because, the miners thought, she had actually seen one.[37]

Being cut off from the outside world for eight months of the year, Forty Mile afforded everyone a captive audience as well as captive company. The subjects of much conversation were the scarcity of provisions and the abundance of gold. Heated conversations often arose over the latter. Oppressed by the boredom of such close living, the miners would, for amusement, pull the most outrageous jokes on each other. In one example of trickery, a miner poured condensed milk into candle moulds, complete with wicks. Once frozen, they looked like the real thing. He sold them to a saloon-keeper, who was short of candles, for a big price. To his embarrassment, and to the entertainment of the customers, when the proprietor opened the box he found a few soggy wicks in the bottom. He returned the favour later, to the delight of everyone, by selling the miner a keg of whiskey for $400. Once he got the keg to his mine, the miner discovered that the only whiskey in the keg was in a much smaller keg, very carefully attached to the spigot from the inside of the larger barrel.[38]

The men of Forty Mile did not attend church frequently. For the twenty or so miners who did, however, there was a special Sunday afternoon service given by Bishop William Bompas. Afterwards, these men could borrow books from the limited supply in the mission library. From this very limited selection, the magazine *Leisure Hour* was the most popular.

The long-time miners could sense the changes in the Yukon valley as both the amount of gold and the population increased. By 1894, they saw that the tradition of equality and fraternity was eroding. To combat this, and to institutionalize their values, they came together to form the Yukon Order of Pioneers (YOOP), an organization which was restricted to those men who came into the Yukon before 1888. Their first formal meeting occurred in Forty Mile on 1 December 1894. Its objectives were: 'The advancement of the Great Yukon Valley, The mutual protection and benefit of its members, and To prove to the outside world that the Yukon

Members of the Yukon Order of Pioneers, Forty Mile, 1895

Order of Pioneers are men of Truth Honour and Integrity.' Their motto was: 'Do as you would be done by.' Sixty-nine men attended the first meeting. Ironically, the first organization to appear in the Yukon valley consisted of a group of men who had prided themselves on their informal, almost anarchistic, social order.[39]

White Women in the Yukon

The White population of the Yukon was almost entirely male. Even when the North was on the verge of the Klondike strike, there were no more than a few dozen White women in the entire region. The first White woman to enter the upper Yukon region was more than likely the wife of the missionary T.H. Canham. She entered the Yukon basin with her husband in the summer of 1888, coming from the Peel River in the North-West Territories and going overland to Tanana Station to establish a mission. The trip overland took five months.

'Dutch Kate,' the first White woman reputed to have come into the Yukon over the Chilkoot Pass, arrived the same year. She was 'one of those poor fallen women, who are often found casting their miserable lot with the mining class.'[40] She accompanied a small party of miners over the pass, dressed in male attire, but when she reached a large Native village farther down the Yukon River 'she arrayed herself in her finest apparel, powdered her face and arranged her bangs in her most bewitching style.' The Native people, never having seen a White woman before, were enchanted by her appearance. Later in the fall, at St. Michael, she was refused passage out on the government revenue cutter and spent the winter on the Alaskan coast. The next spring, she was able to gain passage on a sealing vessel, and eventually made it back to the United States.[41]

Charlotte Bompas, the bishop's wife, arrived at the Buxton Mission in Forty Mile in August 1892 and stayed there for the next four years. On Christmas day 1892, a deputation of miners presented her with a gold nugget, weighing about three ounces, in honour of her being the first White woman to winter over so far north.[42]

In 1893, several other White women reached Fortymile, including Mrs. Matheson,[43] Mrs. Healy and her servant, Bridget Mannion, and Mrs. Callahan, who gave birth to a baby boy on Davis Creek a tributary of the Fortymile River.[44] The following year, several more White women came into the Fortymile area. One of them was a fifty-five-year-old woman named Anna DeGraf. She crossed the Chilkoot Pass on crutches in search of her son, who had gone north in 1892 and disappeared. Another White woman who was among the first to cross the Chilkoot Pass was Emilie Tremblay, who wintered over on Miller Creek with her husband, Jack. By the winter of 1894-5, there were reported to be twenty-eight White women living in the Yukon amongst a thousand men.[45]

These women faced extreme conditions, unlike anything that they had met with before coming to the North, and there was no clearly defined niche for them. This caused many to comment on the astounding qualities of these pioneers. In general, they were treated with considerable respect.[46] One exception to this, however, is indicated in the memoirs of Anna DeGraf, who lived in Circle for two years before moving to the Klondike. DeGraf had to defend herself from one man by hitting him with a heavy stick and, in another instance, she scared off a number of drunken miners (who were abusing a 'dance-hall girl') by firing shots at them. Only a resolution of a miners' committee finally put an end to the men molesting the women.[47] These women encountered much loneliness and deprivation. They were, at first, the wives of traders and missionaries, then they were the wives of miners and, finally, assorted others arrived: theatre troupes, prostitutes, travellers, and those hoping to find their fortune.

One of the pioneer women from the second group, Emilie Fortin, was born in Quebec and later moved to New York state. It was here, in 1893, that she met and married Pierre-Nolasque (Jack) Tremblay, a Miller Creek miner who had come outside that summer to visit his family in the east. The following spring, they departed for the Yukon, crossing the Chilkoot Pass and arriving in Forty Mile on 16 June 1894. After organizing their affairs in town, they made the sixty-mile journey upriver and over the hills to Miller Creek. Jack hired several Natives to carry their luggage and outfit over the trail. The weather Emilie Tremblay encountered was typical of the Yukon summer: hot, with countless mosquitoes. Without complaint, she walked the entire distance, impressing others they met along the way with her endurance.

Her new home was a one-room sod-roof cabin with a single window made from bottles. The cabin had been previously occupied by her husband and his partners; on the walls were the primitive bunks in which they slept. Already several years old, it had a floor partially covered with wood. A single pole in the centre of the cabin supported the roof. At the foot of this post was a thick, black layer of spit – the men, tired from

Emilie Tremblay in front of her cabin on Miller Creek, 1894

working on their claim, would lie in their bunks and spit at the post in the centre of the room. (Tobacco chewing was a widespread indulgence throughout the Yukon. As one man said: 'It is impossible to keep anything clean. Nothing is sacred to him ... If a miner happens to have a clean stove about the place, and a man drops in with his cud in his mouth, the first thing he invariably does is to spit on the stove. It is a sort of recognized salutation – an informal way of starting conversation!')[48] Tremblay took a shovel and started her clean-up at the centre of the room and, in the following days, cleaned it from top to bottom. The cabin was equipped with the barest of essentials along with crudely built furniture.

For Emilie Tremblay, it was a difficult adjustment. There were no other women on the creek, which the other miners felt was no place for them, and she was further isolated by the fact that she did not speak any English. Tremblay started working on her grammar and vocabulary.

Being the only woman on Miller Creek during the winter of 1894, she decided that she should offer a Christmas dinner to the miners living nearby. This, in itself, proved a challenge, as there were none of the usual amenities available to make a Christmas dinner a success. So she improvised: the invitations were written on birch bark, the guests had to bring their own utensils, she could only cook dishes which were small enough to fit into their tiny twenty-two-inch square oven, and she found an unused long skirt to serve as a table cloth.

The Christmas menu consisted of stuffed rabbit, roast caribou, brown beans in broth, King Oscar sardines, evaporated potatoes, sourdough bread and butter, cake, and a plum pudding with blueberry sauce. Just before the end of the meal, a latecomer arrived with a bottle of rum to add to the festivities. He had walked all the way to Forty Mile and back to obtain the liquor. After the meal, they played cards and filled the cabin with tobacco smoke and good cheer.

While her husband burned his way slowly into the frozen placer gravels, she cared for the household. By the end of the winter, supplies were running short, and they had to exchange food with the other miners to ensure a more varied diet, which, by spring, consisted of beans three times a day, sardines, powdered evaporated potatoes, and sourdough bread and butter. They learned to appreciate beans in every conceivable variation.

As her English improved, more socialization was possible. Father Francis P. Monroe, the Roman Catholic priest from Forty Mile, made occasional visits. In the spring of 1895, she was joined on Miller Creek by the French-Canadian wife of one of the Day brothers, whom she had met the previous spring in Juneau. She planted a garden on the roof of her cabin to improve their diet. At the end of the summer the clean-up proved most satisfactory, and they returned to New York state, leaving their cabin and the remainder of their provisions in the custody of the Days. The Tremblays returned to the North to live out the remainder of their lives in the Klondike. She looked back on the first year she spent on Miller Creek as the best time she ever had.[49]

Because there were few White women in the Yukon, the miners married Native women or, more frequently, entered into less formal, short-lived liaisons with them. These women were of considerable advantage to the early miners because of their familiarity with the country and their ability to look after themselves.[50] Attitudes towards Native partners were quite variable. Some of the men looked on their wives as equal partners and took measures to send their children outside to get their schooling.[51] Other liaisons were not so complete. Some men abandoned their Native wives and offspring when overcome by wanderlust.[52] Others could not resist the allure of the White women (who were starting to arrive before and during the Klondike gold rush) and simply abandoned their old partners.[53] Sometimes peer pressure was applied to make the miners into 'honest men.' One Circle man impregnated a Native woman, and a miners' committee determined that he should either give her $500 towards the upbringing of the child or he should marry her. He chose the latter, and the marriage produced several more children.[54]

There were also social pressures that created a distance between White women and Native women, placing the latter much lower on the social ladder. The teacher in Circle, Anna Fulcomer, later described a fund-raising dance held there and attended by both White and Native women. Though some men would dance with members of either group, the women would not dance together in the same sets.[55] The lines distinguishing the two groups were, nevertheless, blurred. In one case, for instance, the proprietor of a Circle dance hall had a common-law wife, a White woman who chose to distance herself from the Native women who attended the dances. Realizing that a sizable number of his customers were men with Native wives and that her attitude was bad for business, he knocked her down.[56] In another instance, a White woman in Circle made a fuss over Native women attending one of the community dances. The men of the community told her that they were not going to exclude these women and that she could stay home if she so desired.[57] Regardless of the perceived social differences between Whites and Natives, relationships with the latter were a commonplace, integral part of the social fabric of pre-Klondike society.

9

THE ARRIVAL OF THE
NORTH-WEST MOUNTED POLICE

In the winter of 1894-5, the Yukon valley was inhabited by a thousand White men, a handful of White women, and one mounted police officer. Staff Sergeant Charles Brown arrived at Fort Cudahy from Fort Selkirk on the *Arctic* on 6 September 1894, just after Inspector Charles Constantine left for the outside. For the next ten months, he was the only representative of Canadian justice in the Yukon, and his major function that winter was to collect several thousand dollars' worth of duty from imported goods. During his stay, he witnessed a number of events which revealed the changes occurring in the miners' society.

In December, a miner named Sailor tried to shoot Frank Bowker, but he failed when someone knocked his gun off target just as he pulled the trigger. Sailor was popular among the miners, so nothing happened to him.[1] Only the previous year, George Matlock and another man were also involved in a shooting incident. And, of course, illicit liquor production was rife. There was a 'whiskey gang' made up of a number of men, including Jack McQuesten and T.W. O'Brien, who later established a brewery in Dawson. Brown was able to locate nearly all of the thirty-five illicit stills operating in the region. He also reported that a couple of individuals were responsible for the importation of hundreds of gallons of liquor. 'There has not been so much drunkenness as I would have supposed among the whites,' he reported in February, 'but quite a lot amongst the Indians.' His opinion on this matter changed, because in June, just prior to his departure, he reported 'a lot of drunkenness ... amongst whites and Indians [in the] spring, but no serious roughs.'[2] With the lure of profits from the Birch Creek diggings downriver in Alaska, many of the hooch-makers departed for greener pastures in the spring.

On 16 January 1895, Brown watched an event which demonstrated the need for law and order in the Yukon. A meeting was called by a female servant working for C.H. Hamilton (the manager of NAT&T Co.) at Fort Cudahy that winter. He had contracted the woman to work for him for a period of one year. After awhile, she began to go out in the evenings to meet her boyfriend. Hamilton first warned her to stop and then fired her.

She complained bitterly, and her boyfriend encouraged the camp to become indignant about the situation. At a miners' committee meeting, it was resolved that Hamilton should give her a full year's wages, her boat fare back to the coast, and enough food to carry her over until her departure in the spring. The crowd was so worked up that the committee openly discussed blowing up the company safe in order to obtain the necessary funds. Hamilton was prepared to stand his ground, which could have led to violence, but Brown advised him to cooperate.[3]

The boyfriend benefited from the young servant's windfall, which amounted to less than $600. Afterwards, some of the older and more seasoned sourdoughs were embarrassed and ashamed by their abuse of the system.[4] NAT&T Co. was noted for not giving credit, to which the miners had grown accustomed in their dealings with McQuesten, and Hamilton was so unpopular that he had been bestowed with the epithet 'the Pope.' The ill feelings which they harboured for the company, however, did not justify the harsh and violent actions which the miners planned.

Before Christmas, Brown patrolled over the hills to Miller Creek, where he found one man coming out with several thousand dollars' worth of gold, which he had recovered after only a short period of work. Brown also collected over $5,000 worth of duty on imported goods, mainly from NAT&T Co. While getting cooperation from Healy's company, Brown got none from McQuesten's, the latter successfully evading the sergeant's efforts to collect duty.[5] Having survived a relatively mild winter, Brown left Fort Cudahy on 20 June 1895 and headed for St. Michael.

Brown reported that 1,500 to 2,000 men were expected to enter the Yukon in the spring because of the good prospects on Glacier and Birch creeks. In fact, there were 400 men camped at the Chilkoot Pass, waiting for break-up. Groups of men were scattered along the trail, and seventy men were waiting at the foot of Lake Laberge for the ice to go out.[6] While these men waited impatiently to start their downriver odyssey, a more important, if smaller, group of men would soon come up the Yukon River from St. Michael.

Establishing a Post in the Yukon

While Brown was executing his duties on the fringe of the Dominion of Canada, the Canadian government decided to establish a detachment at Forty Mile, with Inspector Charles Constantine in command. Although he had said that a force of forty men would be required, he was given twenty, including Inspector D'Arcy Strickland, Assistant Surgeon A.E. Wills, two staff sergeants, two corporals, and thirteen constables (who were recruited in early 1895).

The men Constantine assembled to accompany him to the Yukon departed Regina on 1 June 1895. Five days later, they embarked from Seattle on the steamer *Excelsior*, headed for Unalaska and St. Michael. Within two weeks, the *Excelsior* was jammed in floe ice in the Bering Sea, off St. Lawrence Island. Hemmed in on all sides by the endless wall of ice, the hapless mounties had to wait thirteen days before they were freed from their frigid prison. They arrived at St. Michael on 3 July, where Brown joined them, and they all left two days later on the *Portus B. Weare*, NAT&T Co.'s double-smokestack river steamer.

The trip up the Yukon River against the current was slow, tedious, and punctuated by frequent stops for firewood. By this time, the excitement of the journey was replaced by boredom.[7] The heat was unbearable and the clouds of insects so thick that they were likened to the Egyptian plague. The 'plague' reached its pinnacle at the abandoned post of Fort Yukon, which was literally black with the tormentors.[8]

The mounties arrived at Forty Mile on 24 July and immediately set to work. First, they unloaded the vessel, as they had brought a large quantity of provisions with them. For this, they became beasts of burden, dragging, hauling, and carrying all supplies ashore, where they were unceremoniously dumped in a disorganized jumble on the bank. Constantine selected the low-lying ground which lay strategically between Fort Cudahy and Forty Mile (near the mouth of the Fortymile River) for the location of the new NWMP barracks. What a feeling of despair these men felt when they gazed upon what was to become their new home: a swamp with a scattering of small spruce and ground covered with a spongy, saturated, eighteen-inch thick layer of moss!

On 26 July they set about building their headquarters. On the *Portus*

Inspector D'Arcy Strickland supervises the milling of lumber
for construction of buildings at Fort Constantine, 1895.

B. *Weare*, Constantine sent Strickland and a squad of eight men thirty miles up the Yukon River to the mouth of the Twelve Mile River. Under primitive conditions, and enduring horrible attacks of mosquitoes, they cut and hauled 400 logs to the bank of the Yukon River. These logs were assembled into three rafts and floated downriver to Fort Cudahy. In the three weeks during which this work was done, Constantine and the remainder of the men were busy preparing the ground upon which the new barracks, named Fort Constantine, were to be built. Brush had to be cleared, drains built to carry away excess water, and the moss covering the surface stripped away. 'All this entailed much hard work,' explained Constantine, 'and was gone on with regardless of the state of the weather. If it was not 90° in the shade, it was pouring rain. At any time the men were working up to their ankles, and sometimes up to their knees in water.'[9]

Constantine rented the sawmill from NAT&T Co., and when the party of men returned from upriver with the logs, they set about cutting the timber. A wooden tramway was extended from the sawmill to the location of the new post, a distance of one-third of a mile. This eased the task of hauling the dressed logs to the site. The work of milling the logs, hauling

Buildings under construction at Fort Constantine, 1895

them to the site, and constructing the buildings was carried out by the officers and men without any outside help.

Fort Constantine was laid out in a square, with eight buildings constructed around the perimeter. The buildings consisted of a guardroom, barracks, storehouse and office, two officer's quarters, a hospital, and quarters for the surgeon and the staff sergeants. The entire perimeter was enclosed within a stockade (essentially a fence), which spanned the space between the buildings and enclosed the front of the square. Bastions ten-feet square were constructed at opposite corners of the stockade, and an entrance and fifty-foot high flag pole were built facing the Yukon River. The men completed the work in early October and moved into their new quarters on 7 October 1895; the officers moved in about a week later.

What the NWMP had established at this little mining community was not only a post for maintaining law and order but also a symbol that the Dominion of Canada extended even as far as this isolated outpost on the very fringe of the British Empire. Sergeant M.H.E. Hayne summed it up:

> Those [buildings] that we now erected were naturally more elaborate than the ordinary run of buildings ... for they were destined to a degree of permanency for which the miner's 'shack' is never intended, and as far as we

Parade square at Fort Constantine

could we studied comfort and convenience, seeing that we had to live there for two years and then be succeeded in two years by others in the same quarters. Our life too, had to be very different from that of the miners. We had all our regular apparatus for cooking and washing, work (clerical and manual) and recreation. We had to keep ourselves clean and tidy. In a word, we had to aim at erecting as near a model as was possible under the circumstances of a decent civilized set of barracks, in which we should be able to conform to the more important of the requirements of discipline and civilization.[10]

Living a 'Civilized' Life

These men represented the encroachment of 'civilization,' and their lifestyle was in stark contrast to that of the miners. The North-West Mounted Police were more like a military force than are the present-day Royal Canadian Mounted Police (RCMP). The men lived together in a military encampment, following a rigid, disciplined routine. The government supplied them with all of their basic needs; room and board, transportation, uniforms, entertainment, and, such as it was, medical care. They could purchase supplementary items at wholesale prices from the canteen.

For their services, they received a wage that appeared small compared to the going rate of six to ten dollars per day for mine labour in the Fortymile region. The salary for an inspector in the NWMP was one thousand dollars per annum. As an agent of the government collecting

North-West Mounted Police at Fort Constantine, 1896

duties from imported goods, they could retain 10 per cent of the duty collected per annum, that is, they could make up to an additional thousand dollars. The staff sergeants received $1.50 per day, the sergeants received $1.00 per day, the corporals received $.85 per day, and the constables received $.50 per day. A northern allowance was provided, amounting to $1.50 per day for officers, $.75 per day for sergeants, and $.50 per day for corporals and constables. Special duty pay was also given for specific assignments, such as an additional $.50 per day for carpentry duties.[11]

The enlisted men were accommodated in barracks, while the sergeants, surgeon, and inspectors had their own quarters. In addition, the officers each had an enlisted man to perform servant duties, which must have relieved them of a substantial amount of the daily burden. The officers were also allowed to bring their wives and children with them at the government's expense.[12]

The daily routine started early. Reveille was at 6:20 AM, roll call was at 7:00 AM, lights out was at 11:00 PM, and a special routine was observed on Sundays. Meals were prepared by a mess cook. The routine included watchsetting roll, kit inspections, and maintenance of arms. The instructions given Constantine stated that the men should be kept proficient in squad and arms drill, and orders were issued for target practice (revolver).[13]

Daily local orders were issued to specify the observance of particular rules, to spell out duty assignments, and to record punishment for infractions. Since fire was a constant and serious problem, standing orders forbade the men to leave lamps lit when unattended and instructed them to clean out the chimneys once a month. As the winter progressed, the men were required to daily consume three ounces of lime juice in front of the non-commissioned officer (NCO) (by this time the medical profession knew how to prevent scurvy, although the miners still did not).

The orders given to Constantine in preparation for the trip to the Yukon provided for promotion, demotion, and various forms of punishment should the need arise. Constantine remarked that the conduct of his men was good; nevertheless, such infractions as having dirty weapons, having weapons loaded in the barracks, sleeping in, being insubordinate, and being absent at roll call did occur. On 3 January 1896, for instance, Constable Angus P. McKellar was fined ten dollars for missing roll call on New Year's Day and being brought in drunk and improperly dressed. Punishments (other than those of a financial nature) included confinement to barracks and admonishment.

North-West Mounted Police at Fort Constantine, winter of 1895-6

Freeze-up occurred on 17 October 1895. The temperature plummeted from minus twenty-three degrees Fahrenheit in mid-December of that year to minus seventy-three degrees Fahrenheit in January.[14] The detachment consumed two cords of wood a day in cold weather, and all men (except the mess cook, carpenter, and orderly) went on general fatigue two days a week to cut their wood supply and haul it one-quarter of a mile to the fort.

During the winter, there were occasional dog-sled patrols to the principle creeks of the region, where the interaction with the miners was peaceful. The officers on patrol had to proceed cautiously until William Ogilvie's survey team determined the precise location of the international boundary. Once that was accomplished, however, they patrolled and collected mining royalties with impunity. When called in at the slightest hint of trouble, their mere presence was sufficient to bring it to an end.

The Quest for Salvation

While the Canadian government was slow to move into the Yukon basin to protect its sovereignty and to collect revenues, the churches had for some years been settled in the communities along the Yukon River, tending to the perceived religious needs of their widespread congregations. There was fierce competition between the Roman Catholic and Protestant (represented by the Church Missionary Society) churches in the drive to find converts to Christianity. In the early years, between 1886 and 1894, the primary interest of the two antagonists was the Native population.

The Buxton Mission was reoccupied by Bishop William Bompas and his wife in 1892. Although they attended his Sunday services, relations between the local miners and Bompas were not entirely cordial. Bompas found that the miners were corrupting the Natives, particularly through the distribution of alcohol and the practice of cohabiting with Native women. To realize any success with the miners in Fortymile, Bompas would have to await reinforcements.

In the year 1894, Father Francis P. Monroe, a Jesuit priest, visited the miners on the creeks of the Fortymile and Sixtymile regions during the summer. In August, Father William Judge was dispatched to Forty Mile in response to some miners' requests for a priest. Judge rented a cabin in the community and obtained the standard supplies necessary for survival during the long winter. However, lacking sacramental wine and unable to obtain any from the Buxton Mission, Judge decided to return downriver in search of a supply. He was unable to return to Forty Mile due to the onset of winter.

The nature of the missionary spirit impeded the success of the Church Missionary Society in winning willing converts among the White population. The early missionaries were devoted to the conversion of the 'heathen' Natives of the Yukon valley and were driven by immense fervour. Though dedicated, they had no interest in the search for gold, and they tended to be rather impractical. Reverend Vincent Sims had worked himself to death some years earlier serving the 'needs' of the Natives, and Ellington had been driven mad by his own naiveté and the cruel jokes played on him by the miners.

The challenge for the missionaries was formidable, because the 'leaderless legion' of miners had little concern for anything but the search for gold. Judge noted: 'Everybody is looking for gold, some finding it and some getting nothing, a few becoming rich, but the greater number only making a living, and all working very, very hard. You would be astonished to see the amount of hard work that men do here in the hope of finding gold ... O if men would only work for the kingdom of heaven with a little of that wonderful energy, how many saints we would have!'[15] Judge returned to Forty Mile in 1895 and spent the ensuing winter serving the community and visiting the miners on the creeks.

Reverend R.J. Bowen arrived from London, England, in August 1895 to join Bishop Bompas at Buxton Mission. He commenced learning the Han language in order to communicate with the Han people in the area. He was sent out that fall, however, to visit the miners on the Fortymile and Sixtymile rivers. This trip shaped the course of his ministry over the next several years. He accompanied a teamster freighting supplies by dog team; his responsibility was to break trail with his snowshoes.

Bowen described his first night in a roadhouse on the Fortymile River:

It was small, dirty and the food, though roughly served, seemed clean and tasted good ... There were no beds or bunks, each man spread his robe or blankets on the floor and rested as well as he could ... This small room accommodated 19 people, the last to arrive kept his feet under the stove. The human smell, with the extra doggy smell was very unpleasant, there were stronger smells that came from a bottle that to me were very obnoxious. I was new to Arctic travel or certainly I would have made camp in the bush, a place where at least, I could have fresh air.[16]

Despite his malodorous first impression, he quickly adapted to the miners he met, and for whom he 'filed a few saws, drew some plans to scale, dressed some wounds, extracted some teeth, and dressed some frozen limbs.'[17]

Later that winter, Bompas charged him with the responsibility of tending to the spiritual needs of the miners. Bowen intuitively understood that to be successful with the miners he would have to meet their standard. He knew that these men were very direct in their actions and speech, and that he would soon be put to the test. During his first visit to Forty Mile after his new assignment, he invited some of the men to attend a service and also invited them to make use of his more secular abilities. The latter invitation was put to the test when Press Ireland, one of the local miners, came to look in on the new 'gospel mill.' Ireland had an infected eye-tooth, and he wanted Bowen to pull it out.

Bowen extracted the offending tooth without incident and refused payment for the service. Ireland retired to a neighbouring saloon, bought a round for the patrons, and proposed a toast to the new preacher. After that, Bowen had no difficulty mixing with the men, nor did they ever allow him to be out of pocket while serving their needs.

Bowen was not immune to the pranks of the miners, and his tolerance was quickly put to the test when some of them paid him a visit and, after stopping up his stovepipe, drove him, coughing, from his smoke-filled cabin. Shortly after this, three miners, bored with the saloons, paid him a visit and talked to him about boxing. Impressed that he could converse intelligently on the subject, they were receptive to Bowen's overture. He said:

'You came here to discuss prize fighting ... However I have a greater battle on my hands than any fought by any of the prize fighters mentioned.' 'What kind of a fight is it?' [one of them asked. Bowen replied:] 'Not a fight to put a man down while a referee counts ten, but a fight to lift a man to face his responsibility to life and his fellow men.' 'When do you begin?' [they asked.] 'That depends upon you gentlemen' [was Bowen's reply. With that invitation, they rose to the bait:] 'Turn loose your guns and open the fight.'[18]

Not one to lose the advantage gained, Bowen opened his impromptu service with music rather than with a sermon. There, in an eighteen- by twenty-foot log cabin, part chapel, part living quarters (with a kitchen, wooden bed, food supplies, and personal effects scattered about), the young missionary picked up a concertina and, singing songs buried in the miners' childhoods, he stirred feelings which these work-hardened men had long stored in their subconscious minds. Song after song from his repertoire lulled them as they joined him, hesitantly, in singing.

Finally, as they were stirring and preparing to leave, Bowen said: 'Now we have passed from the prize ring back to the home circle and feel the presence of mother and God nearer than for some time past, as we think of home and parents, let us have a word of prayer together.'[19] To the minister's surprise, the men kneeled down beside him and joined him in prayer. These men remained Bowen's constant friends throughout his stay in the North.

Through this peculiar sequence of events, Bowen (unlike his Anglican predecessors) earned his entry into the society of miners. For the next year and a half, he travelled throughout the Yukon valley serving the Lord and spreading His Word, while always earning his keep by providing many secular services to those who needed them. During the winter of 1895-6, the services in Bowen's improvised chapel were well attended. Christmas, however, ended up being one of the most bizarre affairs he experienced while in the North.

First of all, the fledgling missionary was trapped in a remote settlement on the Yukon, surrounded by ice, snow, and silence; no mail would reach him until the spring. The Native people clustered at the mission had little interest in the rituals surrounding Christmas – Santa Claus had little appeal for them. At the Buxton Mission, therefore, Bompas made no change in either routine or menu for this hallowed event. Both Charlotte Bompas and Margaret MacDonald, the school teacher who was stationed at the mission, longed for something special.[20] Even a visit to the wives of the NWMP inspectors (due to the short but hazardous journey over the river ice) was considered unsafe. The visits were therefore infrequent.

In contrast to the barren celebration at the mission, the miners attacked the holiday with gusto. The preacher was invited to partake in the specially prepared feasts of wild game, but it was impossible to honour all of the invitations. Liquor was everywhere amidst the celebration, which led to the one sorry event which marred the festivities. According to Bowen, 'One Indian was seen standing on a pile of wood swinging a revolver around and around with bullets going no one knew where. It was fortunate that no one was near. The shooting attracted attention and when re-loading time came, the gun was taken away ... and he was ordered away. Thus ended the strangest Christmas day of my life.'[21]

The next spring Bowen was sent down to St. Michael to get mission supplies which had been shipped from San Francisco. While he was there, he learned that his services had been offered to the American, Bishop Peter Rowe of the Episcopal Church, who sent him to the rapidly growing community at Circle. There, he occupied a former saloon and served the miners until they were siphoned away to the Klondike in the spring of 1897.

William Judge, the Jesuit, was also dispatched to Circle, but on 6 October 1896 he found himself trapped in Forty Mile due to the oncoming winter and the haphazard transportation. Consequently, he tended to his dwindling flock until Spring 1897, when he followed them to Dawson, 'a solitary, feeble old man with a single sled rope over his shoulder, and a single dog helping the load along.'[22]

Freighting to the Gold Fields

With the increasing gold production and the expanding number of miners in the Yukon, a new industry developed to service them – freighting. The first horses were brought into the territory in 1891 by Jack Dalton and E.J. Glave, at which time they explored the southwest corner of the

Yukon and went as far inland as Kluane Lake. The first animals to be brought down to Forty Mile arrived in the spring of 1893 with Pete Mac-Donald. These animals were used to haul logs out of the river as well as for packing.[23] They were either herded in over the Dalton Trail to the mouth of the Nordenskiold River, or they were taken farther downstream to Fort Selkirk to be put onto rafts and floated down to Forty Mile. The beasts of burden learned very quickly to stand still on the rafts during the day and to walk on and off them in the morning and evening, respectively.

Horses were also brought in over the Chilkoot Pass, which was difficult compared to the trip over the Dalton Trail. They had to be hoisted up the steepest part of the Chilkoot Pass in rope slings and on their sides; then they had to slide down the other side to Crater Lake on their backs.[24] They were then herded aboard rafts and floated downstream from the headwaters of the Yukon River to their destination. Horses were a considerable novelty when they first arrived in Forty Mile. Al Mayo had not seen horses in twenty-one years;[25] the Native people had never seen them at all. They gathered with their dogs on the shore of the Yukon River when the horses arrived at Forty Mile. When the first horse came ashore, he 'started up the bank, galloping and neighing and made straight for the Indians, kicking up heels. The dogs, together with the natives, fled in terror, to the brush and woods, and it was days before some of them returned.'[26] Though in demand, horses never fared well. They were plagued by swarms of mosquitoes and suffered from the cold.[27] Feed was always a problem. They relied largely upon feed supplied by the trading companies. Arthur Harper, who had horses at Fort Selkirk, fed them on local fodder, but they never came through the winter in suitable working condition.[28]

Dogs constituted the preferred means of transporting freight. Canines were used in the summer (when they carried packs) and in the winter (when they drew sleds). Sleds were the most economical means of hauling freight, the cost of winter hauling being one-third that of summer hauling. Professional freighters started to operate around 1892,[29] and the service increased thereafter until the gold rush.

With respect to dogs, on observer commented, 'if their values are great, their vices are many.'[30] Fights were constant, and if one should start to howl, the entire dog community would join in. Despite being prized for their economic value, they were not always treated well. In the summer, when they were not working, they were poorly fed; as a consequence, they were constantly foraging for food. Some men actually bragged that their dogs were experts at stealing from others.[31] They sought any means of getting into cabins to invade the larder and could open tin cans to get at their contents. They ate anything, including greasy dish rags, soap, snowshoes, and leather harnesses. One dog was seen to consume a candle, flame and all. They even turned upon each other and occasionally resorted to cannibalism.[32] Perhaps the most heart-wrenching scene ever witnessed in the Yukon valley occurred in Circle, when a Native infant died. While it was being prepared for burial, a dog snatched the corpse and made off with it through the heart of town, with the howling mother in hot pursuit. Soon, a number of White men also gave chase in an effort to catch the dog and relieve it of its morbid prize.[33]

Tending a dog team was hard and unpleasant. The work, of course, was performed outdoors and most commonly occurred when the temperatures were lowest. Dog mushers put in long hours preparing their teams, breaking up fights, freeing tangled lines, and feeding their dogs. All of these matters had to be taken care of before the musher could even think of himself. There was often a battle between the musher and his dogs to keep them away from the food until is was time for them to have it. At one place on the Birch Creek Trail, there was a stopover which had a dog-corral made from logs, and into which the sleds were pushed to keep them and their contents away from the hungry howlers.

A musher's day would start at 5:00 or 6:00 AM. First, the dogs had to be caught and harnessed. Then the provisions, bedding, mess-box, and other gear were lashed onto the sled and the team would be off for their next stop, twenty miles away. When the musher did retire for the day, it was usually after 11:00 PM. If a snowstorm swept down onto the musher and his team, they would have to stop on the trail, often in less than ideal locations. The dogs could curl up in a compact ball in almost any conditions and have a pleasant sleep; the best the man could hope for was to build a campfire and stay up all night guarding the sled.[34]

A dog team usually consisted of six or seven large, heavy dogs harnessed single file to a seven-foot sled which ran on runners only sixteen inches apart (this was so it could easily navigate narrow, wooded trails). The top of the sled extended about two inches on each side of the runners, and two long lash-ropes were attached to its front end. The freight was wrapped in a large canvas on the sled, and the two lash-ropes were then woven back and forth between side-ropes to secure the load. A little water sprayed on the knots kept everything from coming undone on the trail.

The normal freight train consisted of three of these sleds, single file, and connected by cross-chains (so that each would follow directly in the trail of the one in front). Extending upwards at an angle from one side of the front sled was a gee-pole, about six feet long and three inches in diameter. The musher walked in front of the first sled with the gee-pole in one hand. This pole made it easy to steer the sled, aided him in keeping it upright, and enabled him to steady it on side hills and around corners. The gee-pole was also used to break the sled free when it became frozen to the ground. On steep hills, the dogs were unhooked and the musher, holding on to the pole and his feet braced forward into the snow, would ease the load down the hill. If the load went out of control disaster could ensue – several mushers were crushed to death by their loads. In one instance, the gee-pole snapped off and the musher was killed, impaled on the sharp lance-like fragment that remained.

There were several advantages to using the triple sled system: (1) they manoeuvred easily over rough terrain; (2) they steered well along narrow forest trails; (3) they spread the load over a large bearing surface so that the sled did not easily sink into the snow; (4) they were easy to right if they overturned on the trail; (5) they could easily be taken up one at a time when hauled up a steep hill; and (6) on a return trip, now empty, they could be loaded on top of each other, making travel faster and more efficient.

Warm spring weather made for a completely different set of conditions. With the daily cycles of freezing and thawing, the ice became smoother. And, with the increasing melt water run off, the water level of the rivers rose under the ice and the ice itself began to arch in the middle, causing water to run off towards the shores (much like the gutters on the sides of a road). The gutter ice was thin and elastic and, thus, very dangerous. Sometimes when crossing this ice a musher with a team of fast-moving dogs could make it safely while leaving a trail of broken ice behind.[35] For this reason, the mushers preferred to travel at night, when it was cold enough to give the ice a chance to reform.

If they had no choice, the mushers resorted to a couple of tactics to improve their chances of getting safely across a river. Sometimes the ice was so thin that the musher would first send the dogs and sled across the thin ice, then he would 'lay down on the ice and wiggle his way across, flat on his face, spread-eagle fashion. This gave him much more bearing surface, and even if the ice did crack under him, he was still on top of the water.'[36] In other instances, they would attach a light pole cross-wise to the harness at the front of the sled and carry a sheath-knife. Should the sled break through the ice, the musher could save himself by cutting the bindings, throwing himself on the cross-pole while holding on to the harness, and letting the dogs pull him to safety.

Bringing in the Mails

Even at the best of times, communication with the outside was unreliable, interminably slow, and utterly dependent upon tenuous transportation links. The round trip for sending a letter and receiving a reply would be anywhere from a year to eighteen months in duration. By the time the response to the original letter was received, the writer had often forgotten what he had written about![37] Except at great expense, mail only came in the summer, by steamer.

Both governments were aware of the need for better mail service to the Yukon gold fields. In 1895, the governor of Alaska wrote to the American postmaster-general, describing the necessity of providing mail service to Circle and proposing delivery six times a year.[38] With the NWMP now posted in Forty Mile, it became even more important that a reliable mail link be established. In 1895, T.C. Healy offered to provide mail service to Forty Mile at a price of $600 per round trip. According to the figures provided by William Ogilvie, this was considered to be a good price, and the offer was accepted in the fall of that year.[39]

Nevertheless, in general, the mail service was extremely limited, and the arrival of mail was the cause of great celebration. Reverend R.J Bowen remembered his excitement upon receiving his first letter at Forty Mile, after having been there for a year. Imagine his disappointment when he discovered that it was a letter from his London outfitter with six samples of cloth and the prices for making a suit from each of the materials![40]

So rare was mail from the outside that to the men on remote gulches in the outback, any glimpse of the written word was cause for celebration. 'A trademark on a pick handle becomes fairly eloquent in that solitude,' noted one observer.[41] Two Alaskan miners received a small bundle of outdated newspapers from a friend in Seattle. This was cause for considerable excitement, and miners from the nearby creeks congregated at their cabin to read both the news and the advertisements. The ecstatic miners made a collection for their Seattle benefactor and sent him $400 in gold nuggets for his gift.[42]

Josiah Spurr, an American geologist, travelled to the upper drainage of the Fortymile River and encountered miners whose library consisted of a small number of books and three-year-old newspapers. He asked one of the miners what they did for entertainment. 'Do!' he echoed with grave humour, 'Do! Why God bless you, we 'ave very genteel amusements. As for readin' an' litrachure an' all that, wy, dammit, wen the fust grub comes in the spring, we 'ave a meetin' an' we call all the boys together an' we app'int a chairman, an' then some one reads from the directions on the bakin'-powder boxes.'[43] Reliable mail service would have to wait until after the Klondike stampede.

10

DEATH OF THE MINERS' COMMITTEE

Flood of '96

The Yukon is exposed to dramatic cycles of change each year, from the extreme cold of winter to the heat of summer. The most obvious harbinger of changes in the weather is the state of the Yukon River: the formation of ice announces the arrival of winter, and the break-up of that ice announces the arrival of summer. Whereas the freeze-up is slow and subtle, the break-up is violent and dramatic.

As autumn arrives in the Yukon, a number of changes take place. The days become shorter as the equinox approaches. The temperatures decline, and by the end of August, the leaves are changing colour. For a period of two to three weeks, the countryside is clad in gold; then the leaves are gone, and the country takes on a rather drab, brown appearance. The first frost occurs in late August. Finally, the mosquitoes and other insects disappear until the following spring, and the tens of thousands of migratory birds wing their way south for the season. A curious calm envelops everything. With the decreasing temperatures, the streams and quiet pools develop a morning crust of ice, which grows thicker as the season progresses. Slowly, the ice forms along the banks of the Yukon River, thickening and growing out towards the current. The shore of the river recedes with the decrease of water in the colder weather, revealing extensive areas of the river bottom.

Arthur Walden described the transition of fall into winter:

Early in October, very thin sheets of ice, about three or four feet in diameter are noticed coming downstream; these are almost as thin as window glass and as they grow thicker and more plentiful, they rub together and turn up the edges like Japanese water-lilies, and gradually turn white ... The ice gradually fill[s] the whole river. The cakes freeze together till the middle of the river is a solid mass of slowly moving ice. This white ribbon breaks at some of the sharper bends and opens, leaving a V-shaped crack of water to be closed later. The ice gets thicker until the final freeze-up when it closes for good.

The final closing of the river is almost as spectacular as the break-up in the spring. Jamming on some island or between ... narrow cliffs, a huge mass of ice is piled higher and higher, and as more is perpetually being pushed down, in some places, it stands more than fifty feet high, in great pinnacles, from bank to bank. The crushing and grinding noise it makes cannot be described, and is quite different from the roaring sound of break-up.

As more ice comes down and crushes itself on this barrier, it freezes back solid, to a distance of twenty or thirty miles, gradually getting smoother until it meets a new barrier that has been formed above, and the whole process begins over again.

This succession of huge barriers, alternating with smoother sheets formed the surface on which we had to travel.[1]

The spring presents the reverse situation and is a season of anxiety for anyone living close to the river. With the warm spring temperatures, the ice gradually 'rots' and creates 'candle-ice,' which melts away from the shores to leave a zone of open water along each bank. As the break-up commences, huge blocks of ice break off and float downstream, piling up against unbroken stretches of river ice, noisily grinding together, and, with ominous rumbles, breaking off masses of solid ice weighing several tons each. Finally, the entire mass dislodges and flows downstream, leaving open water. Similar floes pass by as tributaries upstream disgorge their own break-ups into the main current. If the ice floes jam in constrictions in the river, the upstream ice continues to build up, forming a huge dam behind which the water rises with alarming speed until the entire mass is freed and continues downstream. Hence, flooding is a constant threat during spring break-up.

By the beginning of May 1896, all eyes looked towards the Yukon River in anticipation of the break-up. Being gamblers at heart, the men of Forty Mile started numerous pools, betting on the day, hour, and

Spring flood at Forty Mile, 1896

minute that the ice would break up. Everyone stayed up late, watching the river and talking about the imminent break-up. A watchman was appointed to rouse the citizens when the river broke, because that is when the danger of flooding is the greatest. Break-up was later than usual, and the wait became monotonous. The watchman sounded the alarm once just to get some company, and then everyone retired and continued their wait. On 14 May, the Fortymile River broke up and dumped its ice onto that which was still locked in place on the Yukon River. Finally, on 17 May the cry went up that the river was moving. Huge masses of ice ground together and gyrated crazily as they moved downstream.

The ice finally jammed a few miles below Forty Mile, and the water level rose eighteen feet in an hour and a half, reaching the sugar bins in the AC Co. store. Everyone prepared to evacuate town. The bridge crossing the slough was washed away. One man, thinking that the end had come, jumped into his boat and paddled up the Fortymile River. Another was forced to climb up onto the roof of his cabin, where he completed the shave that was interrupted by the sudden rise. The mission, which was located on an island, was prone to flooding; when the water finally rushed in, the mission party was forced up into the loft to await a drop in the water level. The jam broke a couple of days later, and the water ran high for a few days before receding, leaving a line of icebergs, uprooted trees, and various debris in its wake.[2]

Life returned to normal very quickly in Forty Mile. On 25 May 1896, an order was given for the detachment of NWMP to parade at noon and fire a 'feu de joie' in commemoration of the Queen's birthday. With the opening of the river came a small armada of boats from upstream, carrying parties of varying sizes. One scow carried two bay horses; other men arrived with scows cut in half, the result of fractured partnerships.[3] From downstream came word of the gold discoveries near Circle, and there was another rush of miners to the new fields. That, and the fact that many of the local miners spent their winters on their creek claims rather than in town, meant that the town of Forty Mile was very quiet indeed. Its hey-day was over.

As the spring of 1896 progressed, the need to keep dry replaced the need to keep warm. The barracks at Fort Constantine leaked during the heavy rains that occurred that spring and summer, and oil sheets and tarpaulins were placed over all of the beds to keep them dry. The men worked on the completion of the existing buildings and added another small building to serve as a recreation and reading room. The stockade was also extended by forty feet on the north and west sides of the fort.

Mindful of the difficulties in cutting and hauling green firewood in the dead of winter, Constantine sent out a detail to cut sufficient dry wood to last them through the season. In all, 130 cords were cut. However, wood was difficult to find; the men scoured the banks of the Yukon River for seventy-five miles upriver and found only one place, an island fifty miles above Forty Mile, which had good dry wood in any quantity. From this island, they were able to cut a hundred cords of wood. Constantine stated that, given these circumstances, firewood would be even more difficult to come by the following year. Ironically, the place where the men cut the wood for their recreation room was the mouth of the Klondike River – within a year, this location would become home for thousands of men and women.

Introducing Law and Order

In the first eighteen months that the NWMP were posted at Forty Mile, they handled, on average, one case every two months. The first case which was heard by Inspector Constantine occurred on 25 August 1895. A man named D.W. Walker charged J.A. Williams with bringing stolen goods into Canada. The goods in question were the affections of Walker's wife. Williams was in the process of being married to her by Bishop William Bompas when he was arrested by Sergeant M.H.E. Hayne and taken into custody at Fort Constantine. This caused some difficulty at the time of the arrest, for there was no proper guardroom or jail in which to detain him. The difficulties in obtaining sufficient evidence to convict him were insurmountable. Although considered to be of questionable character, he was allowed to escape downriver by boat.[4]

In December 1895, Gus Clements was convicted on the charge of selling liquor to a Native and was fined $100 and costs. In March of the following year a case of theft against Clements was dismissed. Two men were sentenced to pay five dollars or to serve thirty days hard labour for breach of the peace, and another man was sentenced to pay $100 or to serve two months hard labour for selling liquor to a Native. However, the first real test of the NWMP's ability to maintain law and order came in 1896, and it marked a significant and irrevocable turning point in the development of the Yukon – it put an end to the miners' committee.

Decline of the Miners' Committee

Over the years, the miners' committee had deteriorated to the point at which the meetings were considered by some to be nothing short of a farce. This came about as a result of increasing population, greater diversity, and the fact that they started holding meetings in saloons. There is no doubt that liquor contributed to the decay of these committees.[5]

Liquor came into the Yukon as early as 1886, when a man named Hawthorne brought in fifty gallons of alcohol and liquor 'presumably to traffic with the Indians.'[6] The saloon was a potent factor in the social changes which were occurring at this time. According to William Ogilvie,

> There was a big profit in whiskey, and some who were going in [to the Yukon] anyway ... took it along and sold it at an enormous advance ... The liquor was sold to the saloon-keepers, who retailed it along with some water at fifty cents a glass. Like the saloons everywhere else, they had their clientele of loafers, and, like all the tribe, they interfered with other people's business more than they attended to their own. After the establishment of saloons, miners' meetings were often held in them, and as all present were generally counted miners ... only some were so when they had to be, seeing it was the only means of employment in the country, so all had a vote.[7]

An example of the problems with the miners' committee is provided by the case of French Joe who, on a trip to town down the Fortymile River, obliged a miner (whose cabin he happened to pass) by taking two ounces of gold to give to Bill Smith. He did so, but Smith complained that the miner owed him an additional ounce and demanded that French Joe produce it. The latter refused, of course, having delivered all that he was given, so Smith called a miners' meeting in Bob English's saloon. Eighty-six men listened to the case and six voted in favour of Smith, five for Joe, while the remainder abstained. In addition to paying the ounce of gold, the defendant was charged twenty dollars for the use of the saloon and had to buy drinks for everyone there. The total amounted to over $100, a large penalty to pay for someone who was simply doing a favour for a stranger.[8]

As the century slipped away, a few White women trickled into the region. This small but significant group had quite an effect on the miners' meetings. Joe Ladue, one of the original sourdoughs in the Yukon, noted bitterly, 'Nobody can get justice from a miners' committee when women [are] on one side.'[9] The 1895 incident concerning C.H.

Hamilton's female servant and her boyfriend (discussed in Chapter 9) was the sort of occurrence which helped to pave the way for the NWMP, as was the farcical 1896-7 trial of May Aiken, a black prostitute in Circle. The woman was encouraged to bring Phil Lester before a miners' meeting on a civil matter. The outcome of the trial was predetermined, and the affair was something of a joke to everyone except May, who did not know what was going on. After two gallons of whiskey had been consumed, the jury came out with the verdict. The joke went sour when George Snow, the judge, assessed a substantial fine against her. This, too, was apparently a joke, although not everyone was aware of the fact.[10] Consequently, the so-called 'coon' trial was also viewed as a miscarriage of justice.[11] The light way in which this trial was conducted reveals that the miners' committees were becoming merely a form of entertainment to allow the idle of Circle to while away the long winter hours.

Even when American government officials were sent into the Yukon basin, their effect upon the administration of justice was somewhat dubious. The Reverend R.J. Bowen describes the actions of an American government official (whom he mistakenly identifies as a US marshal) in Circle in 1896:

> The only government protection we had in Circle City was embodied in a United States marshal. I never really understood his duties but they seemed to embrace all government duties as required as each problem arose. His conscience seemed as elastic as his office. Although there were very stringent laws in reference to liquor being sold in Indian territory, and its disposition ordered as follows: It had to be poured into a hole in the ground ... underneath the hole in the ground into which the whiskey was poured, there was a larger hole ... which held a barrel, to which the liquor poured was led through a funnel and tube.[12]

The same year another observer, William Douglas Johns, noted similar corruption in a US government official (possibly the same one identified by Bowen):

> His [Tex Richard's] side kick in Circle was a young fellow who came in as a revenue officer and collected twenty five dollars a month from the saloonkeepers – as he could have made a nuisance of himself – for they could be heavily penalized for selling liquor as the A.C. Co. were the only ones who had a government permit to sell.[13]

The government officials at Circle were not respected by the miners in the camp. Josiah Spurr, a government geologist conducting a survey of the gold fields in the Yukon basin, experienced this disrespect when he stayed with two customs officers while passing through in 1896. The officers, who had just confiscated two kegs of contraband whiskey, were besieged by 'whiskey-dry' miners, whom they kept at bay only by force of arms. Spurr described a tense night of sentinel duty, during which shadowy figures lurked outside the cabin.[14] The situation could easily have been the same on the Canadian side had it not been for the NWMP.

Showdown on Glacier Creek

From the first moment they arrived in Forty Mile, the NWMP were on a collision course with the rough and tumble style of justice to which the miners were accustomed. Inspector Constantine set about collecting mining royalties from the miners on the Canadian creeks once the boundary was established. They grumbled, but they paid.[15]

If there was any doubt at all about the right of Canadian justice to rule, it was eliminated in a final incident in the spring of 1896. The action resulted from a resolution made by a miners' committee. A miner who had a 'lay' on claim #19 Above Discovery on Glacier Creek defaulted on paying his men. The local miners' committee supported the labourers' demand that the original owners pay up, and it sold the latter's claim off to the highest bidder. F.D. Van Wagener and another miner named Hestwood, the owners, protested to Constantine, who advised the committee in writing on 19 June 1896 that their actions were illegal. The committee disregarded this warning and sold the claim at a public auction. On the morning of 1 July, Fred Hutchings and Dudley McKinney, two of the most vocal opponents of the NWMP, took possession of the property. Terry Baker, the new 'owner,' came to Fort Constantine to register the bill of sale with Constantine, but the inspector refused to recognize the transaction or register the transfer of the claim. Baker left Forty Mile 'breathing defiance, and saying that the miners would see him through.'[16]

Constantine decided that it was time to act.[17] He sent Inspector Strickland, with a force of twelve officers and men armed with Lee-Metford rifles and side arms, to Glacier Creek with orders to settle the issue once and for all. Strickland and his men departed Fort Constantine the morning of 4 July. Guided by Natives familiar with the terrain, the mounties worked their way thirty miles up the Fortymile River, beyond the swift water of the Fortymile Canyon and the rapid current above it. The men pulled the boats against the current while their Native guides, standing aboard, poled them through the difficult waters. They stopped about fifteen miles upstream at approximately 4:00 AM, rested until 1:00 PM, and then continued to the mouth of Moose Creek, which they reached after another nine hours of pulling and a constant battle with the worst mosquitoes of the season.[18]

After getting a night's sleep, the mounties, each armed with forty rounds for their rifles, twelve rounds for their pistols, and carrying haversacks, ascended Moose Creek to Glacier Creek. They occupied the disputed claim, ejected Baker's agent, and refused to talk with the miners' committee.[19] After two days, the miners caved in to the mounties without a shot being fired in the process. The NWMP never received any complaints from the disputants in the case.[20]

Those who felt that their democratic rights had been infringed upon retreated to Circle, where the miners' committee still ruled supreme. The NWMP now turned to the task of maintaining law and order in the Yukon. The serenity was to be short-lived, for a man named George Carmack would soon dramatically change the course of events.

11

CIRCLE: THE LARGEST LOG
CITY IN THE WORLD

In just two years, Circle was thriving on the banks of the Yukon River and became the supply centre for the Birch Creek gold diggings. Originally established twelve miles farther upstream in 1893, it moved down to its final location in the spring of 1894 after the break-up of the Yukon River washed away several of its cabins.[1]

Because of uncertainty about the new gold finds, in the summer of 1894 the town consisted of a cluster of tents and a few small, quickly erected, log cabins. By September 1894, two trading posts were under construction, and as many as 300 men spent the winter at the newly established post.[2] Circle continued to grow; the following year saw the construction of a saloon and gambling centre, and the population rose to 700.[3] By the summer of 1896, Circle had eclipsed Forty Mile as the major mining centre in the Yukon basin and claimed the title of largest log city in the world.

By 1895 the gold recovery potential of the Fortymile and Sixtymile regions had stabilized. There seemed little opportunity for new discoveries, so when word was received of new finds down the Yukon River, many men immediately moved on to greener pastures. In addition, the presence of the NWMP (and the concomitant establishment of British justice on the Canadian side of the border) scared many Americans and whiskey traders away to the new gold camp. Circle was the beneficiary of this migration, and because of the increased gold production the population rose to nearly one thousand. Circle had another advantage, that of being 200 miles closer to the port of St. Michael on the Alaskan coast than was Forty Mile. Thus, not only was Circle easier to reach from the outside, but the transportation costs were considerably lower as well. The increased affluence of this town brought greater diversity than had hitherto been the case. More of the miners brought their wives from the outside to stay with them year-round. There were more children and a greater assortment of amenities.

A steep bank fronted the Yukon River, with an abundance of boats moored along the shore; piles of logs stood atop the bank, waiting to be whipsawed into lumber or cut into lengths to feed the hungry boilers of the steamers that plied the river. The city was surveyed and laid out on a grid. The main street, which was fifty feet wide and faced the river from atop the bank, was dominated by the trading posts and warehouses of the rival North American Transportation and Trading Company (NAT&T Co.) and Alaska Commercial Company (AC Co.). These were flanked by several saloons and dance halls (there were said to be twenty-eight of the former and eight of the latter in Circle that year).[4] One of these, a two-room log building, which had been both a gambling hall and a saloon, was occupied by two customs officers (the only American government officials in the wide-open town). Meals could be obtained in any of three restaurants, and fresh baked goods were available from a number of bakeries. In addition, Circle could boast several laundries.[5]

Surrounding this core of buildings was an array of log residences, each with its anti-mosquito smudge in front of the door during the summer. One of these was occupied by Julius Guise, the tinsmith, who made good, solid barrel stoves for the miners at sixteen dollars each;[6] one was owned by a Black man who operated a barber shop and bathhouse;[7] others were occupied by prostitutes and miners; one housed the local school; and one was home to the schoolteacher. Tapering off to the edge of the community, where the muskeg began, were the 'Indian shacks.'[8] Among the amenities which the town had to offer were two theatres, two churches, a hospital, three blacksmith shops, and a library containing 2,000 volumes (brought from Forty Mile by Jack McQuesten).[9] It was, in fact, 'as complete a town as one could expect on the Yukon, founded as it was but two years before, and rising so suddenly to importance in 1896.'[10]

This was a curious setting for a bustling community – on the outer fringe of the frontier. One visitor described the most outstanding feature of the busy town – the silence:

Circle, Alaska, 1894

Pack trains plodding through the soft muck of the streets; there was no paving; no wagons; no factories, no church bells ... There was little or no wind in this part of the country. The screech of a steam boat's whistle in the summer, sometimes weeks apart, and the occasional howl of the dogs were only part of the great silence. In winter time the silence was still greater. Even the scrape of a fiddle playing for the 'squaw' dances was bottled up, and everything was hushed by the snow.[11]

Still, for all its amenities, Circle, like Forty Mile, had its share of eccentrics. The winters were long and cold, and many of the cabins had been erected in haste, so they were never entirely free from frost no matter how hot the stove might be. One man described the neighbours from an adjacent cabin, musicians from one of the dance halls, who were all negligent about cutting firewood. They stayed at the dance hall as long as they could, delaying the return to their cabin, as the first one to return had to cut firewood and get a fire going in the stove. In the morning, they all delayed getting out of bed, as the first one up had the same duty.[12] Two other men shared a cabin, despite having developed an intense dislike for each other. It was too late for them to make other arrangements for the winter, and neither would move out. They split up their supplies, each cooked for himself, and neither talked to the other. If one was reading in the light from the other's candle, the latter would extinguish the candle and go out just to leave the reader in darkness.[13]

One man, known as the 'Old Maiden,' carried so much gear with him that whenever there was a stampede, he was too burdened down to arrive in time to stake. He always packed forty or fifty pounds of old newspapers with him, even in the roughest country, because he thought they were handy in settling disputes. Some of these men were scholars, educated at Harvard, Yale, and Oxford. One of these, an Oxford man and a younger son, was married to a Native woman with 'blondined' hair. He could quote Greek poetry by the hour when liquored up.[14] Others were uneducated or self-taught. They all lived together, people of many nationalities, in a town with no formal government, no taxes, no courthouse or jail, no post office, and no sheriff; yet they lived, generally speaking, in harmony.

There were, for the first time, a significant number of White women in the community. In addition to Mrs. Healy, the trader's wife, there was Mrs. Yates (the doctor's wife); Mrs. Guise (the tinsmith's wife); Anna Snow, and her daughter, Crystal. Mrs. Spencer was married to the saloon keeper. The school teacher, Anna Fulcomer, was there, too. Others included the wives of miners: more than a dozen lived in Circle by 1896. There were also the theatre women and the prostitutes, like May Aiken, 'Black' Kitty, Lottie Burns, and Esther Duffy.

Perhaps the most striking woman was a Mrs. Wills, a poverty stricken widow from Tacoma, Washington, who went first to St. Michael and then to Circle to work. There, she set up a bakery and sold loaves of bread to the miners at one dollar a loaf, twenty-four loaves per day. She filled in her spare time washing, ironing, and mending, and was in great demand. This hard-working woman was one of the lucky ones; she later left the North with a quarter of a million dollars.

The Traders

The most influential citizens in this community were the traders. Since the arrival of prospectors in the Yukon basin, there were always traders to provide them with the supplies essential to their quest for gold. After each new discovery along the Yukon River, the traders were quick to move to the new location to supply the needs of the miners. Under the grubstake system, the traders ensured that every miner received his share of available provisions. This process was egalitarian and ensured that no one starved at another's expense.[15] Prospecting for gold is like a gigantic lottery; as a consequence, the traders extended credit to many of the prospectors, carrying the debt for years, against the time when they would make a strike which would clear the ledger. The down side to this credit system was that many men were in perpetual debt to the trading companies and were virtually trapped in the North, unable to discharge their obligations.[16]

Gold was the universal currency in the North. At seventeen dollars per ounce, anything could be bought with it. Every business had a set of scales on its premises and, in keeping with the tradition of the North, fairness in all business dealings was expected. It was therefore considered bad manners if a miner did not display his trust by turning his back to a shop proprietor who was weighing out a payment of gold from his poke.[17] By 1896, the extensive system of credit in the Yukon basin was breaking down; the AC Co. no longer liked to extend credit to transients on the lower river because such courtesies were too often abused. The large influx of newcomers was slowly changing the standards of trust fostered by the earlier pioneers.

The grubstake credit system of the early traders made sense. Only when gold was found would it be possible for them to make any kind of profit. It was to their benefit, therefore, to have as many prospectors searching for gold as possible. This system increased the chances for making a big discovery. The supplies were distributed to the pool of prospectors to ensure that they had enough to allow them to continue their quest, while, at the same time, no one was given more than needed or allowed to corner the market in some commodity. Traders like Harper, Mayo, Ladue, and McQuesten made sure that everyone could continue prospecting, while also ensuring that none of their customers would go into competition with them. Unfortunately, the miners had to suffer high costs and poor quality goods until competition, mainly from J.J. Healy, forced the prices down.

In Circle Jack McQuesten was king. The senior trader in the territory, and the patriarch of the miners, it was said that half the town of Circle was in debt to him.[18] According to one observer, 'he ... outfitted, supported and grub-staked more men and kept them through the long winters when they were down on their luck, than any other person in the Yukon. Hundreds of men now on the river all owe the success they have to his help, and they know it and appreciate it.'[19] McQuesten, whose store dominated the waterfront of Circle (serving not only as the trading centre but also as the local post office and library), was even honoured by the Native women of the community. Whenever these women took part in the moose-skin toss, he was the first one to be thrown. This tradition continued for more than twenty years and did not stop until McQuesten was more than fifty years old.[20]

McQuesten's competition in Circle came from J.J. Healy, who had also located there to take advantage of the expanding market. Healy, who hated McQuesten, was his opposite in many ways. Healy believed in bills being paid promptly. Instead of extending credit to the miners as did his nemesis, he believed in promptly billing for his services and, as previously mentioned, the miners hated him for it. He was a strong character and intensely vindictive. Healy told one witness that 'he never felt right unless he had a fight on his hands and he usually had more than one – and that ... he never forgot and never forgave.'[21]

Healy would not sell anything to McQuesten's regular customers. One miner who had been grubstaked by McQuesten, for example, was left short of condensed milk. McQuesten gave him the money to buy the milk at Healy's store, but Healy threw the miner off the premises. Nor did Healy reserve his wrath solely for his competition, having once accused Captain Dixon, the skipper of the company steamer *Portus B. Weare*, of stealing from the ship's stores. The two men came to blows in the trading post and had to be restrained. Healy fired Dixon, but the latter appealed to the miners' committee, who found in his favour and made Healy pay up Dixon's three-year contract.

At the same time, Eli Gage, the profligate son of one of the investors in Healy's company, tried to kill a bartender in Bob English's saloon, thus raising the ire of the miners. Gage returned to Chicago with stories of lawlessness and called for the presence of the army to maintain law and order. Healy and his company provoked troubles and then profited from them. The influence of the company investors in Chicago was enough to get troops sent to the Yukon River, and the company made money supplying the army with provisions.[22] Healy had also lobbied the Canadian government to send police in to Forty Mile, where there, too, his company supplied provisions to the NWMP.[23]

Circle Gets a Teacher
With the North becoming increasingly 'civilized,' and with the gradual arrival of White women and children at Circle, the demand for access to formal education grew. On 7 January 1896, the town held a mass meeting at which a petition was prepared to send to the Department of

Education, requesting the presence of an experienced schoolteacher in the town. They promised to have a schoolhouse ready by September. In the meantime, they would provide a volunteer teacher and raise $1,200. All the women of Circle were made members of the Board of Education.

By the summer, however, enthusiasm had evaporated even among those who had children. A schoolhouse had not been constructed, and the funds fell short of those required to complete the job. Some people wanted the remaining funds diverted to the construction of a dance and meeting hall.[24] The Bureau of Education in Washington provided for the salary of the schoolteacher, fuel, and coal oil for lamps; the people of Circle were to provide a schoolhouse and furniture. The AC Co. loaned the town the money to construct the schoolhouse. During the course of the winter, five dances were held, and the sum of $1714.55 was raised to repay the loan. The remainder of the debt, $544.27, was never repaid – the stampede to the Klondike put an end to it.

The school was constructed (by local labour) of hand-hewn logs chinked with moss, and it was roofed with sod. On 1 October 1896 the sod was on the roof, and classes commenced amidst the continued construction activity. 'I opened school,' reported Anna Fulcomer, the newly arrived school teacher, 'despite the fact that for two weeks the carpenter worked among us, planing benches and doors, putting in a partition, and, of course, driving nails.'[25] The conditions in the school were barely adequate, and it was so cold inside the classroom that despite the 'good-sized' wood heater, Fulcomer occasionally became so cold that her teeth chattered. Due to a fortunate turn of good weather, the last steamer of the season was able to reach Circle, delivering four windows to the school to replace the cotton drill that had been covering the window openings.

In November, the temperature dropped to minus thirty degrees Fahrenheit. The school trustees hired a man, at forty dollars per month, to keep the fire going in the stove and to provide water for the class. The room was never warm, despite the ferocious fire in the heater, around which the children huddled in their parkas and mitts. The children would take turns standing closest to the stove so that they could all stay warm. When they breathed on the slates to erase their lessons, it instantly turned to ice! After the local literary society held a couple of meetings in the school, they realized how cold it was inside the building. Within a few days, the miners had replaced the inadequate stove with a roaring barrel furnace, which, once stoked, lasted half the day.

Anna Fulcomer had a curious assortment of pupils in her classroom. Where she had expected a dozen to attend, she had thirty-six. They were a mixture of White, Native, and Inuit, ranging in age from five to thirty. Some were unable to speak English, while others were well advanced in their schooling, having attended classes at Buxton Mission. Some were intent upon gaining an education, while others, including a fifteen-year-old White boy who was eventually expelled for misbehaviour, were not. Fulcomer was convinced that some of the Native children who attended were in school because it was the only place where they could get warm.

The classroom was ill-equipped. For example, each seat had to be shared by three pupils, and still there were not enough. Worse yet, the Department of Education had neglected to include primers for the students. Fortunately, Reverend R.J. Bowen loaned Fulcomer a collection of slates, pencils, and books, among which were included six primers and first readers. 'I doubt' she said, 'if such a medley of books was ever before seen in a school room.'[26] The books included geography texts, a world history, English readers, spellers, arithmetic books, half of a copy of the New Testament, a hundred pages from Wilkie Collins's *The Woman in White*, parts of four other novels, and scraps of newspapers. Some of the books were yellow with age.

Like many things in this land of perpetual winter darkness, time became rather distorted. The teacher would be up early and arrive at the school at 9:00 AM, either in darkness or crystal moonlight. It was so early that smoke would be coming out of only half a dozen or so of the chimneys in the community. Students would begin to straggle into the lamp-lit room at about 10:00 AM and would continue to appear until 12:30 PM. Other adults in the community would sleep late into the morning. When Fulcomer was walking home for lunch, she would be invited by friends to join them for breakfast.

By 1:30 PM, it was time again to light the coal-oil lamps. Since there were not enough of these to go around, the students would gather around each of them to conduct their studies in the faint light. By 3:30 PM, the youngest children were sent home for the day. As winter progressed, and the sun began to return, spirits picked up. Students began coming to class earlier in the day, and there were more frequent opportunities to play outdoors. During the colder weather, however, a small corner of the classroom was set aside as a playground so that the younger students could wear off the excess energy that is universally found in small children. This also made them better learners when they were finally given their lessons.

Unfortunately, before Circle ever had a chance to reach its peak, it became a victim of the Klondike gold rush. By March 1897, some of the older students had departed for the new gold fields. By the beginning of May, with nearly constant daylight, the number of students attending class was halved. The arrival of the first steamer headed for the Klondike was witnessed on 27 May. The settlement was in an uproar; everyone wanted to go to Dawson. The next day, only six children answered roll call. School was closed on 4 June. Said Anna Fulcomer: 'I closed the most enjoyable year of school work that I had ever known.'[27]

While Fulcomer was tending to the community's educational needs, a member of the clergy was tending to its spiritual needs. Needless to say, passing on Christian ideals to a community wholly obsessed with the pursuit of gold was a futile undertaking.[28] Reverend R.J. Bowen was loaned to the American Episcopal Church by Bishop William Bompas upon the request of Bishop Peter Rowe. He occupied a log structure which was acquired from Robert Ambold, a trader, and which had formerly been a saloon and gambling house. From here, Bowen provided service to a constituency which extended from Circle to the Birch Creek diggings and down the Yukon River to Fort Yukon. During the winter of 1896-7, he travelled throughout this constituency, lending assistance to miners and Natives alike. In addition to his travels, Bowen operated a small two-bed hospital, offered some instruction to visiting Natives, conducted regular church services, Sunday school, and religious meetings in the school house, and did general parish work as well as maintaining his own household.

High Life of Circle

As winter closed Circle off from the outside world, its social life went into high gear. As most log cabins were hastily erected, drafty, dark, lonely shelters, the men of the town were drawn to the saloons, which, as previously indicated, were the centres of social activity. They were warm, comfortable places with lights and music. Even if a man spent nothing, he was still welcome, because, in the great game of chance known as prospecting, today's pauper might well be tomorrow's king.

The men went to either the dance hall run by Billy Leake and Oscar

Ashby or to Harry Ash's opera house. Both operated with a string of 'dance-hall girls' brought in from Juneau. Harry Spencer, Frank Densmore, and Bill McPhee had a saloon with a large room next to the bar for dances or meetings. McPhee was not universally admired, because he was reputed to encourage men to drink themselves into insolvency. Bob English had a higher-class saloon, complete with billiard table. Other establishments were run by Billy Lloyd, Casper Ellinger, Fritz Miller, Billy Moran, John Burke, Al Shaw, Pete Nelson, Fred Bullie, Jim McCauley, and Jim White. Many of these men had been early pioneers in the Yukon.[29]

Well dressed and fed, the saloon-keepers, gamblers, and 'dance-hall girls' were at the centre of Circle's social life. The professional gamblers were a new element in the Yukon basin; they made their living off the miners, many of whom were themselves inveterate, if not accomplished, gamesters. The 'dance-hall girls' were treated with much respect, as they were the only single White women around.

Gambling went on in every saloon but not with the feverish intensity that was later found in Dawson. In addition to poker games, some of the establishments had faro layouts and roulette wheels. Faro was considered the game with the most favourable odds, but whichever game they chose, the miners would inevitably find themselves broke at the hands of the professional gamblers.[30]

Of all the gamblers, the most well known and respected was 'Silent' Sam Bonnifield, a barkeeper in Leake and Ashby's saloon. He was considered the best gambler in Circle. He never drank and was as straight as an arrow; so much so that even the likes of J.J. Healy trusted him. All the other gamblers wanted to beat him but could not do it. When playing his game, in the words of one observer, he 'gave one quick look at his cards, ran them together and kept his eyes on the other players, his own face – win or lose – as expressionless as a wooden Indian's.' Later on, Bonnifield won a saloon in a card game in Dawson. When he moved to Fairbanks, Alaska, he opened a commercial bank, his integrity and honesty obviously standing him in good stead.[31]

Circle had a number of prostitutes, who, although considered to be a notch lower on the social ladder than were the 'dance-hall girls,' were thought to be a necessity by the predominantly male community. They maintained a low profile and did not frequent the dance halls. They provided, for many men, the only female companionship that they had since coming to the North to look for gold. One of them, Esther Duffy, was renowned for her good heartedness and generosity. Another, Lottie Burns, was notorious for her delight in ruining men.[32] These women were often the brunt of cruel jokes, perhaps the most renowned of which was the infamous 'coon trial' of May Aiken.[33]

Circle had two theatres in the winter of 1896-7. The Tivoli was constructed in March 1896. The first professional troupe to perform there consisted of six women and five men who had been hired to play the winter. The Tivoli was touted as being the most northerly 'temple of amusement' in the world; the price of admission was two dollars and fifty cents.[34] Despite the novelty of having live theatre in Circle, the patrons soon tired of the performance, as the same program was offered nightly for seven months. It became 'so threadbare from repetition it was rotten.'[35]

One evening, the audience took it upon itself to change the performance:

> It was agreed by all to encore a different way. At a climax of a scene the Malamute howl was given by nearly every bean eater in the audience. Fiddle, piano and xylophone were put out of the running. Soon quiet returned and at it they go, when another ki-yi stopped the works. But here the leading lady showed to be in fine tragic form. The sourdoughs for once heard what that professional group thought of them.
>
> As an opening prelude: 'You s— of b——, look at that girl cry. You like it do you?' And, sure enough, the Virgin was crying. 'Gumboot, bean bellied scrawny Malamutes, we're doing our best to give you an evening of amusements, and now to be Malamuted!'
>
> [The stage manager climbed up to the stage and addressed the audience:] 'If there is any in the vast audience not satisfied with this clean and legitimate show, step to the box office and get your money back.' Next night a big advertising poster showed that the A.C. [Co.] brown wrapping paper and marking pot had been made use of.
>
> Miss M— Head Queen Artist in a New Role All in Cast of 'The Puyallup Queen' [read the poster, but the performance was virtually identical].[36]

By this time, it did not matter: the population was rapidly being siphoned off to the Klondike, as word of rich discoveries trickled back to Circle.

Meanwhile, George T. Snow brought his own family troupe to Circle and operated out of the Grand Opera House. Snow and his partner, Byron Allison, started building the theatre in the spring of 1895 and eventually formed a partnership with the AC Co. in order to complete its construction.[37] Patrons were treated to Snow, his wife, and his son performing such classics as *Uncle Tom's Cabin*, *Old Kentucky*, *The Newboy*, and *Camille*. In addition, the Circle City Miners' Association had their own log 'opera house,' where they sponsored minstrel shows and other entertainment presented by such people as 'Nigger Jim' Daugherty (thus named for his black-face performances) and Casey Moran.

The miners of Circle were not above abusing the performers as a form of entertainment. One night they lit a bonfire outside the Tivoli Theatre and called in a false alarm, which caused panic among the women, who, scantily clad, exited down a conveniently prepared slide and into the arms of the waiting men (much to the ire of Mr. Chase, the stage manager).[38] As one observer noted of that winter: 'Although legitimate drama of the blood-curdling type found many admirers, the dancing saloons were infinitely more popular.'[39] Furthermore, in the stillness and boredom of the long, dark winter, it seems that everything, including justice, became a form of entertainment in Circle.

For those who did not frequent the saloons and dance halls, they could always attend regular dances. Scheduled every two weeks, these dances were sponsored by the married women of Circle. They were ostensibly for the purpose of raising funds for worthy causes such as the school or hospital. At these dances a collection was taken to pay for the musicians, and the hall was provided free of charge. The musicians included Jim Bullard (fiddler), Sam Kelly (banjo), and one-legged Joe Twan (violinist).

During his stay in Circle, Josiah Spurr saw one of the first of these dances. It was held in the building occupied by the customs officers, and a 'pock marked vagabond' acted as master of ceremonies. Two unwashed miners from the creeks provided a string duet of fiddle and guitar music. The men wore high boots, rubber boots, moccasins, and mukluks. Flannel shirts without vests were common, although some men wore a corduroy coat or a red- and green-checked mackinaw. One man wore blue overalls (which, being much too large, were rolled up at the bottom) and a green and yellow abomination of a necktie; he also had greased down hair and seemed to be a favourite with the women. One new arrival to town wore a black cut-away suit and polished shoes.

The dance occurred in candle light. A row of shy, partnerless miners sat along the walls, hunched up and spitting tobacco juice 'until the dance floor [became] a sort of an island.' The couples gyrated in concentric curves around the floor in obedience to the caller's commands, and all agreed that they had a 'Haioo' time. At midnight, the women served cake, and the dance continued until a late hour.[40]

Both White and Native women were admitted to the dances but Native men were not. Although the Native women were dressed as well as the White women, they did not dance in the same sets. The men in attendance took members of both groups as dance partners and, all the while, 'little half-breed children ran about among the dancers and their baby brothers and sisters slept, or cried, in a corner.'[41]

Boxing matches also provided a form of entertainment for the men of Circle, the most notable of which was a contest arranged between Jerry Heater, who was six and a half feet tall, and a 'dwarfish' opponent, who was less than five feet tall. What the latter lacked in size, he apparently made up for in spunk.[42]

The Rush to Dawson

The discovery of gold in the Klondike came just when Circle seemed to be reaching its pinnacle of success and growth. When the suspicions were confirmed in late January 1897, the life-blood of the community, the miners, slowly trickled away, inflicting an injury from which the town never recovered.

In late January, Hugh Day arrived in Circle from Dawson, carrying word of the new rich finds to Harry Ash's saloon. At first, no one believed him, but a few hours later, Arthur Walden arrived from Dawson with the mail. Disregarding Walden's plea for a drink of beef tea, Ash sorted through a bundle of letters until he found one addressed to himself. Meanwhile, as word of the mail spread around town, men poured into the saloon to hear for themselves.

As Ash finished his letter, he exclaimed: 'Boys! Hughie is right! Help yourselves to the whole shooting match. I'm off for the Klondike!' Walden described the pandemonium that followed: 'Then began the wildest excitement as man after man got his letter and thought he was rich for life. Harry's invitation was promptly accepted and a wild orgy began. Corks weren't even pulled, and necks were knocked off bottles.'[43]

Within twenty-four hours, the price of a cabin in Circle had dropped from $500 to nearly nothing, while the price of dogs sky-rocketed. As the supply of dogs dwindled, so did the size of the teams that were being run. Those lacking dog teams pulled their own sleds – a numbing and heartbreaking task. By the time any of these men arrived in Dawson, hundreds of claims had already been staked and the prime ground had already been claimed.

THE DISCOVERY OF GOLD

IN THE KLONDIKE

The discovery of gold in the Klondike is the single most important event in the history of the Yukon. The circumstances of the discovery are surrounded by controversy and dispute as to who was the true discoverer of gold in the Klondike. There are several players in this drama, with personalities as unlike each other as possible. The traditional story tells us that Robert Henderson, a Canadian from the Maritimes, was the first person to discover gold in the Klondike region, and that George Carmack, who staked the discovery claim on Bonanza Creek, denied Henderson his share in the discovery.[1]

The 'Squaw Man'
George Carmack was born in Contra Costa County, California, on a wheat farm near Pacheco on 24 September 1860. At the age of two, he accompanied his parents east to Harvard, Illinois, where his mother died a short time later.[2] He returned with his father to Stockton, California, in the fall of 1865 and then went to Hollister, California, in 1869. At the age of twelve, Carmack was orphaned. He lived with his married sister for nine years. Eventually, his wanderlust took him north to Alaska. In the spring of 1885, he headed first for Juneau and then for Dyea. He spent the summer prospecting the upper reaches of the Yukon River, coming back out for the winter to work at Juneau. He signed on as a second mate on Healy and Wilson's schooner *Charlie,* and then helped the traders erect their first building in Dyea.

The following year, 1886, he accompanied miners named Barney Hill and Muldoon into the Yukon, prospecting down the Yukon River as far as the Big Salmon River. Discouraged by high water, he sold his outfit and hiked out across country to Dyea with three others. Subsisting on rabbits and fowl, they were near starvation. At one point, they found a Native cache with beans in it, which they ate; they then encountered Bishop Charles Seghers and his party on their way into the Yukon. Seghers provided them with a substantial meal of beans and enough food to get them to Dyea.

Carmack stayed at Dyea for the winter of 1886-7. It was here that he met a Tagish man named Keish, who was also known as Skookum Jim. They explored the White Pass together, and Carmack claimed to have been only the second White man to have done so. Carmack was at Dyea when Tom Williams delivered to Healy and Wilson his dying message concerning the Fortymile discovery. The following spring, Carmack did good business helping pack goods over the Chilkoot Pass (among those he helped were William Ogilvie and his party). Carmack spent the winter of 1887-8 trapping west of Tagish Lake.

For a while, in the spring of 1888, Carmack hauled freight over the Chilkoot Pass for other miners. Then he took trade goods over the pass himself and down to the Big Salmon River, with Skookum Jim and his nephew Kaa Goox (also known as Charlie), to trade with the Native people. Each of them obtained a good set of furs for their efforts. They tried their luck rocking for gold on the bars of the Yukon River. Carmack did fairly well from this, but did not find anything when he prospected the hills back of the river.

In September, the three men cached their boat and walked to Marsh Lake, where they found a small boat and paddled up the string of lakes to the Chilkoot Pass. Having lived on meat and fish all summer, the bread and bacon which they were given by some Tagish on Lake Bennett constituted a memorable event. Carmack sold his furs when he arrived at the coast and then returned to the Yukon to spend the winter of 1888-9 in the mountains west of what is now Carcross. Living for months on caribou, mountain sheep, and moose, he bivouacked under a canvas tarpaulin, using an open fire for heating and cooking. Carmack went back to Dyea in March 1889 'in good health and as tough as a piece of sole leather.'[3]

Carmack sold his furs to finance another trip into the interior in the spring of 1889. He travelled overland from the lower end of Marsh Lake to the Teslin River, picked up the boat which had been cached the year before, and travelled downstream to the Salmon River, which he ascended to the forks. He wanted to prospect the country between the Salmon and the Pelly rivers, as it had not been done before. Since the local Natives had convinced Jim and Charlie, his companions on this journey, that it was not a good idea to go into this country, Carmack proceeded on his own – without prospecting equipment and without success. He wintered downriver (below Fort Yukon) in a primitive cabin with H.H. Hart.

The following three summers, 1890, 1891, and 1892, Carmack mined on the Fortymile River and one of its tributaries, Nugget Gulch. In the fall of 1892, he went back upriver to Fort Selkirk and worked with Joe Ladue that winter, sawing lumber for William Bompas at one hundred dollars per thousand feet. In spring 1893, Carmack cut and hewed the logs for a large mission building. That summer, he hauled two tons of food and supplies twenty miles above the Five Finger Rapids and traded with the Tagish.

In the spring of 1894, he went downriver to help at the mission at Fort Selkirk. The steamer did not arrive in time to allow him to go back upriver to his trading post for the winter, so instead he floated down to Ladue's post at Ogilvie. From there, he spent the winter prospecting on Indian River and Quartz Creek, as well as in Sixtymile, without finding any pay. He worked at Ladue's sawmill the next summer and returned to Fort Selkirk to look after the post for Arthur Harper until the latter arrived on a steamer. Unfortunately, this steamer did not arrive until late in the season, so Carmack found himself again stranded at Harper's post for the winter, which he spent comfortably with Harper, Stewart Menzies, and two others.

Carmack led a life which was, in several ways, unlike that of the typical miner. He had married Skookum Jim's sister and, when she died, Tagish tradition dictated that her sister, Shaaw Tláa (Kate), take her place. Thus Jim and Carmack had strong ties through marriage. George could speak a couple of Native dialects (as well as Chinook), and he lived a life not so very unlike that of the average Tagish male. He liked the independence of his lifestyle and took it as a compliment when someone said to him: 'Why, George, you're getting every day more like a Siwash!'[4] He was widely known as 'Siwash George' and 'Stick George,' and, although many of the miners in the Yukon valley had taken Native wives, Carmack lived in closer association with the Native people than the miners found acceptable.[5] He was also given another name, 'Lying George,' because he always tended to colour his stories to place himself in the best light.[6] His lifestyle was eclectic: he had, at various times, been a sheepherder, a marine (he deserted the marine corps), a trapper, a trader, a labourer, a packer, and a prospector. Although he had looked for, and at least once found, gold, he was not regarded as a true prospector; for that reason he had no credibility amongst the miners.

Carmack's Dream

In late May 1896, while still at Fort Selkirk, Carmack tossed a coin and decided to go downriver. When he arrived at Forty Mile, he still had not resolved what his next move would be. That night, he had a very vivid dream. He dreamt about two beautiful fish, which were covered with gold nuggets rather than scales and which had twenty-dollar gold pieces for eyes. He interpreted this to mean that he should go fishing.[7] On 18 July, he loaded up his boat and started upriver with a prospector named Cooper, who was investigating some quartz outcrops opposite the mouth of the Klondike River.

After arriving at the mouth of the Klondike River with Kate, he was soon joined by Skookum Jim and his two nephews, Charlie and Patsy. They had not heard any word from Carmack in over two years and had become concerned over his whereabouts.[8] They established their camp on the shore of the Yukon River on the future townsite of Dawson and set their nets at the mouth of the Klondike River. Special fish-smoking structures had been constructed to cure the fish in Tagish fashion. It was here that Robert Henderson met them in early August 1896, as he returned to his mining prospects up the Klondike valley.

The Prospector

Robert Douglas Henderson was a stereotypical prospector. The tall, lean, blue-eyed, thirty-seven-year-old son of a Nova Scotia lighthouse keeper, he had been stricken with the lust for gold as a very young man. He had given up a secure career in the carriage-making business to wander the world from one gold rush to another, be it in Australia, New Zealand, or the United States. He lost his first opportunity to make a fortune when he gave up 160 acres of valuable property near Grand Junction, Colorado. Gripped by the quest for gold, it seemed, for him, that the seeking of this substance was more important than was the finding of it. After recovering

Native encampment at the mouth of the Klondike River, c. 1895

A fish-smoking operation, run by Fritz Kloke, at the mouth of the Klondike River, 1894

from a serious illness, he had returned to Nova Scotia, married, and settled down to a successful life of farming and fishing.[9] But he gave it all
up to head for the Yukon.

Henderson was drawn to the Yukon by glowing reports of gold in the
Fortymile region. He arrived at Ogilvie, Joe Ladue's post at the mouth of
the Sixtymile River, without a dollar in his pocket. Ladue was an opti-
mist. Confident that a big strike would eventually be made, and sure that
it would be nearby, he encouraged all of those who stopped at his post to
try the nearby tributaries of the Yukon River. Enthusiastic about prospects on Indian River (where an Englishman from Devonshire named
Billy Readford had found promising prospects), Ladue grubstaked Henderson and sent him to try his luck in the waters of Indian River.
Abandoning his original partners, Henderson struck out for Indian
River with a new partner, Jack Collins. Eventually Collins, too, left
Henderson, who remained at Indian River to find his paystreak.

Henderson spent the winter of 1894-5 alone on Indian River, thawing
holes to bedrock. For a lone man, this was incredibly tedious, slow work.
For his efforts, he recovered only a few colours.[10] In March 1895,
Henderson went further up Indian River to test a tributary called
Australia Creek. It took him sixty days just to transport his supplies from
his previous camp. Up Australia Creek, he found nothing to encourage
him, although he was able to live off the land; he killed some moose and
caribou and made a skin boat in which to float down Indian River.

It was while he was on Australia Creek that Henderson had another
stroke of bad luck which he described:

> In order to bridge the stream, I felled a large tree, and during the process
> of climbing it, held a stick in my left hand to steady myself. This unfortu-
> nately snapped off to the right and the broken jagged end penetrated the
> calf of my leg, thereby causing a bad wound and tearing the muscle of my
> calf. It was naturally very painful and I had to crawl back into camp, where
> I lay for 22 days only being able to creep on my hands and one knee to a
> nearby hole in order to bathe the wounded limb in the ice cold water. My
> leg would puff up and become much inflamed, but the cold water gave a
> great deal of relief.
>
> Not having any medicines, I used thin slices of bacon as a salve, and
> when these had done duty, I would throw them under the flap of my tent,
> from whence they would be devoured by prowling wolves of which there
> were hundreds in close proximity.[11]

Robert Henderson

Henderson lost forty pounds while recovering from the injury. He was also the victim of snow blindness and, in another instance, he capsized his boat and nearly drowned.[12]

When he was well enough to travel, he floated down to Quartz Creek in his skin boat. He travelled up this creek for a day and a half, then spent over two weeks building a dam to raise the water for sluicing. At the end of one and a half days of sluicing, he cleaned up only sixteen dollars' worth of gold. Disheartened by this and the continuing discomfort of his wound, which was still healing, he returned to Ogilvie, where he picked up more provisions and a new partner, Billy Readford. They returned to Quartz Creek, where they ground-sluiced in preparation for the following season.

Again, Henderson returned to Ogilvie for more supplies, then returned to Indian River alone for the winter. He spent his time burning holes to bedrock and making preparations for the spring clean-up. This time he made $620, which was poor pay for a hard winter's work. In the spring and summer of 1896, he eventually worked his way over the summit above Quartz Creek and down onto a tributary he called Gold Bottom Creek, which flows into the Klondike River. Here he started getting good prospects, eight cents to the pan.[13] He invited three men (Ed Munson, Frank Swanson, and Albert Dalton),[14] who were working on the bars at the mouth of Quartz Creek, to join him; between them, they shovelled out $750 worth of gold.[15] Running short of supplies, Henderson went back down Indian River and up to Ogilvie to replenish his outfit. Because Indian River was low, he decided to float down to the mouth of the Klondike River and return to Gold Bottom Creek from that direction. He left the word of his new discoveries with Joe Ladue, who, immediately and enthusiastically, spread the news.

Henderson touched shore at the mouth of the Klondike River. Surveying the small camp, the nets, and the fish curing, he saw George Carmack. 'There,' he said, 'is a poor devil who hasn't struck it.'[16] He walked over to greet Carmack.

The Encounter

Henderson hailed Carmack with news of his journeying from Joe Ladue's post to the mouth of the Klondike River. He explained that he was mining a tributary of the Klondike River, and that he was receiving a good return for his efforts. He and his friends were digging an open cut down to bedrock on Gold Bottom Creek, and he invited Carmack to join them and try his luck. Henderson also told Carmack that his Tagish relatives were not welcome. He did not like 'Indians,' particularly those from the upper Yukon River. This was not the most hospitable thing for Henderson to say about Carmack's relatives, and it cost him dearly. Having passed on word of his find, Henderson pressed on to join his partners on Gold Bottom Creek.

The next day, Carmack, Jim, and Charlie prepared small packs of provisions (mainly fish), shovels, and pans and set out to see Henderson's find. Rather than follow the Klondike River for several miles to where Henderson's creek flowed into it from the south, they turned off at the first tributary, a small stream known as Rabbit Creek, and ascended it, prospecting and fighting the dense underbrush and the thick clouds of mosquitoes as they went. At a point not far from what later became the discovery claim, Jim and Charlie panned out ten cents' worth of gold from the stream bed. The men discussed this and decided that if they found nothing better on Gold Bottom Creek, they would come back to test the gravels more carefully.[17]

George counselled Jim and Charlie not to say anything about their find; they would pass the word along to the Henderson party if the prospect panned out. They continued up the creek bottom until they reached a fork; here, they chose the southerly fork. After following this fork for some distance and finding the travel difficult, they ascended the ridge above it and travelled to the east to where another ridge joined it from the north. They did not know it then, but the creek they had just left was later to become known as Eldorado Creek. From the point where these two ridges met, they looked down into the canyon below and, in the distance, saw a wispy column of smoke rising from a tiny camp. They descended the valley until they reached Henderson's camp. Here, they tested the prospect and, though finding nothing as promising as what they had just found on Rabbit Creek, they staked claims on Gold Bottom Creek near Henderson's quarry on 11 August 1896 and then left.[18]

Before leaving, however, Henderson had an encounter with Jim and Charlie which sealed his fate. Being nearly out of supplies and sorely wanting some tobacco, they offered to buy some from Henderson, who declined. Henderson was still bitter about a perceived wrong which had occurred the year before, and which he blamed on 'Indians.' He had returned to a cache in which he had stored a good quantity of supplies, found everything gone and, as a consequence, nearly starved. He was convinced that the thieves were Natives, as he had been the only White man in the region at the time.[19] As Carmack said later, 'his childish unreasoning prejudice would not even allow him to stake on the same creek with the despised "Siwashes" so his obstinacy lost him a fortune.'[20]

Carmack, Jim, and Charlie climbed back over the ridge separating the waters of Gold Bottom Creek from those of Rabbit Creek. They slowly worked their way down Rabbit Creek, prospecting while they went. After three days, they had run out of supplies. At this point, Jim was fortunate enough to kill a moose. He signalled the others and, while he was waiting for them to arrive, went to the creek to get a drink. He saw gold in the bottom of the creek in greater quantities than he had ever seen before.[21] Here they tested the gravel and were able to fill a shotgun cartridge with gold. The next day, after having tested the stream up and down for some distance, Carmack flattened the sides of a small spruce tree in the middle of the valley, and on it he wrote in pencil: 'TO WHOM IT MAY CONCERN: I do, this day, locate and claim, by right of discovery, five hundred feet, running up stream from this notice. Located this 17th day of August, 1896. G.W. Carmack.'[22] Carmack took the discovery claim and another one above it (#1 Above Discovery) for Jim, the claim below discovery for himself, and #2 Below Discovery for Charlie.

Carmack and his partners immediately headed down the valley at top speed, floundering through the swampland and arriving at the mouth of Rabbit Creek looking like 'human pin cushions.' There they encountered four prospectors who had been directed to the Klondike River by Joe Ladue. Carmack redirected them up Rabbit Creek. At the mouth of the Klondike River, he met two Frenchmen, whom he also directed to Rabbit Creek. He sent Jim back up to start working the claim while he and Charlie headed for Forty Mile. He passed the word to more miners along the way, but he never sent word back to Robert Henderson, who, oblivious to the excitement just over the ridge, was still working with his partners on Gold Bottom Creek.

The two discoverers arrived in Forty Mile on 20 August 1896 with word of their new discovery, first making their announcement in a saloon and then crossing over to the NWMP post to file. The news of their discovery took root and consumed the passions of the miners. By the next morning, the town of Forty Mile was empty. Ironically, Carmack was unable to file his claim at that time due to insufficient funds. Inspector Charles Constantine told him that if he had indeed found gold, he could go back to get enough to pay his fees.[23] After rushing to Forty Mile, he and Charlie had to turn around and struggle back upstream to pan out their winter grubstake and their filing fees.

The effect of the stampede upon the denizens of the mining camp was electric. Everyone was gripped by the fever to gamble on the untested ground of a newly discovered creek. Suddenly, the value of boats sky-rocketed while that of real estate plummeted. In the winter, the value of dogs surpassed that of boats. The race to stake a claim on the new creek was, indeed, frantic.

The fever spread faster than an epidemic. Those who were mining up Fortymile River noticed that men who had gone down to McQuesten's post to get supplies had not returned. Suspicions aroused, they floated into Forty Mile without having received any news of the strike. Their deductions were correct, and they, too, became infected with the fever. Boats which had been left in Forty Mile in the custody of friends were 'borrowed,' leaving the owners stranded on the shore when they arrived in town, eyes straining upriver, waiting for signs of a returning launch.

Even the NWMP were gripped with the fever and were granted leave to go up and stake ground. Constantine and Strickland remained at their posts, immune to the plague, although Alfred Wills (the surgeon), a staff sergeant, and several of the men were infected. Within a few days, they had taken leaves of absence and joined the stream of hopeful men dragging their boats upriver to the Klondike. Even before Carmack had reached Forty Mile, word had spread among the men already near the Klondike River. On 22 August 1896, twenty-five of them met on a hillside one and a half miles below Carmack's claims. There, they renamed Rabbit Creek 'Bonanza Creek'[24] and appointed Dave McKay to serve as a mining recorder.[25] Someone produced a measured length of rope with which to measure the lengths of the claims. This was later to create problems which William Ogilvie had to straighten out. In the meantime, they started removing and relocating stakes according to the 'measured rope,' thus reducing the length of the claims.

Carmack and Charlie returned to Bonanza Creek as soon as they could and commenced to mine their claims. They constructed a low dam from which the water flowed down a ten-foot long sluice box which had pole riffles in the bottom. The two Tagish hauled gravel on their backs in two small, home-made boxes from a bank fifty feet away, while Carmack tended the sluice box and removed the small amount of tailings which were produced. Passers-by would stop and, by accepted practice, pan a sample of the paydirt, while Carmack glowered at them as he laboured at his sluice box. Most of the gold was lost from this primitive recovery system; nevertheless, Carmack was recovering about five ounces per day and, within three weeks, had recovered $1,400 worth of the precious metal[26] – more than enough to cover the cost of his filing fee and his winter grubstake.

Sluicing on Bonanza Creek, #2 Below Discovery

The weather that fall was unusually cold, and snow fell early. Despite the discomfort, there was a constant stream of men moving up and down the Yukon between the Klondike River and Forty Mile to obtain food and supplies, file claims, and then frantically return to their claims to start work. The silence of this tiny valley was broken by the hurried

Drift mining on Eldorado Creek, winter of 1896-7

activities of 300 men, who moved up and down Bonanza Creek looking for open ground and opportunity.

By tradition, they started staking below the discovery, then rapidly filled in the ground above. Others staked on the tributaries, including a tiny stream called Whipple Creek, which was renamed Eldorado Creek and which entered Bonanza Creek about half a mile above Carmack's claim. The confluence of these two creeks soon became known as Grand Forks and served as the focal point for the mining activity in the gold fields. The first bench claim was staked in December 1896 by George Bounds. By 20 November 1896, 338 claims were filed with Inspector Constantine. William Stanley staked claim number 500 on 6 January 1897; by 14 June 1897, just before the new tide of prospectors arrived from the outside, 584 claims had been staked.

Unfortunately for Robert Henderson, word did not reach him until a couple of weeks after Carmack's discovery, and he was not able to take advantage of the Bonanza Creek discovery. He eventually filed a claim on Hunker Creek, not even being able to take advantage of the right to a discoverer's claim (which is double the normal size) because of changes in mining regulations. Eventually, Henderson left the Yukon for a short time, dispirited, profitless, and in ill health.

Joe Ladue, who followed quickly on Henderson's heels, was one of the

Joe Ladue, trader and founder of the city of Dawson

first to arrive in the Klondike River valley. Sensing from experience that a town would spring up at the mouth of the Klondike River, he staked a townsite of 160 acres and, realizing that there would be a tremendous demand for lumber, sent his land application to Forty Mile by messenger. He then went back to his post at Ogilvie to move his sawmill and supplies downstream to the new townsite. Meanwhile, the AC Co. steamer *Arctic* pushed up through the ice to the new townsite to drop off a hundred miners[27] and a small amount of supplies. In less than a month from the time of Carmack's discovery, a new townsite was created which would soon be the hub of the greatest gold rush in Canadian history. William Ogilvie named it after George Dawson, with whom he had explored the Yukon in 1887.

Who made the Discovery?

There has long been a dispute as to who should claim the title as the discoverer of the Klondike gold deposits.[28] In 1904, an affidavit was sworn by the most prominent and senior officials of the Yukon, which states that Bob Henderson was the real discoverer.[29] The claim is based upon the work he had done on Indian River and Gold Bottom Creek just prior to Carmack's discovery. Joe Ladue, in fact, was directing everyone who passed his post in August 1896 to try the waters of the Klondike River. He, himself, was on his way to the Klondike River (on Henderson's word) to stake ground, when he turned back to bring his sawmill down the Yukon River. Carmack passed the word of his discovery to others whom Ladue had sent to the Klondike River. These men were eventually to reap immense profits for their brief and chance encounter with him on the banks of the Klondike River on 18 August 1896. It is obvious that these men were entering the area on the basis of information supplied by Henderson. But Henderson does not deserve the credit for the first discovery of gold on either the Klondike River or on Indian River.

Numerous men had been around the Klondike River before Henderson, including McQuesten and Ladue.[30] In fact, it was Ladue, along with John Nelson, Dan Sprague, and Pete Nelson, who first found gold on the upper reaches of the Klondike River in 1886. Sprague and Nelson found twenty-five- to thirty-cent prospects on one bar, but they did not consider it worthwhile.[31] George Carmack did not claim that he was the first person to find gold in the Klondike River region – just that he was the first to find it in paying quantities. He gave credit to Andrew Madden for having

Dawson, 1897

178
0.97.

found gold on the Klondike River in 1889.[32] What happened on Bonanza Creek was typical of what happened elsewhere in the Yukon; it was a chance discovery on ground that others had already passed over as worthless. The traders had a system which maximized the number of prospectors working in the Yukon. Each prospector was grubstaked for the supplies that he needed to carry on but not for those that would enable him to be idle. By 1896, Ladue was diverting everyone possible to the new region reported by Henderson in the hope that their sheer number would create a better chance for one of them to find the paystreak.

With respect to the discovery of gold in the Indian River region, that distinction goes to Billy Readford, who preceded Henderson into the area.[33] Even Carmack had mined on Quartz Creek the winter of 1894-5.[34] In fact, it was widely felt that a big discovery was imminent. That year, for example, Jack McQuesten cautioned Henry Davis not to leave Circle for the outside: 'No, Henry, you stay here, somebody is going to make a big strike here soon for sure.'[35] Perhaps it was just McQuesten expressing the eternal optimism that all the traders shared, but these men had been in the region for more than two decades and had seen the gradual growth of the placer mining industry.

What is certain is that Henderson dealt himself out of the benefits of the discovery because of his attitude towards Native people. He committed a serious mistake when he insulted the men with whom Carmack had lived and worked for ten years, and into whose family he had married.

It has also been said that Carmack had broken the miners' code by sharing word of new discoveries with others, but Henderson's prejudices had not helped matters.[36] Henderson, too, was guilty of violating the rigid moral code of the gold camps, for he had refused to share supplies with someone who was in need The prospectors were accustomed to sharing their last crust of bread if they came upon someone who had none.

The claims to discovery were also based upon national pride. Canada had a choice between recognizing an Englishman (Readford), an American (Carmack), or a hard-working, if luckless, Canadian from Pictou, Nova Scotia. National pride regarding so important an event would not allow credit for the discovery to go to anyone but a Canadian. So the Canadian government gave Henderson a yearly pension to prove that he was the rightful owner of the title. In fact, if neither Carmack nor Henderson had made the crucial discoveries, it was inevitable that someone else would have. Within a year of Carmack's find, the stampede was on.

13

EPILOGUE

During the years when the gold-seekers of the Yukon were searching out the large placer deposits hidden in the frozen gravel, great events were happening around the world. Nations went to war, and battles were won and lost. Great Britain was reaching its ascendancy under the reign of Queen Victoria, and the British Empire was expanding around the world. Great literature was being penned. Mark Twain, Henrik Ibsen, Oscar Wilde, and Leo Tolstoy were publishing their works, while Karl Marx's works were published posthumously.

In medicine, scientists were just beginning to understand the importance of bacteria and sterilization. George Eastman perfected his Kodak box camera, Rudolph Diesel patented his internal combustion engine, Karl Benz and Henry Ford began producing automobiles, and Wilhelm Roentgen discovered X-Rays. Chicago hosted the Colombian exposition, Jack the Ripper gained notoriety, haunting the streets of Whitechapel, London, and the Canadian Pacific Railway was completed. Events which shaped the course of world affairs were occurring all over the globe.

And in the Yukon, a small army of ordinary men struggled with the elements in the fevered search for gold. Little that went on in the 'outside' really affected them, so isolated was their world. Only near the end of the century did something happen which overnight catapulted this obscure corner of the globe onto the centre stage of world events – the great Klondike gold rush. Yet the figures who furthered the developments leading up to this event were dwarfed by the sheer enormity of the tide of humanity which flowed over the Chilkoot Pass in 1898.

What happened to the places which were the focus of activity before the great stampede? Fort Reliance was abandoned when McQuesten and Harper moved to the mouth of the Stewart River; it was never reoccupied. Slowly, the remains of the settlement disappeared (as did those of many other settlements during that period) into the hungry boilers of the small steamers that transported goods up and down the Yukon River. Today, it consists of a few depressions in the bank beside the Yukon River, of interest only to archaeologists.

Fort Nelson, at the mouth of the Stewart River, never really grew at all. Its short-lived existence ended when the miners stampeded to Forty Mile. Slowly, the Yukon River eroded the ground on which it stood until it disappeared. Forty Mile, too, diminished gradually after the Klondike gold rush until it was finally abandoned. Both it and Fort Selkirk exist today as small clusters of abandoned log and frame buildings, under the protection of the territorial government but victims, still, of the harsh elements.

And what of the pioneers who played such an important roll in the search for gold? Jack McQuesten, the king of Circle City, retired to San Francisco, where he lived in relative comfort until his death in 1909.

Both Arthur Harper and Joe Ladue cashed in on the Klondike gold rush by investing in real estate. Ladue selected 160 acres of prime land on the moose pasture that became Dawson. His lots sold at high prices and he became incredibly rich. Having left New York state more than a decade before with a vow that he would become rich enough to return and marry his sweetheart, Ladue was finally able to fulfil his dream. Worn out by the years of hard living in the North, and exhausted by the demands of the gold rush, he succumbed to tuberculosis in 1901 in his home in Plattsburgh, New York. Harper, too, did not live long enough to enjoy the fruits of his labour. He died, also of tuberculosis, in Arizona in November 1897 – just as the stampede to Dawson was reaching its pinnacle. At the time of his death, he left his wife and seven children an estate worth over $200,000, which, at that time, was no small sum.[1]

Fred Hart, who came into the country at the same time as did Harper and McQuesten, also died during the gold rush, without even the comfort of having made a fortune. He was buried on 12 November 1897, in the Yukon Order of Pioneers cemetery on Eighth Avenue in Dawson. His grave is still there.

Chris Sonnickson never made it rich mining. In 1897, he took up freighting and ranching. He died in Dawson of a heart attack in 1901, leaving a wife, five children, and an estate worth forty to fifty thousand dollars.

William Ogilvie became the most trusted civil servant in the Yukon and, when the scandal of corruption tainted the administration of the first commissioner of the new gold rush centre, he took over and served with distinction from 1898 to 1901. He returned to the Yukon briefly in 1908 as the president of a dredging company located on the Stewart River. Always a dedicated and honest public servant, he died in poverty in Winnipeg in 1912.

Both Skookum Jim and Tagish Charlie had their lives ruined by the gold rush. Never totally accepted by White society, and no longer able to return to their traditional ways, they both lost their families and lived out their years looking for another Bonanza Creek. Charlie drowned in 1909, after falling from the bridge in Carcross. Jim contracted Bright's Disease and died in 1916.

George Carmack fared well after the Klondike gold rush. He left his Tagish wife, Kate, and in 1900 married Marguerite Laimee, who operated a cigar store in Dawson. The couple moved to Seattle, and while George searched for another Bonanza Creek in the Cascade Mountains of Washington state, Marguerite managed various properties in Seattle. In 1917, Carmack purchased and worked mining property in California, but never again did he experience the heady thrill of a big strike. Carmack contracted pneumonia after giving a speech to the Yukon Order of Pioneers and died, in Vancouver, on 5 June 1922. He left behind an estate valued at $150,000. His wife and daughter battled over the disposition of the estate and, in the end, lawyers got most of it.

Doctor Alfred Ernest Wills, who so ably served the sick in Forty Mile while with the NWMP before the Klondike gold rush, resigned his post in February 1898 and remained in the Klondike region for several years, operating a partnership (which was considered to be the largest private mining operation in the gold fields) on Gold Run Creek.

Jack Dalton made money supplying cattle to the Klondike region (over the trail that bears his name) during the gold rush. Going on to projects in other parts of the North, he led an adventurous life and died in San Francisco in 1945 at the age of eighty-nine.

Bob Henderson never did find the wealth which he sought. Plagued by bad luck, he did receive a small pension from the Canadian government in recognition of his contribution to the discovery of the Klondike gold fields. Still seeking another big strike, he lived for several decades after the gold rush.

Reverend R.J. Bowen continued to serve his church for many years, establishing the first Anglican Church in Dawson and serving the congregation in Whitehorse.

Father William Judge did not survive to see the new century. Suffering ill health from overwork and constant strain, he tended to the sick and needy during the gold rush, establishing the first hospital in Dawson. Dubbed the 'Saint of Dawson,' he died on 16 February 1899. He was recognized by the Historic Sites and Monuments Board of Canada in 1991 for his contributions to the people of Dawson.

The Yukon Order of Pioneers still exists, although its membership requirements have changed over the years. Today, any man who has lived in the Yukon for more than twenty years may apply for admission. In recent years, the male tradition of the organization has been challenged. Madeleine Gould, a long-time resident of Dawson, applied for membership in the all-male organization, and, when refused, she appealed to the Human Rights Commission. The case is currently before the Supreme Court of Canada.

In later years, the American Episcopal missionary, Hudson Stuck, recorded an encounter on the Yukon River with one of the pre-Klondike pioneers. Stuck was travelling upriver on one of the steamers when he passed an older prospector poling his way upstream to one of the river's tributaries. An offer was made to give the man a lift, thereby making his journey much easier and faster. The man declined and continued to pole against the heavy current by himself. The behaviour of this solitary argonaut exemplifies the hardiness of those early pioneers.

In *Klondike: The Last Great Gold Rush, 1896-97*, Pierre Berton wrote the following about the stampeders on the trail of '98:

> In the years that followed, they [the stampeders] tended to run their lives as if they were scaling a perpetual Chilkoot, secure in the knowledge that any obstacle, real or imagined, can be conquered by a determined man. For each had come to realize that the great stampede, with all its searchings and its yearnings, with all its bitter surprises, its thorny impediments, and its unexpected fulfillments, was, in a way, a rough approximation to life itself.[2]

Like the argonauts to whom Berton referred, the early miners and prospectors proudly carried the badge of their experiences as a symbol of what they had done in the early days on the Yukon River. Though most of them never became rich as a result of their search, the communal/ independent ethic which evolved during their early search for gold in this northern wilderness formed the measure by which most of these men gauged the rest of their lives. They suffered hardships that were almost unimaginable, and they overcame them. The experiences and hardships of the Klondike stampede were modest compared with those endured by the men who came before.

The early adventurers established a society which served as a model for those who followed during the great gold rush. In many ways, the northern frontier seems different from the western frontier. The harsh climate, the distances, and the isolation compelled the prospectors to cooperate. This legacy was inherited by the Klondike mob and, in con-junction with the presence of the NWMP, made the great Klondike gold rush a peaceful and orderly event. The early pioneers sought for nearly twenty-five years to locate the mother lode. Their quarter-of-a-century quest culminated in the discovery which completely changed the face of the Yukon wilderness and thrust it, on the eve of the birth of the twenti-eth century, onto the main stage of world events.

APPENDIXES

Appendix A: Mining Methods and Terms

Prized since ancient times, gold is a soft, yellow, virtually indestructible element with a melting point of 1,994 degrees Fahrenheit and a density more than nineteen times that of water. It is commonly found in hard rock deposits, where it is incorporated into the rock, or in concentrations of more or less free particles (*nuggets*), which are found in unconsolidated gravels. In the latter form, it is known as placer gold, and the recovery of gold in such deposits is known as *placer mining*.

Ranging from tiny, almost microscopic granules (dust) to large nuggets weighing many ounces, its density causes it to settle quickly to the bottoms of streams, even when the water is moving at a rapid speed. It tends to concentrate in small backwaters or eddies and can lie in these deposits for tens of thousands of years, awaiting discovery.

A prospector will investigate stream beds looking for gold, testing the bottom materials with a gold pan, which has a circular, flat bottom and broad, sloping sides. Mixed with water, the gold in the gravels will, when agitated vigorously, settle to the bottom of the pan. The pan is normally agitated at a slight incline, so that the dense yellow particles will be trapped in the angle formed by the bottom and sides of the pan. After centuries of mining, this is still the first basic step in the gold refining process.

Once concentrated deposits are found in a stream bottom, the material is trapped in a *sluice box*, which is a long, narrow, open-ended box, slightly inclined so that water will flow through it. The placer gravel is excavated and dumped in the upper end, where it is mixed with generous quantities of water. As this mixture flows down the incline, the gold falls to the bottom of the box and is trapped between rows of ribs, or *riffles*, that are placed in the bottom of the sluice box at right angles to the current. The sluice box is still incorporated into every complex mechanical device used for gold recovery.

Another form of gold recovery involves the use of the *rocker*, a box-like device, handmade, which is rocked back and forth like a child's cradle. While rocking this device with one hand, with the other a placer miner scoops water (using a small homemade ladle) into a hopper, through the screened bottom which the finer material passes with the water. In the lower portion of the rocker, gold is trapped on a canvas apron or in riffles. During a *clean-up* the introduction of water and gravel is stopped, and the riffles are removed. The material trapped between the riffles, which contains a large concentration of gold, is scooped up and taken away to be panned.

Gold is given different names, according to its granular size. *Flour* or *dust* are terms used to describe the finest particles normally recovered. *Flake gold* consists of discrete granules, up to about one-eighth of an inch in size. *Nuggets* are the next size of particle and range from a fraction of an ounce to several ounces in weight, the latter being several inches in diameter. The shapes of these nuggets vary, and they are often incorporated into fragments of quartzite. In the Yukon, the appearance of gold nuggets varies in purity and appearance from one creek to another.

The gold found in the Yukon valley is usually trapped in ground which is permanently frozen. Before the gold can be removed, the ground has to be thawed. This can be achieved naturally, with water or the heat of the sun; or it can be achieved artificially, with fire. In the period covered in this account, fire was often used to thaw permafrost.

The majority of gold found in the earliest explorations was in the bars of the large rivers (*bar claims*). As time went on, particularly after the discovery of coarse gold on the Fortymile River in 1886, gold was found in the bottoms of the creeks and smaller tributaries (*creek claims*). *Bench claims* consist of gold found in placer deposits on hillsides above the creeks. Extraction of gold from these deposits required the miners to find some way of getting water from the creek up to the bench deposits. This was usually done through the use of ditches or flumes, which diverted water upstream to the claims along the contours of the hillside.

In some instances, wheels were used to raise the water level. These usually consisted of a continuous chain of buckets, placed on a raft, which would be powered by the current of the very creek or river from which the water was being drawn. There are some accounts of these being used, but they seem to have been limited. There are virtually no references in the early accounts to suggest that steam equipment was being used in any aspect of placer mining – whether for thawing, powering engines, or for pumping water (although, in one instance, Al Mayo is recorded as having used a pump from the *New Racket* to raise water to mine the banks of the Stewart River).

Once a deposit was discovered by an individual, it was *staked*, or marked out, and then *claimed*, or documented. The size of the claims was prescribed in the government mining regulations and was subject to occasional change. Before the presence of the government was felt in the Yukon, the size of the claims was established by consensus at meetings convened by the miners. Usually, one individual was designated as the mining recorder, whose duty it was to keep track of the ownership of these claims.

When the claim was staked, the miner might either work his claim or form a partnership with others. In some cases, another would take a *lay* on a claim. This meant that he could work the claim for the registered owner for a share of the gold.

Every miner dreamed of finding the *paystreak* in a placer deposit. This is the zone in which the gold is most heavily concentrated and, thus, the richest. The paystreak was seldom near the surface, however, nor was it always found beneath the existing stream bed. To locate it, the miners had to excavate large quantities of gravel from an open pit. This work, which was performed in the summer, was both extensive and expensive (and was often hampered by the presence of permafrost). Once a method of thawing frozen ground was perfected, miners could work through the winter, sinking slender shafts down into the frozen ground, then excavating small adits, or drifts, horizontally until the paystreak was intercepted. This method, known as *drift mining*, was efficient, as it did away with the necessity of removing extensive quantities of overburden. By thawing ground and working through the winter, the miner could accumulate a large amount of gravel, known as a dump, by spring. With the spring run-off, this material would be sluiced in a spring *clean-up*.

Water was essential to the sluicing process and, since sufficient supplies were not always immediately available, it could be obtained by building small dams or by diverting water from nearby streams through flumes or ditches. In some cases, water was used to remove the overburden (or even placer gravels), leaving the gold concentrated on the washed ground. This was known as *ground sluicing*. Pressurized water was supplied to some claims so that it could remove overburden through a process known as *hydraulicking*. In this process, the ground would be cut away along a vertical exposure by the pressure of the water. (Hydraulicking was not common before the Klondike discovery.)

Appendix B: Roll Call: Names of the Early Yukon Pioneers

PIONEER MEN

Adams, Jim (also McAdams, J.W.)
Addison, Charlie
Ainsley, Bob
Albasine, Steve
Albrecht, John
Ambold, Robert A.
Amcher, Cash
Anderson, ——
Anderson, A.H. (Abraham?)
Anderson, Bernard
Anderson, Capt. ——
Anderson, Charles A.

Anderson, Charlie (H.C.)
Anderson, Gabriel
Anderson, Henry
Anderson, John
Anderson, J.J.
Anderson, Louis P.
Anderson, Theodore
Andrews, Charlie
'Arkansas' Jim
Ash, Harry (also Ashe)
Ashby, Oscar (Tommy's brother)
Ashby, Tommy

Atkins, Francis A.
Atkinson, Mark
Atwater, Ben
Austin, Al
Aylward, Frank (also Elwood, Frank)

Baird, Robert
Baker, Frank
Baker, George
Baker, I.J.
Baker, Jim
Baker, Terry
Baldwin, ——
Banfield, F.
Barnes, George Washington
Barrett, Dennis
Bartlett, John
Bates, ——
Bauman, Peter
Beach, Benjamin
Bean, Edmund
Bean, James
Bean, Rob
Bear, Frederick
Beatty, Fred J.
Beatty, Fred R.
Beaudoin, Joseph
Beaudreau, Jo(seph)
Beaumont, Thomas Henry
Beaune, N.
Bedoe, N.A.
Becker, F.E. (Frank)
Beecher, ——
Belanger, F.
Belanger, T.H.
Belcher, Jim
Bell, Harry
Bell, O.C.
Bell, Timothy
Bellonger, —— (Belanger?)
Bemis, George
Bender, Jim
Bengler, Jim (Bender?)

Bennett, Ben
Bennett, Frank
Bent, W.N.
Bergeron, Joseph
Bergevin, Joseph
Bergholt, N.
Bermland, Nils
Berndt, ——
Berry, C.J.
Berry, Fred
Berthold, Jeremiah
Bertrand, D.
Bertrand, Jerry
Best, Bill
Betro, Charles
Bettles, Gordon
Bettleson, Joe
Big Dan
Big Dick
Bigelow, W.A.
Biggs, Orville R.
Biggs, Walter H.
Bigham, Frank
Binet, J.E.
Bismo, Tom
Black, Oscar
Blackburn, ——
Blake, Thomas
Blanchard, A.S.
Blick, Jack
Blodgett, Jim
Blythman, Clement
Boker, George
Bomier, Alex
Bompas, Wm. Carpenter
Bonnifield, 'Silent' Sam
Bordwine ——
Boss, Billy
Boswell, —— (Thomas's brother)
Boswell, Thomas
Boucher, James E.
Boulene, John
Boulet, ——

Boulet, Philimon (sp.?)
Boullais, Fred (Bullie?)
Bounds, George
Bourke, John
Bourne, John
Bowen, R.J.
Bowker, Frank
Boyle, Jack
Bozeman, Bill
Braddae, W.S. (Braddock?)
Braises, Charlie
Brand, Fred
Brand, Joe
Brandham, Frank
Brannan, Peter
Brebean, Gill
Bremner, John
Brenier, John E.
Brennan, Charles
Brewenes, Henry
Brooker, Frank
Brother, Const. Johnathan
Brown, Charlie
Brown, St. Sgt. Charles
Brown, Daniel
Brown, George T.
Brown, Gus
Brown, J.J.
Brownlie, James S.
Bruseth, Fred
Bullard, Jim
Bunt, George
Bunyan, John
Burke, John
Burke, Thomas
Burns, Archie
Burns, Cameron
Burroughs, James
Buteau, Frank (Taffy)
Butler, George
Butler, Richard (Dick)
Byrne, George H.
Cadieux, Jos. (James?)

Cain, Jim
Calamity Bill
Callahan, ——
Cameron, ——
Campbell, ——
Campbell, Daniel
Campbell, John A.
Canham, Rev. Thomas H.
Cannell, Joseph
'Cannibal' Ike
Carey, George
Carey, M.B.
Caribou Bill
Caribou Johnny
Carleson, Charles
Carlson, Oscar
Carmack, George Washington
Carr, ——
Carr, A.E.
Carrell, Frank
Carter, Dr. Charles
Carter, Henry
Cary, George (also Carey, George)
Castle, William
Cauthier, William
Cazelars, Joseph (Cazelais?)
  (also Gazerlais, Joseph)
Chabot, Laurence
Chamberlain, Dr. ——
Chambers, Dr. J.J.
Chaplin, Jim
Chapman, ——
Chapman Jr., ——
Chapman, Ernest
Chapman, J.P.
Chapple, Wm.
Chase, ——
Cherosky, —— (also Syrosca)
Chilean George
Christianson, Charley
  (also Christiansen, Charles)
Christopher, Martin
Chronister, Jim (also Connister)

Churchill, Const. S.R.
Circle City Mickey
Claffey, John
Clark, ——
Clements, Gus
Clemmins, Jim J. (also Clements)
Clifton, Talbot
Clinton, ——
Cloudman, ——
Cloudman, Press
Cobb, F.W. 'Papa'
Codiga, Frank
Codiga, George
Cody, L.
Coffman, Billy
Cohuler, Matt
Collins, Jack
Colombe, Charlie
Conalley, Pat (also Kanaly, Pat)
Cone, Edward C.
Coniff, P.
Conley, ——
Conners, John
Conners, T.
Connister, —— (also Chronister, Jim)
Connor, Roger
Conrad, Frank
Constantine, Inspector Charles
Conway, Thomas J.
Cook, Arthur
Cook, J. Thomas
Cooper, ——
Cooper, Joe
Cooper, Loren E.
Corbeil, Camille
Corbin, ——
Cormier, Frank
Cornell, W.F.
Corwin, ——
Cotey, Louis (Cody?)
Cotica, Chrissiann
Cox, L.
Cowley, W.M.

Criss, ——
Cromeau, Frank (also Cormier, Frank)
Cronister, —— (also Chronister, Jim)
Crooked Leg Louie
Crow, Chas.
Crowley, Timothy
Crutcher, Earl
Cummings, Bill
Curney, Thomas
Currie, John
Currier, Jack
Cushman, Fred
Custer, Stephen
Cut Throat Johnson
Czernofsky, —— (also Zarnowsky, John)

Dahl, Conrad
Dale, Richard
Dalk, ——
Dalton, ——
Dalton, Albert
Dalton, Jack
Dancing Bill
Daugherty, 'Nigger' Jim
Daughtry, James M.
Davis, 'Crooked Leg'
Davis, Henry
Dawson, Dave
Dawson, George Mercer
Dawson, J.V.
Day, Albert
Day, Hugh
DeHaas, W.A.
Delgarn, John
Demers, George
Denhart, Paul
Densmore, Frank (also Dinsmore, Frank)
Desroches, Joseph
Devine, Jack
DeYoung, ——
DeYoung, Martin
Dickson, Charlie 'Baggage'
Dinker, Bill

Dinsmond, J.

Dinsmore, Frank (also Densmore, Frank)

Dion, Ed

Dionne, Gilbert

Dixon, Capt. ——

Dodson, John R.

Dody, ——

Donahue, Hugh

Donald, John O.

Donnelly, Michael

Donovan, Chris

Donovan, Jack

Dotery, Charles (Daugherty, Daughtry?)

Dotey, Joe (Dody?)

Dougan, John

Dougherty, Dan

Doughty, ——

Douvall, Michael (also Duvall, M.)

Dron, Alex.

Dryden, Billy

Dubuque, Ed

Duggan, Robert A.

Dupreau, Napoleon (also Dupras)

Dusel, J.J.

'Dutch' Bill

'Dutch' Ed

'Dutch' Fritz

'Dutch' John

'Dutch Kid,' (the)

Duval, ——

Duval, Eugene

Duval, M. (also Douvall, Michael)

Eagle, Bill

Eaton, Charlie

Eckardt, R.

Edgar, G.T.

Edgar, R.E.

Edmunds, Cornelius

Edmunds, Tom (Edmonds)

Edwards, Dave

Ekre, O.J.

Ellinger, Casper (Ellingen?)

Ellington, Rev. J.W.

Elliott, ——

Elliott, J.F.

Elliott, Wm. H.

Ellis, ——

Elwell, Bill

Elwood, Frank (also Aylward, Frank)

Empkins, Louis

Engel, Charles F.

Engel, Corporal P.I.

English, Robert J.

Erikson, John

Evans, Fred

Evans, Tom

Everette, Willis

Ewen, Fred W.

Fallon, James

Fancio, Phillip

Farcint, Charlie

Farrel, William

Farrell, Larry

Farshaw, Charles O.

Fawcett, Adam

Fay, Fred

Feddis, ——

Fensted, Olaf

Fenzer, John

Ferguson, H.A.

Fetch, Clinton

Fettes, 'Old Man'

Finch, George

Flack, Thomas

Flewelling, Frederick Fairweather

Flure, Rudolph

Foley, ——

Folger, John

Follett, Julius

Fortier, 'Hootch' Albert

Foster, William

Fox, Albert

Fox, Lewis W.

Fox, Robert

Franklin, Howard
Fraser, Alex
Fraser, Francis
Fraser, J.
'French' Curly
'French' Joe
'Frenchy'
Frew, A.D. 'Sandy'
Friend, George
Fuller, A.D.
Fuller, Frank

Gage, Eli
Gaisford, Uly
Galazzi, Victor
Galvin, Pat
Gates, Humboldt
Gates, 'Swiftwater' Bill
Gauvin, Alfred
Gauvin, Wilfred
Gauvin, William
Gay, Emil (Emile)
Gazerlais, Joseph (also Cazelars, Joseph)
Gedna, Joe
Gee, Joseph H.
Geitler, ——
Gibson, Ian
Gilbert, Charles
Gillis, D.
Giordano, Carmel
Giwouard, Oliver
Glaus, Albert
Glenton, Dr. ——
Goderich, ——
Goff, Nick
'Goldie'
Goldsmith, Joe
Goodman, G.P.
Gordon, A.A.
Gordon, Abe ('Dutch' Bill,
  'Missouri' Bill)
Goutier, William
Gowler, Const. Matthew R.

Grainger, Chet
Gray, A.
Gregor, Jack
Grignon, Ed
Grubb, Thomas G.
Guise, Julius
'Gus the Greek'
Guyer, John

Hagen, Lee (Hagan)
Hall, Jim
Hall, Matt
Halstead, Knut
Halterman, ——
Halterman, J.J.
Hamilton, C.H.
Hamilton, Howard
Hamilton, Marcus L.
Hampshire, Cash
'Handshaker' Bob
'Happy' Jack
Hare, ——
Harkrader, George
Harper, Alfred
Harper, Arthur
Hart, Andrew
Hart, David
Hart, Frederick
Hart, Howard Hamilton
Hart, W.R.
Hartwell, John
Haskell, Wm. B.
Hasser, Joe
Hatch, J.
Hawley, Frank
Hawthorne, ——
Hayes, M.A.
Hayes, William
Hayne, St. Sgt. M.H.E.
Healy, John J.
Heator, Jerry
Hebert, Andre H.
Hellwinkle, John A.

Henderson, Robert
Henry, ——
Henry, Sam
Herman, George
Heron, S.J.
Herrington, Chris
Hess, D.
Hess, Michael E.
Hester, E.
Hestwood, ——
Higgins, B.
Higgins, Lee
Hill, Barney
Hill, Bernard (Barney?)
Hill, Charlie
Hill, Mannie
Hines, Fred
Holden, Ed
Hollingshead, J.B.
Holmes, ——
Holmes, Anthony
Holmes, J.
Holt, George W.
Honge, Andrew (Andru?)
'Hootch' Albert (Fortier?)
Hopkins, J.F.
Horn, Jack
Horn, John
Howard, B.
Howard, Johnny A.
Howard, Wm.
Howe, George A., Jr.
Hubbard, Dick
Huffman, James
Hughes, John
Hulbert, Harvey
Hunker, Andrew
Huot, Napoleon
Hutchins, Fred
Hutchinson, Fred
Hyde, Henry

Ireland, Press

Ironmonger, A.E.

Jackson, Jeremiah
Jackson, Jimmie
Jackson, Oscar
Jackson, Waldron
Jakeman, William
Janes, Byron E.
Jenkins, Const. Eldon W.
Jenkins, Const. H.L
Jenott, J.T.
Jensen, Ike
Jimmy the Pirate
Johansen, Joe
Johanson, George
Johanson, Frank
Johns, William Douglas
Johnson, ——
Johnson, A.E.
Johnson, Albert
Johnson, Andrew S.
Johnson, Charles M.
Johnson, Gus
Johnson, Jeremiah
Johnson, Nels
Johnson, Pete
Johnson, Sandy
Johnson, Victor
Jones, Frank A.
Jones, Tom
Juneau Joe

'Kaiser' Bill
Kanals, Tom
Kanaly, Pat (Keneller?)
  (also Conalley, Pat)
Kansellar, Andrew
Karlson, Charles
Karlson, Robert
Keithly, C.L.
Keller, Frank
Kelly, John
Kelly, Sam

Kendrick, ——
Keneller, Pat (Kanaly?)
Kennedy, ——
Kennedy, James D.
Kenney, Barney
Kernan, Tom
Kerr, ——
Kerrigan, T.
Kerry, Jimmy
Kiernan, Thomas
Kimball, C.
King, ——
King, Tom
'Kink' Miller
Kinnealy, Pat
Kirkpatrick, Thomas W.
Kittleson, ——
Kloke, Fritz
Knight, S.A.
Kroll, John
Kroll, Josef (Joseph)
Kronstadt, ——
Krook, Robert
Kuhl, John
Kuley, William
Kuttinger, 'Sheep Creek'
  (Shorty's brother)
Kuttinger, 'Shorty'

Laackman, Herman
Lacerte, Aime
Ladouceur, Frederick
Ladue, Joseph
LaFlem, L.
Lafond, Joseph
Lahtinen, Adolf
Lamarre, George
Lamb, Charley
Lambert, Nick
Lamie, Joe
Lamont, ——
Lamont, Neal
Lamore, F.

Landreville, Max
Landsing, G.S.
Langford, ——
Langlow, Knut
Langlow, Louie (Louis)
Langlow, Nels
Langtry, George G.
Lanier, Noi
Lapierre, Alphonse
Laplant, Louis
Laroche, ——
Larry, Johnny
Larsen, Chas.
Laumeister, J.P.
Lauzon, —— (Loozon?)
Lavois, Louis (Lavoy?)
Lawrence, Frank
Lawson, Frank
Leak, Billy
Leautaue, L. Baptiste
Ledger, —— (John?)
Lee, John
Legault, Noah
Legget, Billy (also Liggett, Bill)
Leindecker, Gus
Lemon, John
Leonard, Frank
Leslie, J. (Lesley?)
Lester, Phil
Levantie, Charles
Levi, Ben (Levy?)
Levy, Herod
Lewin, Eddie
Lewis, Ellis
Lewis, Henry
Liberati, ——
Liggett, Bill (also Legget, Billy)
Lind, John Grieve
Lindgaard, August
Lindig, Ed
Lindig, Frank
Lindquist, ——
Lineham, Thomas

Linsem, Matt
Lippy, Percival
Lippy, Thomas
Lloyd, W.R. (Billy?)
Londreville, Max
'Long' John
'Long' Shorty
Loper, Mark
Lord, Victor
Love, Bill
Loveland, Charlie
Lovett, ——
Lowe, Dick
Lowrie, R. (Bob)
Lowry, Ed
Lumpkin, Webb M.
Lying George (Carmack?)
Lynch, Pat
Lyons, ——

MacDonald, Walter
Machiel, Joseph
MacNulty, Richard
Madden, ——
Madison, ——
Madison, Harry
Madison, Henry
Madsen, H.
Magaw, Albert (also McGaw, Albert)
Maiden, Andrew
Maloney, E.S.
Manberg, Solomon
Manly, Frank
Manley, Tom
Manning, ——
Manook, John (also Minook)
Marlow, Owen
Marks, Antone
Marks, John
Marpak, Solomon
Martin, J.
Masson, J. Newton
Matheson, Robert (also Mathison, Bob)

Mathews, Samuel
Matlock, George H.
  (Madlock, Medlock?)
Matson, Henry
Mattfieldt, Fred K.
Matthews, S.B.
Mauck, George
Maynard, Charles
Mayo, Al H.
Mayon, Matt
McAdams, J.W.
McArthur, Neil
McCabe, ——
McCabe, Augustine F.
McCann, Bill
McCartney, John
McCarty, Jim
McCauley, Jim
McClarity, ——
McClinchey, Patrick
McCloud, John
McCluskey, James
McComber, Alexander
McConkey, Charles (also McCoskey, C.)
McConnell, ——
McCord, George
McCormack, Jack
McCormack, John
McCormick, Jack
McCoskey, C. (also McConkey, Charles)
McCue, ——
McCue, George (also McHugh)
McCullough, H.
McCullar, 'Old Man'
McDonald, Alex
McDonald, Alexander ('Big Alex')
McDonald, Andy
McDonald, Dick
McDonald, Pete I.
McGaw, Albert
McGillivery, Dan
McGrath, Pete
McHugh, —— (also McCue, George)

McKay, Albert
McKay, Dave
McKay, James J.
McKellar, Const. Angus P.
McKenzie, John
McKinnes, 'Colonel' Willis
McKinney, Dudley
McKinnon, Alexander
McKnipp, James
McLean, Hector
McMahon, James
McMears, ——
McMoran, Billy
McNamee, Jimmy
McNamera, James
McNeil, James
McPhee, William
McPike, Jim
McQuesten, Leroy Napoleon 'Jack'
McQuesten, Richard
McQuirk, Nick
Mean, ——
Menier, Fred (also Meunier, Fred)
Menzies, Stewart
Mer, Wm.
Mercier, F.
Mercier, M.
Meunier, Fred (also Menier, Fred)
Meyers, H.G.
Midboe, ——
Miller, 'Buckskin'
Miller, Fred
Miller, Fritz
Miller, Harry
Miller, Henry
Miller, James
Miller, Joe
Miller, John P.
Miller, Kink
Miller, Mike
Miller, Oliver
Mills, Fred
Miner, ——

Miner, A.
Minook, —— (also Manook, John)
'Missouri' Bill (also Gordon, Abe)
'Missouri' Frank
Mitchell, Archie
Mitchell, S.S. ('Skiff')
Moffat, Frank
Moffat, J.
Moffat, John J.
Molinari, J. David
Monohan, Edward
Monroe, James 'Curly'
Monroe, Father Francis P., S.J.
Monson, ——
'Montana' Pete
'Montana' Red
Montgomery, Frank
Montgomery, Jim
Mooney, John
Moore, J.T.
Moore, Capt. William
Moran, Billy
Moran, Casey (Bernard H.)
Moran, Pat
Morancy, Al
Morford, Judge S.A.
Morgan, Capt. ——
Morphat, Frank (Francis, also Moffat?)
Morris, William
Morrison, H.
Mosher, ——
Muldoon, ——
Mulhern, A.M. (also Mulhorn, A.M.)
Mulligan, George
Munro, 'Curly' (Monroe?)
Munroe, Charlie
Munroe, James
Munson, K.
Murphy, Padrick
Murray, Alfred
Murray, Const. Johnathan
Myers, Charlie

Nabidon, Nabidon
Nash, A.D.
Navarroo, Joe (Navarro?)
Naylor, Rev. H.A.
Nedeau, Fred
Neebur, Henry F.C.
Nelson, Andrew
Nelson, E.
Nelson, Sgt. Edward William
Nelson, Fred
Nelson, John
Nelson, John
Nelson, Pete
Nelson, Thomas C.
Ness, Andrew
Newbrook, Corporal Eli
Newman, George
Newman, Rudolph
Nicholson, G.
Niela, Azel F. (Nida?)
Nigger Jim (Dougherty?)
Nollner, A.R. (Nowlen? Nollnes?)
Nonteman, Preston
Norcross, M.S.
Nordstrom, Andrew
Norman, ——
Norman, Ed

Oblasser, John
O'Brien, James
O'Brien, Thomas Miller
O'Brien, Thomas W.
O'Donell, J.
O'Leary, John
O'Neil, James
O'Sullivan,
O'Sullivan, J.
Ogilvie, Ezekiel
Ogilvie, William
Oksvig, L.P.
'Old' Herman
'Old' John
'Old' Maiden

'Old' Solomon
Oler, J. Winfield
Oleson, Andrew
Oleson, H.
Olmstead, W.E.
Olsen, ——
Olson, C.
Orr, Alex
Osborne, Howell
Overhiser, C.B.

Park, Ed
Patch, Sam
Pate, Al
Pate, ——
Patterson, Jack
Pelkey, Thomas
Penlein, John
Perkins, Dick
Perry, Arthur
Pete the Pig
Peter, H.E. (Peters?)
Peters, ——
Peterson, Capt.
Peterson, Dankert
Peterson, Henry
Peterson, J.P.
Peterson, Swan
Petrie, D.
Petroes, ——
Phiscator, Frank
Pichon, Frank
Picotte, N.E.
Pickarts, Frank G.
Pielow, Ed
Pierce, Mark
Pierce, W.H.
Piggot, Frank
Pinkerton, Const. Arthur
Pitka, ——
Pitts, Buffalo
Poot, Simon
Poplin, Richard (Popland?)

Powell, Charles
Powers, Capt.
Powers, George
Powers, Ike
Powers, Isiaah
Powers, Isaac
Powers, J.
Powers, Napoleon
Preido, William C.
Prescott, Charley
Prevost, Rev. Charles
Price, Frank
Price, Frederick
Pross, Felix
Proteau, J. Henry
Provost, Antoine
Putto, ——

Qualley, Thomas T.
Quigley, Joe
Quinlan, Johnnie

Raap, John
Rabideaux, ——
Ragaru, Aloysius, S.J.
Ramsay, ——
Ramsey, George
Ramsey, 'Sorehead'
Randall, Jack
Raymond, Charles R.
Raymond, Henry
Raymur, Jack (Raynor?)
Readford, William 'Billy' (Redford?)
'Red-Handed' Mike
Redmond, William A.
Reed, John
Remillard, George
Reynolds, G.H.
Reynolds, Jack
Rhodes, Louis B.
Ribot, ——
  (also Robaut, Father Aloysius)
Ricards, —— (Ricardo?)

Richardson, P.C.
Rickard, 'Tex'
Riggin, Herbert
Riley, ——
Riley, John
Riter, W.S.
Rivers, Henry
Robaut, Father Aloysius
Robertson, A.
Robertson, D.A.
Robertson, Donald
Robertson, Robert
Robinson, Dick
Robbin, Fred
Roblin, Peter
Rockwell, ——
Rogers, John
Roselle, Desire R.
Ross, ——
Ross, David
Ross, George
Rosswell, Tom
Roux, Victor
Rowan, James
Rowe, Bishop Peter Trimble
Roy, Francois
Roy, Joe
Russell, ——
Russell, Isreal C.
Russell, Mark

Saffron, ——
Sailor, ——
Sailor John
Sajan, Thomas L.
Salt Water Jack
Sather, ——
Sather, E.A.
Saur, Ephraim
Sawbury, Charles
Scales, M.
Scals, Hans
Schafer, Henry

Schanz, A.B.
Schaska, H.G.
Scheehey, John
Schieffelin, Edward
Schieffelin, Eff
Schell, H.A.
Schonborn, Louis K.
Schrader, ——
Schuler, Matt
Scofiel, Piter
Scott, A.E.
Scott, Billy
Scott, John
'Scottie'
Scouse, William 'Bill'
Sears, Silas
Seghers, Bishop Charles John
Sedgewick, Leonard
Seguin, Frank
Senenza, John
Seymore, Henry
Shequin, Lewis E.
Shaw, Al
Sheehy, John
Sherman, W.A.
Sherwood, Thomas
Shorty
Shumack, ——
Shute, Jerome
Sibistone, ——
'Silent' George
Silvero, Nick (Silvers? Silver?)
Sims, Rev. Vincent
Sinclair, Const. D.
'Siwash' George (Carmack)
'Slim' Jim (Winn?)
Singleton, Ebin
Slater, Andrew
Sloan, William
'Slobbery' Tom
Smith, A.L.
Smith, Bill
Smith, Ira

Smith, Harry
Smith, Jack
Snider, ——
Snow, —— (George Snow's brother)
Snow, George T.
Solomon, Joe
Sonnickson, Chris
Soule, C.M.
Speckter, Otto
Spence, Billy
Spencer, ——
Sperry, Charles
Spingerburgh, George (Spongeburgh?)
Spotts, A.L.
Sprague, B.C.
Sprague, Dan
Spurr, Josiah Edward
'Squaw' Cameron
St. Louis, Jean Baptiste
Stafford, Jim
Stander, Antone
Stanley, Samuel L.
Stanley, ——
Stanley, William
Stanton, William Nicholas
Stay, E.
Stearns, L.C.
Steele, ——
Steele, H.N.
Steele, R.
Stella, George
Stevenson, O.
Steward, Jack
Stewart, ——
Stewart, Bill (William)
Stewart, George
Stewart, Greg
Stewart, J.
Stewart, Ray
Stills, ——
Stillwater Willie (Gates?)
Stites, Al
Stitt, J.

Stolder, William B.
Stoll, Caspar
Stough, Emil
Strauss, Theodore B.
Strickland, Inspector D'Arcy, A.E.
Strong, Robert E.
Strong, Wm. G.
Stuart, Bill
Stumph, George
Sullivan, E.M.
Sullivan, J.W.
Summers, Hank
Swanson, Frank
'Swiftwater' Bill (Gates)
Swinehart, John
Syrosca, —— (also Cherosky)

Talbert, Jeff
Tarter, A.
Telford, Const. Edw.
Tessino, Arsene
Tetu, O.
Thayer, Alfred
Thibert, ——
Thibbert, 'Old Man'
Thomas, George
Thompson, A.K.
Thompson, Joe
Thompson, M.F.
Thompson, 'Whiskey'
Thornberry, L.M.
Thornton, Const. Johnathan
Thorpe, Edward A.
Thorpe, Wm. Lee
'Three Finger' Jack (Miller?)
Thurlow, Henry J.
Thyson, Mike
Tilly, Carlo
Timonen, Charles
Tin Kettle George
Tom, Dr. J.T.
Toman, Ed
'Tommy the Fiddler'

Totty, Benjamin
Tozee, Father Pascal (Tosi? Tosey?)
Traub, C.G.
Treasure(r), B.
Treasure(r), J.H.
Tremblay, Nolasque (Jack)
Turgeon, Charles B.
Turner, Ellis
Twan, Joe
Tweed, James

Van, J.
Van Alstine, Con (also Alstyne)
Van Iderstan, Johnny
Van Iderstine, Johnny C.
Van Wagoner, F.D.
Vogel, Barns
Voses, G.W.
Voss, ——
Voss, George R.

Wade, Jack
Walden, Arthur T.
Walker, ——
Walker, D.W.
Walker, H.P.
Walker, Percy
Wall, Ben
Wallis, Rev. Geo. C.
Walsh, ——
Warburton, H.
Ward, Const. Everett J.
Warner, Jack
Washburn, ——
Watts, C.V.
Waugh, Harry J.
Weare, Eli
Webster, Const. Fred
Welch, ——
Welch, Charles (Welsh)
Wells, Dick
Wells, E. Hazard
Welsh, Dick (also Wells, Dick)

Welsh, R.
Wendling, ——
Wentzell, ——
Westfall, H.J.
Westbrook, George G.
Weymouth, O.E.
Wheeler, H.
Whipple, Jay
White, Jim
White, John I.
Whitechurch, —— (also Whitchurch)
Whitney, John
Wiborg, Peter A. (Weiberg? Wyborg?
  Wilboring? Wybourg?)
Wick, John
Wigg, Marcus
Wigg, Robert
'Wild Cat' Bill
Wilkins, L.J.
Wilkinson, John
Wilkinson, Samuel
Wilkinson, W(ilfred?)
Willett, Erwin
Willett, Henry
Williams, ——
Williams, F.A.
Williams, Evan
Williams, Gus
Williams, J.A.
Williams, J.J.
Williams, John
Williams, Thomas
Wills, Alfred E.
Wilson, Floyd
Wilson, Frank
Wilson, George. A.
Wilson, H.R.
Wilson, Peter
Wilson, Sed (Sid?)
Wilson, Tom
Wilson, Veazzie
Wilton, ——
Windy Jim

Winn, James 'Slim Jim'
Wold, Ben
Wolfe, Austin
Woods, ——
Woods, Dr. Benton S.
Woods, Jeremiah
Worden, C.
Worden, Caggie
Worden, Charles
Wright, C.
Wright, Fred
Wright, H.D.
Wright, Hank

Yager, Charlie
Yantiss, S.A.
Yates, Bill
Yates, Dr. ——
York, Jim
Young, Andrew
Young, Jack
Young, Thomas

Zarnowsky, John (also Czernofsky)
Zilly, Carroll K.
Zoble, William

PIONEER WOMEN

Aiken, May
Andrews, —— (Mrs. Charlie)
Aylward, Bridget Mannion
Baker, —— (Mrs. Thomas D.)
Barker, Amanda
Beaumont, ——
Beaumont, Marie Louise Yukonia
Berry, Ethel Bush (Mrs. C.J.)
Black, Kitty
Bompas, Charlotte Selinas
Bowen, Susan Mellett (Mrs. R.J.)
Burns, Lottie
Canham, —— (Mrs. T.H.)
Carlson, —— (Mrs. Oscar)

Carter, Annie
Constantine, —— (Mrs. Charles)
Dahland, —— (Mrs. Con)
Davis, Viola
Day, —— (Mrs. Albert)
Day, —— (Mrs. Hugh)
Debney, —— (Mrs. Charles)
DeGraf, Anna
Drummond Sisters
Duffy, Esther
'Dutch' Kate
Fulcomer, Anna
Galvin, Mary Ellen
Guise, —— (Mrs. Julius)
Healey, —— (Mrs. John J.)
Lamore, Gussie
Langlow, —— (Mrs. Louie [F.])
Lippy, Salome
Lloyd, —— (Mrs. Billy)
Lyons, Esther (also Robinson, E.L.)
MacDonald, Margaret
Mannion, Bridget (also Aylword,
   Bridget Mannion)
Matheson, —— (Mrs. Bob)
McGrady, Julia
McGrath, Julia
Mellett, Susan
Naylor, —— (Mrs. H.A.)
O'Neil, Bridgett (also Andrews, ——
   [Mrs. Charlie Andrews])
Philips, Rose
Robinson, Mrs. E.L. (also Lyons,
Esther)
Snow, Crystal (daughter of G.T. Snow)
Snow, Anna (Mrs. George T.)
Spencer, —— (Mrs. Harry)
Strickland, —— (Mrs. D.A.E.)
Totty, Selina Mayo
Tremblay, Emilie
Turner, —— (Mrs. Howard)
Wallis, —— (Mrs. Geo. C.)
Wentzell, ——
Williams, —— (Mrs. J.A.)

Williams, Matilda
Willis, ——
Wills, —— (not related to A.E. Wills)
Wilson, Cad (also Lyons, Esther)
Yates, ——

NATIVE STAKERS

Albert, Indian
Essau, Indian
Filas, Alfred's Boy
Indian Ben
Indian John
Indian Thomas
Indian Peter
Indian Sandy
Isaac, Indian
John, Simon's Boy
Johnathan, Indian
Paul, Peter's Boy
Schwatka
Snider, Billy
Tagish Charley
Tagish Patsy
Tagish Jim

$$\boxed{\text{N O T E S}}$$

Chapter 1: Early Days

1 Josiah Edward Spurr, *Through the Yukon Gold Diggings* (Boston: Eastern Publishing 1900), 82-3.

2 For other descriptions, see M.H.E. Hayne, *The Pioneers of the Klondike: Being an Account of Two Years Police Service on the Yukon* (London: Sampson Low, Marsten & Co. 1897), 33-4, 52; Spurr, *Yukon Gold Diggings*, 85-6; Frederick Schwatka, *A Summer in Alaska* (Philadelphia: John Y. Huber 1891), 263; Will Chase, *Reminiscences of Captain Billie Moore* (Kansas City: Burton Publishing 1947); William B. Haskell, *Two Years in the Klondike and Alaskan Gold Fields* (Hartford, CT: Hartford Publishing 1898), 155-6; Arthur Walden, *A Dog-Puncher on the Yukon* (Boston: Houghton Mifflin 1931), 26; William Douglas Johns, 'The Early Yukon, Alaska, and the Klondike Discovery as They Were Before the Great Klondike Stampede Swept Away the Old Conditions By One Who Was There,' typescript, Coutts Collection, 78/69, box F-89, folders 20 and 21, Yukon Archives, Whitehorse, n.d., pp. 71-2.

3 A prospector is one searching for a deposit (prospect) of gold which can be mined profitably. Once such propects are found, an individual might settle down to work the deposit, extracting the gold. This work, in the early days of the Yukon mining industry, might last only a few days, or a few weeks. Once the deposit was worked out, the miner would once again set out prospecting. Thus someone could change from one role to another quite quickly.

4 Accounts vary. Harold B. Goodrich, 'History and Condition of the Yukon Gold District to 1897,' in Josiah Edward Spurr, *Geology of the Yukon Gold District, Alaska*, 103-33 (Washington: Government Printing Office 1897), 108, states that various dates have been given regarding Holt's travel into the Yukon, including 1872, 1874, 1875, and 1878. Allen Wright, *Prelude to Bonanza* (Sidney, BC: Gray's Publishing 1976), 133, states that Holt made a trip into the Yukon sometime between 1875 and 1878. Alfred H. Brooks, *Blazing Alaska's Trails* (Fairbanks: University of Alaska 1953), 32, says that it occurred in 1875. The *Sitka Alaskan*, 2 October 1897, states that the trip

occurred in 1874, and that, in 1876, a second man, Levi Herod, repeated Holt's trip in order to verify his assertions.

Chapter 2: The Chilkoot Pass and Early Transportation

1 Alfred H. Brooks, *Blazing Alaska's Trails* (Fairbanks: University of Alaska 1953), 323-5; Allen Wright, *Prelude to Bonanza* (Sidney, BC: Gray's Publishing 1976), 135-7.
2 G.T. Emmons, *Sitka Alaskan*, 19 June 1886, 1.
3 John Grieve Lind, untitled manuscript, 81/58, Yukon Archives, Whitehorse, n.d., pp. 1-2.
4 Arthur Walden, *A Dog-Puncher on the Yukon* (Boston: Houghton Mifflin 1931), 8, 9.
5 Ibid., 19.
6 William Ogilvie, *Information Respecting the Yukon District from the Reports of Wm. Ogilvie, Dominion Land Surveyor* (Ottawa: Government Printing Bureau 1897), 15.
7 R.C. Coutts, *Yukon Places and Names* (Sidney, BC: Gray's Publishing 1980), 98.
8 W.H. Pierce, *Thirteen Years of Travel and Exploration in Alaska, 1877-1889* (Anchorage: Alaska Northwest Publishing 1977), 58.
9 Walden, *Dog-Puncher*, 25.
10 Israel C. Russell, 'A Journey up the Yukon,' *Bulletin of the American Geographical Society* 27, no. 2 (1895):154-5.
11 Josiah Edward Spurr, in *Through the Yukon Gold Diggings* (Boston: Eastern Publishing 1900), 136, stated that, while tracking up the Fortymile River, he and his party managed seven or eight miles a day. W.A. Redmond, in *Down the Yukon*, PAM-1891-7, Yukon Archives, Whitehorse, 1891, p. 612, said that the trip from Forty Mile to the outside took from 28 to 35 days. Brooks, *Blazing Alaska's Trails*, 415, gives a range of 10 to 30 miles per day, depending upon the load being transported.
12 William B. Haskell, *Two Years in the Klondike and Alaskan Gold Fields* (Hartford, CT: Hartford Publishing 1898), 193-4.
13 Spurr, *Yukon Gold Diggings*, 124.

Chapter 3: Early Developments on the Yukon River

1 Melody Webb, *The Last Frontier: A History of the Yukon Basin of Canada and Alaska* (Albuquerque: University of New Mexico Press 1985), 68.
2 William Ogilvie, *Early Days on the Yukon and the Story of Its Gold Fields* (Toronto: Bell & Cockburn 1913), 106.
3 Snow Papers, 'Snow Papers of the Yukon,' Chris Sonnickson handwritten manuscript, Dartmouth College, Hanover, NH, 7.
4 Edward Schieffelin, 'Ed Schieffelin's Trip To Alaska [1882-1883],' manuscript P-K 43, Bancroft Library, Berkeley, CA, 1888, p. 7.
5 Ogilvie, *Early Days on the Yukon*, 107.
6 Vincent Sims, 'Journal of Trip on the Yukon, 1883,' manuscript, Dawson City Museum.
7 Ogilvie, *Early Days on the Yukon*, 108.
8 George W. Carmack, *My Experiences in the Yukon*, pamphlet (published privately by Marguerite P. Carmack 1933), 10.

9 This is probably the same man identified as Frank Moffat, or Morfeat, in other sources.
10 William Ogilvie, *Information Respecting the Yukon District from the Reports of Wm. Ogilvie, Dominion Land Surveyor* (Ottawa: Government Printing Bureau 1897), 109-10.
11 Carmack, *My Experiences in the Yukon*, 11.
12 Francois Mercier, *Recollections of the Yukon: Memoirs from the Years 1868-1885*, Alaska Historical Commission Studies in History, no. 88 (Anchorage: Alaska Historical Society 1986), 59; *Sitka Alaskan*, 30 October 1986, 3.
13 Snow Papers, George T. Snow personal account, 118.
14 Ibid., 119.
15 Gerard G. Steckler, *Charles John Seghers, Priest and Bishop in the Pacific Northwest, 1839-1886: A Biography* (Fairfield, WA: Ye Galleon Press 1986), 240.
16 Snow Papers, George T. Snow personal account, 118.
17 Fr. Marcel Bobillier, *Une Pionnière du Yukon, Madam Emilie Tremblay*, Publications de la Société Historique de Saguenay, no. 13 (Chicoutimi: La Société Historique de Saguenay 1948), 35, 36; Madame Emilie Tremblay citing Ray Stewart.
18 Steckler, *Charles John Seghers*, 241.
19 Frank Buteau, 'My Experiences in the World,' in *Sourdough Sagas*, edited by Herbert L. Heller, 93-118 (Cleveland: World Publishing 1967), 117.
20 For further reading on the murder of Bishop Seghers, refer to Sister Mary Calsanctius, *The Voice of Alaska: Memoirs of a Missioner* (Lachine, PQ: St. Ann's Press 1947), 31-43; William R. Hunt, *Distant Justice: Policing the Alaska Frontier* (Norman: University of Oklahoma Press 1987), 36-41; Steckler, *Charles John Seghers*, Chapter 15; and Melody Webb, *The Last Frontier: A History of the Yukon Basin of Canada and Alaska* (Albuquerque: University of New Mexico Press 1985), 175-6.

Chapter 4: The Miners' Code

1 Israel C. Russell, 'A Journey up the Yukon,' *Bulletin of the American Geographical Society* 27, no. 2 (1895):158-9.
2 Russell, 'Journey up the Yukon,' 152-3.
3 Rev. Charles Judge, *An American Missionary: A Record of the Work of the Rev. William A. Judge, S.J.* (New York: Ossining 1907), 162; Tappan Adney, *The Klondike Stampede* (New York: Harper Bros. 1900), 271.
4 John Richard Bowen, 'Incidents in the Life of the Reverend Richard John Bowen among the Natives, Trappers, Traders, Prospectors, and Gold Miners in the Yukon Territory Before and After the Gold Rush of the Year 1898,' MG 29 C92, National Archives of Canada, Ottawa, 1950, p. 76. See also descriptions by Frederick Palmer, *In The Klondyke* (New York: Charles Scribner's & Sons 1899), 69; Adney, *Klondike Stampede*, 273; Bowen, 'Reverend Richard John Bowen,' 68; Alfred H. Brooks, *Blazing Alaska's Trails* (Fairbanks: University of Alaska 1953), 333-4; Josiah Edward Spurr, *Through the Yukon Gold Diggings* (Boston: Eastern Publishing 1900), 227-8.
5 William Ogilvie, *Early Days on the Yukon and the Story of Its Gold Fields* (Toronto: Bell & Cockburn 1913), 293.

6 See, for instance, William Ogilvie, *Lecture on the Yukon Gold Fields (Canada), Delivered at Victoria B.C.* (Victoria: The Colonist Presses 1897), 39.

7 Spurr, *Yukon Gold Diggings*, 125.

8 Ibid., 141, 146-7.

9 Ogilvie, *Early Days on the Yukon*, 247.

10 Will Chase, *Reminiscences of Captain Billie Moore* (Kansas City: Burton Publishing 1947), 11.

11 Chase, *Captain Billie Moore*, 132-3, 136-7.

12 Leroy N. McQuesten, *Life in the Yukon, 1871-1885* (Whitehorse: Yukon Order of Pioneers 1952), 11.

13 William B. Haskell, *Two Years in the Klondike and Alaskan Gold Fields* (Hartford, CT: Hartford Publishing 1898), 178.

14 James Wickersham, *Old Yukon: Tales, Trails, and Trials* (Washington: Law Book 1938), 125.

15 Pierre Berton, *Klondike: The Last Great Gold Rush, 1896-97* (Toronto: McClelland & Stewart 1972), 28.

16 John Grieve Lind, untitled manuscript, 81/58, Yukon Archives, Whitehorse, n.d., pp. 4-5. Ogilvie, *Early Days on the Yukon*, 271-2, describes a similar conflict between an Englishman and an American. It is probable that both stories are based upon the same instance. Jack London also describes a similar tale in his short story 'Men of the Fortymile.' See also *Alaska Searchlight*, 3 October 1896, 1.

17 According to the Snow Papers, Chris Sonnickson typescript, Dartmouth College, Hanover, NH, 11, one of the priests analyzed the food which was poisoned by Leslie, and he determined that it was strychnine.

18 Ogilvie, *Early Days on the Yukon*, 43-51. See also *Alaska Free Press*, 12 February 1887 and 19 March 1887, letter from J.C. Stitt to P. Corcoran.

19 Snow Papers, Sonnickson typescript, 9. See also 'Latest from the Yukon,' *Alaska Free Press*, 28 May 1887, which depicts the shooting of Dick Welsh and a man named Manning.

20 Snow Papers, Peter Roblin manuscript, 1. W.A. Redmond, *Down the Yukon*, PAM-1891-7, Yukon Archives, Whitehorse, 1891, p. 615, encountered Leslie on the Chilkoot Trail and heard that three Whites and five Natives had been shot.

21 The *Sitka Alaskan* carried a small article in the 4 June 1887 issue, p. 3, which stated that a man named McManus had been killed at the Stewart River.

22 Ogilvie, *Early Days on the Yukon*, 267-71.

Chapter 5: The Fortymile Stampede

1 William Ogilvie, *Early Days on the Yukon and the Story of Its Gold Fields* (Toronto: Bell & Cockburn 1913), 111, states that Franklin and Madison were the discoverers. Frank Buteau, in 'My Experiences in the World,' in *Sourdough Sagas*, edited by Herbert L. Heller, 92-118 (Cleveland: World Publishing 1967), 101, states that the discoverers were Franklin, O'Brien, Lambert, and Madden. Snow Papers, Chris Sonnickson typescript, Dartmouth College, Hanover, NH, 11, states that the four men were Franklin,

T. O'Brien, Lambert, and McAdams, while Tappan Adney, *The Klondike Stampede* (New York: Harper Bros. 1900), 238, states that the four were Franklin, Mickey O'Brien, Jim Adams, and Lambert. The actual number and identities of the discoverers may never be known with certainty. Most chroniclers have accepted Ogilvie's account, but Sonnickson and Buteau were both in the Yukon the fall that the discovery was made. The *Alaska Free Press*, 19 March 1887, also mentions Franklin, Lambert, and O'Brien in a letter sent by T. Kerrigan.

2 Buteau, 'My Experiences in the World,' 99.

3 Adney, *Klondike Stampede*, 238.

4 W.A. Redmond, *Down the Yukon*, PAM-1891-7, Yukon Archives, Whitehorse, 1891, p. 615; R.N. DeArmond, 'A Letter to Jack McQuesten: Gold on the Fortymile,' *Alaska Journal* 3 (Spring 1973):114-21.

5 Buteau, 'My Experiences in the World,' 96.

6 Ibid., 98.

7 Ibid., 101-2.

8 Snow Papers, Sonnickson manuscript, 11.

9 Snow Papers, Cooper manuscript, pp. 1,2; William Ogilvie, *Information Respecting the Yukon District from the Reports of Wm. Ogilvie, Dominion Land Surveyor*, (Ottawa: Government Printing Bureau 1897), 31; Snow Papers, Roblin manuscript, 2; Snow Papers, Sonnickson manuscript, 26.

10 Buteau, 'My Experiences in the World,' 116.

11 Redmond, *Down the Yukon*, 623.

12 Snow Papers, Matlock manuscript, 3.

13 Redmond, *Down the Yukon*, 623.

14 Buteau, 'My Experiences in the World,' 102.

15 Ibid., 103.

16 Redmond, *Down the Yukon*, 622.

17 Ibid., 625.

18 Henry Davis, 'Recollections,' in *Sourdough Sagas*, edited by Herbert L. Heller, 28-83 (Cleveland: World Publishing 1967), 49-50.

19 Redmond, *Down the Yukon*, 627; J. Bernard Moore, *Skagway in Days Primeval* (New York: Vantage Press 1968), 80; William Ogilvie, *Yukon District*, 44.

20 Buteau, 'My Experiences in the World,' 103. This was not the only party to traverse the Chilkoot Pass in the winter of 1887. George Stella and Joe Miller crossed the pass after lengthy delays due to the weather ('Out from the Yukon,' *Alaska Free Press*, 31 December 1887).

21 William Ogilvie, *Yukon District*, 9. See also *Sitka Alaskan*, 12 February 1887.

22 Ogilvie, *Yukon District*, 39; Redmond, *Down the Yukon*, 620. Redmond reported that there were several mining parties at the mouth of the Hootalinqua River, and that men were also working on several old claims below here on the Yukon River. He stated that Cassiar Bar had been worked out. The water was too high to mine here earlier in the season, so by 24 June the remaining men were leaving.

23 Ogilvie, *Yukon District*, 41.

24 Ogilvie, *Early Days on the Yukon*, 117.

25 Ogilvie, *Yukon District*, 39-40.

26 Ibid., 18.

27 Ibid., 142-4.

28 *Sitka Alaskan*, 1 September 1888.

29 Ogilvie, *Yukon District*, 18; *Sitka Alaskan*, 1 September 1888.

30 Ogilvie, *Yukon District*, 18; Snow Papers, Sonnickson manuscript, 26.

Chapter 6: Strangers in a Strange Land

 1 Frank Buteau, 'My Experiences in the World,' in *Sourdough Sagas*, edited by Herbert L. Heller, 93-118 (Cleveland: World Publishing 1967), 118.

 2 Buteau, 'My Experiences in the World,' 117.

 3 *Klondike Nugget*, 11 March 1899, 4; letter from Chris Sonnickson.

 4 M.H.E. Hayne, *The Pioneers of the Klondike: Being an Account of Two Years Police Service on the Yukon* (London: Sampson Low, Marsten, & Co. 1897), 51-2.

 5 William B. Haskell, *Two Years in the Klondike and Alaskan Gold Fields* (Hartford, CT: Hartford Publishing 1898), 189: 'The monotony of the ordinary Alaskan diet is something that requires a strong stomach and the patience of Job.'

 6 Buteau, 'My Experiences in the World,' 109: 'We had not had any fresh potatoes during our six or seven year sojourn in the interior, so you can imagine our enjoyment when we were served a large platter of French fried potatoes soon after our arrival at Dyea.' Henry Davis, 'Recollections,' in *Sourdough Sagas*, edited by Herbert L. Heller, 28-83 (Cleveland: World Publishing 1967), 68, comments that he joined a trader for dinner in 1889 and had the first potatoes he had eaten in two years.

 7 Esther Lyons, comp., *Esther Lyons' Glimpses of Alaska* (Chicago: Rand McNally & Co. 1897), 41; Tappan Adney, *The Klondike Stampede* (New York: Harper Bros. 1900), 283.

 8 Jim Bender, 'Early Days in Alaska,' in *Sourdough Sagas*, edited by Herbert L. Heller, 85-92 (Cleveland: World Publishing 1967), 91; Davis, 'Recollections,' 33-54.

 9 A.E. Wills, 'Extract From Assistant Surgeon A.E. Wills' Report for 1895,' in William Ogilvie, *Information Respecting the Yukon District from the Report of William Ogilvie and Other Sources*, 64, 65 (Ottawa: Government Printing Bureau 1897), 65.

10 Ibid., 65.

11 W.H. Pierce, *Thirteen Years of Travel and Exploration in Alaska, 1877-1889* (Anchorage: Alaska Northwest Publishing 1977), 92.

12 J.G. MacGregor, *The Klondike Rush Through Edmonton, 1897-1898* (Toronto: McClelland & Stewart 1970), 236-42; Pierce, *Thirteen Years of Travel*, 92; Will Chase, *Reminiscences of Captain Billie Moore* (Kansas City: Burton Publishing 1947), 128.

13 Arthur Walden, *A Dog-Puncher on the Yukon* (Boston: Houghton Mifflin 1931), 61-2, describes a man freezing to death on the trail to Preacher Creek.

14 Leroy N. McQuesten, *Life in the Yukon, 1871-1885* (Whitehorse: Yukon Order of Pioneers 1952), 14.

15 See James Wickersham, *Old Yukon: Tales, Trails, and Trials* (Washington: Law Book 1938), 121; and Francois Mercier, *Recollections of the Yukon: Memoirs from the Years*

1868-1885, Alaska Historical Commission Studies in History, no. 88 (Anchorage: Alaska Historical Society 1986), 25, 27, 55.

16 See the comments about the early buildings at Forty Mile in Chapter 5.

17 Snow Papers, Chris Sonnickson manuscript, Dartmouth College, Hanover, NH, 9; *Klondike Nugget,* 11 March 1899, 4. See also Davis, 'Recollections,' 39.

18 See Davis, 'Recollections,' 50: 'We had to make a furnace as there are no stoves here yet.' See also William Ogilvie, *Early Days on the Yukon and the Story of Its Gold Fields* (Toronto: Bell & Cockburn 1913), 300.

19 Chase, *Captain Billie Moore,* 182, describes a rock stove built in a cabin at Forty Mile in 1886. As the furnace warmed up the cabin it also thawed the permafrost, and the whole thing started sinking into the ground.

20 Davis, 'Recollections,' 61.

21 For a good description of a log cabin of the era, refer to Ogilvie, *Early Days on the Yukon,* 297-301.

22 See Haskell, *Two Years in the Klondike,* 176-81, for a comparison of the temporary and the permanent log building.

23 Pierce, *Thirteen Years of Travel,* 92, reports using moose, caribou, and bear oil for illumination, while Josiah Edward Spurr, *Through the Yukon Gold Diggings* (Boston: Eastern Publishing 1900), describes the use of seal oil.

24 Spurr, *Yukon Gold Diggings,* 158, 159; Pierce, *Thirteen Years of Travel,* 92; Hayne, *Pioneers of the Klondike,* 91.

25 Buteau, 'My Experiences in the World,' 102-3.

26 Hayne, *Pioneers of the Klondike,* 74.

27 Chase, *Captain Billie Moore,* 130; Ogilvie, *Early Days on the Yukon,* 290.

28 Ogilvie, *Early Days on the Yukon,* 291.

29 Davis, 'Recollections,' 54.

30 Snow Papers, Sonnickson manuscript, 19, 20.

31 See Davis, 'Recollections,' 62-3, 76.

32 Snow Papers, Roblin manuscript, 2.

Chapter 7: Years of Change

1 Snow Papers, George T. Snow manuscript, Darmouth College, Hanover, NH, 118.

2 Ibid., 119.

3 Snow Papers, Sonnickson manuscript, 21-9.

4 Ibid., 29-30.

5 According to several sources (Jim Bender, 'Early Days in Alaska,' in *Sourdough Sagas,* edited by Herbert L. Heller, 85-92 [Cleveland: World Publishing 1967]; Henry Davis, 'Recollections,' in *Sourdough Sagas,* edited by Herbert L. Heller, 28-83 [Cleveland: World Publishing 1967]; Will Chase, *Reminiscences of Captain Billie Moore* [Kansas City: Burton Publishing 1947]), members of the party who were named included: Gordon Bettles, Jim Bender, Caribou Johnny, Henry (Crooked-Leg) Davis, John Minook, Pitka, William Moore, Matt Hall, Hank Wright (or Anderson – he used both names), John Folger, E. Chapman and his son, George Carey, John Boardwine, and

other men named Clinton and Kerr.

6 For various accounts of the events, refer to Bender, 'Early Days in Alaska,' 87-9; Erinia Pavaloff Cherosky Callahan, 'A Yukon Autobiography,' *Alaska Journal* 5 (Spring 1975):128; Chase, *Captain Billie Moore*, 147-53; Davis, 'Recollections,' 55-8.

7 The reader might also consider the effect that Jack Leslie's false account of an 'Indian massacre' had on several of the prospectors who were travelling into the Yukon, as described in Chapter 4.

8 See Melody Webb, *The Last Frontier: A History of the Yukon Basin of Canada and Alaska* (Albuquerque: University of New Mexico Press 1985), 80-1, for a brief discussion of this incident.

9 *Mining and Scientific Press*, 2 October 1889, 286.

10 Information regarding Ellington comes from: Marjorie Almstrom, 'A Century of Schooling: Education in the Yukon, 1861-1961' (Whitehorse: Privately published manuscript 1990), 25; and Linda Johnson, 'Reverend Canham's Contribution to the Cultural and Historical Record of the Yukon Valley, 1888-1916,' manuscript, 1988, 13.

11 William Ogilvie, *Early Days on the Yukon and the Story of Its Gold Fields* (Toronto: Bell & Cockburn 1913), 112, states that, as a consequence of poor supply, two-thirds of the miners in the Yukon made their way out of the country each year. J.E. McGrath, 'The Alaska Boundary Survey,' *National Geographic* 4 (1892):188, stated: 'It is a very risky venture trying to live on the country in the interior of Alaska.'

12 Chase, *Captain Billie Moore*, 168-75.

13 Frank Buteau, 'My Experiences in the World,' in *Sourdough Sagas*, edited by Herbert L. Heller, 93-118 (Cleveland: World Publishing 1967), 104-5.

14 Lewis Green, *The Boundary Hunters: Surveying the 141st Meridian and the Alaska Panhandle* (Vancouver: University of British Columbia Press 1982), 33.

15 The *Mining and Scientific Press*, 3 December 1892, states that Neil McArthur was the discoverer. Tappan Adney, *The Klondike Stampede* (New York: Harper Bros. 1900), 456, states that the gold was discovered by O.C. 'Kink' Miller in 1892.

16 J.E. McGrath, letter to Mendenhall, 16 February 1892, RG 23, ser. 22, vol. 620, Coast and Geodetic Survey, National Archives (US).

17 *Sitka Alaskan*, 16 July 1892.

18 Both the *Sitka Alaskan*, 29 August 1891, and William Douglas Johns, 'The Early Yukon, Alaska, and the Klondike Discovery as They Were Before the Great Klondike Stampede Swept Away the Old Conditions By One Who Was There,' typescript, Coutts Collection, 78/69, box F-89, folders 20 and 21, Yukon Archives, Whitehorse, n.d., p. 95, illustrate the drop in price.

19 *Mining and Scientific Press*, July 1894. McQuesten's son, Richard, is quoted as saying that Healy's store had more stock than did his father's.

20 Veazzie Wilson, *Guide to the Yukon Goldfields*, PAM-1895-3C, Yukon Archives, Whitehorse, 1895, p. 36; William Ogilvie, *Information Respecting the Yukon District from the Reports of Wm. Ogilvie, Dominion Land Surveyor* (Ottawa: Government Printing Bureau 1897), 30.

21 Claus M. Naske, 'The Fortymile Country: A Historical Study of the Fortymile Mining

NOTES TO PAGES 61-75 177

District,' report prepared under contract for Fairbanks District, Bureau of Land Management, US Department of the Interior, 1973, 11.
22 *Mining and Scientific Press*, 7 July 1894, 2.
23 *Mining and Scientific Press*, 10 November 1894, 292.
24 Arthur Walden, *A Dog-Puncher on the Yukon* (Boston: Houghton Mifflin 1931), 27.
25 A.E. Ironmonger Sola, *Klondyke: Truth and Facts of the New Eldorado* (London: The Mining and Geographical Institute, Broad Street House 1897), 77-80, describes typical mining methods in the region at this time.
26 Buteau, 'My Experiences in the World,' 103-4.
27 Ibid., 106. See also Chase, *Captain Billie Moore*, 195.
28 Ogilvie, *Yukon District*, 40.
29 Sola, *Klondyke*, 66.
30 Webb, *Last Frontier*, 89-90.
31 Snow Papers, McCloud typescript, 1, 2.
32 Snow Papers, anonymous account.
33 Davis, 'Recollections,' 74.
34 Adney, *Klondike Stampede*, 459.

Chapter 8: Forty Mile: Anatomy of a Gold Rush Town
1 A.E. Ironmonger Sola, *Klondyke: Truth and Facts of the New Eldorado* (London: The Mining and Geographical Institute, Broad Street House 1897), 69.
2 *Sitka Alaskan*, 31 August 1895, 3.
3 *Sitka Alaskan*, 20 July 1895, 1.
4 Tappan Adney, *The Klondike Stampede* (New York: Harper Bros. 1900), 456-7.
5 Annex 'B' to PC 2344, 29 November 1893. Copy on file, Mining Recorder's Office, Dawson.
6 Annex 'C' to PC 1201, 16 May 1893. Copy on file at Mining Recorder's Office, Dawson.
7 Annex 'A' to PC 1201, 26 May 1894. Copy on file in Mining Recorder's Office, Dawson.
8 Insp. Charles. Constantine, 'Report of Inspector Charles Constantine, 10 October 1894,' in *Report of the Commissioner of the North-West Mounted Police Force, 1895*, 69-85 (Ottawa: Queen's Printer 1895), 76.
9 Ibid.
10 *Sitka Alaskan*, 6 October 1894, stated that 800 men were to winter in the Yukon that year. The issue of 16 October 1894, quoting Veazzie Wilson, stated that 1000 miners were wintering in the region.
11 Marjorie E. Almstrom, *A Century of Schooling: Education in the Yukon, 1861-1961* (Whitehorse: Privately published manuscript 1990), 28.
12 William Ogilvie, *Information Respecting the Yukon District from the Reports of Wm. Ogilvie, Dominion Land Surveyor* (Ottawa: Government Printing Bureau 1897), 52.
13 Harry DeWindt, *Through the Gold Fields of Alaska to Bering Strait* (London: Chatto and Windus 1898), 139-40.
14 *Alaska Searchlight*, 18 February 1895, 4.
15 William Douglas Johns, 'The Early Yukon, Alaska, and the Klondike Discovery as

They Were Before the Great Klondike Stampede Swept Away the Old Conditions By One Who Was There,' typescript, Coutts Collection, 78/69, box F-89, folders 20 and 21, Yukon Archives, Whitehorse, n.d., p. 85.

16 Ibid.

17 *Mining and Scientific Press*, 7 July 1894, front page. Article quotes Richard McQuesten.

18 Various authors described the services available in Forty Mile: Sola, *Klondyke*, 68; S.A. Archer, *A Heroine of the North: The Memoirs of Charlotte Selina Bompas* (London: Society for Promoting Christian Knowledge 1929), 138; DeWindt, *Gold Fields*, 140; Henry Henderson, *True Story of the Discovery of the Klondike by Bob Henderson* (Edmonton: H.H. Hull Printing, n.d.), 12; William B. Haskell, *Two Years in the Klondike and Alaskan Gold Fields* (Hartford, CT: Hartford Publishing 1898), 149; Esther Lyons, comp. *Esther Lyons' Glimpses of Alaska* (Chicago: Rand McNally & Co. 1897), 48-51; Veazzie Wilson, *Guide to the Yukon Goldfields*, rev. ed. (Seattle: Calvert 1897), 41; H.A. Cody, *An Apostle of the North* (London: Seeley & Co. 1910), 167; Rev. Charles Judge, *An American Missionary: A Record of the Work of the Rev. William A. Judge, S.J.* (New York: Ossining 1907), 165.

19 Constantine, 'Report of Inspector Charles Constantine, 1894,' 84; Haskell, *Two Years in the Klondike*, 149; M.H.E. Hayne, *The Pioneers of the Klondike: Being an Account of Two Years Police Service on the Yukon* (London: Sampson Low, Marsten, & Co. 1897), 43; Wilson, *Guide to the Yukon Gold Fields*, 43.

20 See Harold B. Goodrich, 'History and Condition of the Yukon Gold District to 1897,' in Josiah Edward Spurr, *Geology of the Yukon Gold District, Alaska*, 103-33 (Washington: Government Printing Office 1897), 119. In 1895, its population was 600, or about 100 less than that of Circle.

21 *Yukon Press*, 1 January 1894.

22 *Sitka Alaskan*, 29 May 1886, 2, states that a man named Hawthorne took fifty gallons of alcohol and liquor into the Yukon, 'presumably to traffic with the Indians.'

23 Constantine, 'Report of Inspector Charles Constantine, 1894,' 76.

24 Hayne, *Pioneers of the Klondike*, 90; Will Chase, *Reminiscences of Captain Billie Moore* (Kansas City: Burton Publishing 1947), 131.

25 Sola, *Klondyke*, 69, said that after the arrival of the steamer *Arctic*, everyone in town got drunk.

26 William Ogilvie, *Early Days on the Yukon and the Story of Its Gold Fields* (Toronto: Bell & Cockburn 1913), 102-3.

27 Hayne, *Pioneers of the Klondike*, 89; Constantine, 'Report of Inspector Charles Constantine, 1894,' 81.

28 Hayne, *Pioneers of the Klondike*, 92.

29 Sola, *Klondyke*, 70.

30 See Josiah Edward Spurr, *Through the Yukon Gold Diggings* (Boston: Eastern Publishing 1900), 124; Ogilvie, *Early Days on the Yukon*, 286-7.

31 J. Lincoln Steffens, 'Life in the Klondike Gold Fields,' *McClure's Magazine*, September 1897, 965; Sola, *Klondyke*, 68.

32 Henderson, *True Story of the Discovery of the Klondike*, 12.

33 Spurr, *Yukon Gold Diggings*, 116-19.

34 Hayne, *Pioneers of the Klondike*, 89.

35 Haskell, *Two Years in the Klondike*, 150; Henry Davis, 'Recollections,' in *Sourdough Sagas*, edited by Herbert L. Heller, 28-83 (Cleveland: World Publishing 1967), 75.

36 C.H. Hamlin, *Old Times in the Yukon* (Los Angeles: Wetzel Publishing 1928), 4.

37 Ibid., 24.

38 Hayne, *Pioneers of the Klondike*, 114; Spurr, *Yukon Gold Diggings*, 116.

39 Copy of minutes of first meeting of Yukon Order of Pioneers organized at Forty Mile, 1 December 1894, records of the Yukon Order of Pioneers, Yukon Archives, Whitehorse, 1894.

40 *Sitka Alaskan*, 23 November 1889, 3.

41 Ibid.

42 Archer, *Heroine of the North*, 139.

43 Johns, 'Early Yukon,' 148, quoting J.R. Howard.

44 Richard John Bowen, 'Incidents in the Life of the Reverend Richard John Bowen among the Natives, Trappers, Traders, Prospectors, and Gold Miners in the Yukon Territory Before and After the Gold Rush of the Year 1898,' manuscript, MG 29 C92, National Archives of Canada, Ottawa, 1950, p. 157.

45 *Sitka Alaskan*, 31 August 1895, 3; *Alaska Searchlight*, 17 December 1894.

46 Constantine, 'Report of Inspector Charles Constantine, 1894,' 81; Haskell, *Two Years in the Klondike*, 81, described them as more than mere women; Arthur Walden, *A Dog-Puncher on the Yukon* (Boston: Houghton Mifflin 1931), 47, said 'men looked up to them, not as their equals, but as their superiors.'

47 Anna DeGraf, *Pioneering on the Yukon 1892-1917* (Hamdon, CT: Archon Books 1992), 28-32.

48 Hayne, *Pioneers of the Klondike*, 45.

49 Fr. Marcel Bobillier, *Une Pionnière du Yukon, Madam Emilie Tremblay*, Publications de la Société Historique de Saguenay, no. 13 (Chicoutimi: La Société Historique de Saguenay 1948).

50 Some of the White men who took Native wives included Tom Evans, Frank Cormier, George Carmack, Frank Buteau, Henry Davis, Al Mayo, George Carey, Arthur Harper, Pete MacDonald, and Chris Sonnickson. Clarence Berry reported that in 1895 at Forty Mile, all the sourdoughs (forty in number) had Native wives, while the Cheechacos did not. The latter were, however, allowed to borrow these women for the occasional 'squaw dance' (C.J. Berry, 'Personal Account, 1894-96,' typescript from the Berry family, California, 6).

51 Examples include Jack McQuesten and Chris Sonnickson. See *Klondike Nugget*, 1 June 1901, with regard to the latter.

52 Israel C. Russell, 'A Journey up the Yukon,' *Bulletin of the American Geographical Society* 27, no. 2 (1895):153.

53 Davis, 'Recollections,' 79. See also DeGraf, *Pioneering on the Yukon*, 22.

54 Johns, 'Early Yukon,' 141; James Wickersham, *Old Yukon: Tales, Trails, and Trials* (Washington: Law Book 1938), 125; Walden, *Dog-Puncher*, 55-6.

55 Anna Fulcomer, 'The Three R's at Circle City,' *Century* 66, no. 2 (1898):225.
56 Johns, 'Early Yukon,' 136.
57 DeGraf, *Pioneering on the Yukon*, 24.

Chapter 9: The Arrival of the North-West Mounted Police

1 Staff Sgt. Charles Brown, letter to Inspector Charles Constantine, 9 February 1895, RG 18, A1, vol. 100, file 17-96, National Archives of Canada, 1895, p. 2.
2 Staff Sgt. Charles Brown, letter to Inspector Charles Constantine, 9 February 1895, part 3, RG 18, A1, vol. 100, file 17-96, National Archives of Canada, 1895.
3 Ibid., p. 5.
4 Ibid. Also, William Ogilvie, *Early Days on the Yukon and the Story of Its Gold Fields* (Toronto: Bell & Cockburn 1913), 257.
5 Brown, letter to Constantine, 9 February 1895.
6 E. Turner, letter to unnamed newspaper, 19 May 1895, in research file on J. Ladue, Dawson City Museum, Dawson, 1895.
7 M.H.E. Hayne, *The Pioneers of the Klondike: Being an Account of Two Years Police Service on the Yukon* (London: Sampson Low, Marsten, & Co. 1897), 31-2.
8 Ibid., 53.
9 Insp. Charles Constantine, 'Report of Inspector Charles Constantine, 20 January 1896,' in *Report of the Commissioner of the North-West Mounted Police Force, 1895*, 7-15 (Ottawa: Queen's Printer 1896), 8.
10 Hayne, *Pioneers of the Klondike*, 64.
11 Brown, letter to Constantine, 9 February 1895, part 3.
12 Ibid.
13 Local orders, Fort Constantine, RG 18, D1, vol. 3055, National Archives of Canada, n.d.
14 Hayne, *Pioneers of the Klondike*, 83.
15 Rev. Charles Judge, *An American Missionary: A Record of the Work of the Rev. William A. Judge, S.J.* (New York: Ossining 1907), 160-1.
16 Richard John Bowen, 'Incidents in the Life of the Reverend Richard John Bowen among the Natives, Trappers, Traders, Prospectors, and Gold Miners in the Yukon Territory Before and After the Gold Rush of the Year 1898,' manuscript, MG 29 C92, National Archives of Canada, Ottawa, 1950, pp. 72-3.
17 Ibid., 75.
18 Bowen, 'Reverend Richard John Bowen,' 107.
19 Ibid.
20 Bowen, 'Reverend Richard John Bowen,' 112-13.
21 Ibid.
22 Judge, *An American Missionary*, 184.
23 Frank Buteau, 'My Experiences in the World,' in *Sourdough Sagas*, edited by Herbert L. Heller, 93-118 (Cleveland: World Publishing 1967), 116; Don Stewart, *Sourdough Ray* (Coos Bay, OR: Gorst Publications 1983), part 5; Henry Henderson, *True Story of the Discovery of the Klondike by Bob Henderson* (Edmonton: H.H. Hull Printing, n.d.), 11.

24 Arthur Walden, *A Dog-Puncher on the Yukon* (Boston: Houghton Mifflin 1931), 6.

25 'Ray Stewart Talks about the Horseless Days,' *Dawson Daily News*, 29 June 1939, 3.

26 John Grieve Lind, untitled manuscript, 81/58, Yukon Archives, Whitehorse, n.d., p. 3.

27 Stewart, *Sourdough Ray*, part 7; William B. Haskell, *Two Years in the Klondike and Alaskan Gold Fields* (Hartford, CT: Hartford Publishing 1898), 195.

28 Haskell, *Two Years in the Klondike*, 195.

29 Stewart, *Sourdough Ray*, part 2.

30 Hayne, *Pioneers of the Klondike*, 104.

31 William Douglas Johns, 'The Early Yukon, Alaska, and the Klondike Discovery as They Were Before the Great Klondike Stampede Swept Away the Old Conditions By One Who Was There,' typescript, Coutts Collection, 78/69, box F-89, folders 20 and 21, Yukon Archives, Whitehorse, n.d., 87.

32 Ibid., 105, 107, 108; Veazzie Wilson, *Guide to the Yukon Goldfields*, rev. ed. (Seattle: Calvert 1897), 42.

33 Walden, *Dog-Puncher*, 57, 58.

34 A.E. Ironmonger Sola, *Klondyke: Truth and Facts of the New Eldorado* (London: The Mining and Geographical Institute, Broad Street House 1897), 71-3.

35 Walden, *Dog-Puncher*, 89-90.

36 Ibid., 80-1.

37 Ibid., 45.

38 *Sitka Alaskan*, 24 August 1895, 1.

39 E.H. Fletcher, letter to postmaster-general, RG 18, A1, vol. 133, file 140-97 (letter from comptroller to commissioner of NWMP also included in this record group), National Archives of Canada.

40 Bowen, 'Richard John Bowen,' 137-8. See also S.A. Archer, *A Heroine of the North: The Memoirs of Charlotte Selina Bompas* (London: Society for Promoting Christian Knowledge 1929), 134, 141; Insp. Charles Constantine, 'Report of Inspector Charles Constantine, 10 October 1894,' in *Report of the Commissioner of the North-West Mounted Police Force, 1895, 69-85* (Ottawa: Queen's Printer 1895), 77.

41 Haskell, *Two Years in the Klondike*, 295.

42 Ibid.

43 Josiah Edward Spurr, *Through the Yukon Gold Diggings* (Boston: Eastern Publishing 1900), 142; See also Haskell, *Two Years in the Klondike*, 142.

Chapter 10: Death of the Miners' Committee

1 Arthur Walden, *A Dog-Puncher on the Yukon* (Boston: Houghton Mifflin 1931), 29-30.

2 Richard John Bowen, 'Incidents in the Life of the Reverend Richard John Bowen among the Natives, Trappers, Traders, Prospectors, and Gold Miners in the Yukon Territory Before and After the Gold Rush of the Year 1898,' manuscript, MG 29 C92, National Archives of Canada, Ottawa, 1950, 134-6; M.H.E. Hayne, *The Pioneers of the Klondike: Being an Account of Two Years Police Service on the Yukon* (London: Sampson Low, Marsten, & Co. 1897), 109-11; H.A. Cody, *An Apostle of the North* (London: Seeley & Co. 1910), 271.

3 Bowen, 'Reverend Richard John Bowen,' 139.

4 Hayne, *Pioneers of the Klondike*, 68-73; Insp. Charles Constantine, 'Report of Inspector Charles Constantine, 20 January 1896,' in *Report of the Commissioner of the North-West Mounted Police Force, 1895*, 7-15 (Ottawa: Queen's Printer 1895), 12; Insp. Charles Constantine, diary, RG 18, vol. 1345, file 190-1895, National Archives of Canada 1895.

5 William Ogilvie, *Lecture on the Yukon Gold Fields (Canada), Delivered at Victoria B.C* (Victoria: The Colonist Presses 1897), 29; see also William B. Haskell, *Two Years in the Klondike and Alaskan Gold Fields* (Hartford, CT: Hartford Publishing 1898), 150; Warburton Pike, *Through the Subarctic Forest* (London: Edward Arnold 1896), 220-1; Harold B. Goodrich, 'History and Condition of the Yukon Gold District to 1897,' in Josiah Edward Spurr, *Geology of the Yukon Gold District, Alaska*, 103-33 (Washington: Government Printing Office 1897), 127.

6 *Sitka Alaskan*, 29 May 1886, 2.

7 William Ogilvie, *Early Days on the Yukon and the Story of Its Gold Fields* (Toronto: Bell & Cockburn 1913), 248.

8 Ogilvie, *Early Days on the Yukon*, 248-9.

9 J. Lincoln Steffens, 'Life in the Klondike Gold Fields,' *McClure's Magazine*, September 1897, 964-5.

10 Jim Bender, 'Early Days in Alaska,' in *Sourdough Sagas*, edited by Herbert L. Heller, 85-92 (Cleveland: World Publishing 1967), 90.

11 William Douglas Johns, 'The Early Yukon, Alaska, and the Klondike Discovery as They Were Before the Great Klondike Stampede Swept Away the Old Conditions By One Who Was There,' typescript, Coutts Collection, 78/69, box F-89, folders 20 and 21, Yukon Archives, Whitehorse, n.d., 155-6.

12 Bowen, 'Reverend Richard John Bowen,' 150-1.

13 Johns, 'Early Yukon,' 138.

14 Josiah Edward Spurr, *Through the Yukon Gold Diggings* (Boston: Eastern Publishing 1900), 188-95.

15 Insp. Charles Constantine, 'Report of the Yukon Detachment, 20 November 1896,' in *Report of the Commissioner of the North-West Mounted Police Force, 1896*, 232-9 (Ottawa: Queen's Printer 1896), 234. Constantine reported that 'a few miners denied Canada's jurisdiction and right to collect fees, on the grounds that there was no joint survey, and a possibility of error in the work. However, I went up to Miller and Glacier Creeks and all dues were paid without any trouble except that of a hard trip.'

16 RG 18, vol. 123, file 467-96, National Archives of Canada 1896.

17 RG 18, vol. 123, file 459-75, National Archives of Canada 1896.

18 Ibid.

19 Ibid.

20 Hayne, *Pioneers of the Klondike*, 124.

Chapter 11: Circle

1 Tappan Adney, *The Klondike Stampede* (New York: Harper Bros. 1900), 459.

2 Veazzie Wilson, *Guide to the Yukon Goldfields*, rev. ed. (Seattle: Calvert 1897), 44, 45; Esther Lyons, comp., *Esther Lyons' Glimpses of Alaska* (Chicago: Rand McNally & Co. 1897), 59, 60.

3 John Richard Bowen, 'Incidents in the Life of the Reverend Richard John Bowen among the Natives, Trappers, Traders, Prospectors, and Gold Miners in the Yukon Territory Before and After the Gold Rush of the Year 1898,' manuscript, MG 29 C92, National Archives of Canada, Ottawa, 1950, 55; Harold B. Goodrich, 'History and Condition of the Yukon Gold District to 1897,' in Josiah Edward Spurr, *Geology of the Yukon Gold District, Alaska*, 103-33 (Washington: Government Printing Office 1897), 119.

4 Thomas Stone, 'The Mounties as Vigilantes: Perceptions of Community and the Transformation of Law in the Yukon, 1885-1897,' *Law and Society Review* 14, no. 1 (1979):86, quoting William B. Haskell, *Two Years in the Klondike and Alaskan Gold Fields* (Hartford, CT: Hartford Publishing 1898), 162, 164, and Pierre Berton, *Klondike: The Last Great Gold Rush 1896-97* (Toronto: McClelland & Stewart 1972), 29.

5 *Alaska Searchlight*, 28 November 1896, 1.

6 William Douglas Johns, 'The Early Yukon, Alaska, and the Klondike Discovery as They Were Before the Great Klondike Stampede Swept Away the Old Conditions By One Who Was There,' typescript, Coutts Collection, 78/69, box F-89, folders 20 and 21, Yukon Archives, Whitehorse, n.d., 138.

7 Ibid., 158.

8 Arthur Walden, *A Dog-Puncher on the Yukon* (Boston: Houghton Mifflin 1931), 42.

9 Stone, 'Mounties,' 86, quoting Haskell, *Two Years in the Klondike*, 162, 164, and Berton, *Klondike*, 29. See also Johns, 'Early Yukon,' 137.

10 Haskell, *Two Years in the Klondike*, 175.

11 Walden, *Dog-Puncher*, 42.

12 Johns, 'Early Yukon,' 132.

13 Ibid.

14 Walden, *Dog-Puncher*, 44.

15 Henry Davis, 'Recollections,' in *Sourdough Sagas*, edited by Herbert L. Heller, 28-83 (Cleveland: World Publishing 1967) 50-1; Johns, 'The Early Yukon,' 131; M.H.E. Hayne, *The Pioneers of the Klondike: Being an Account of Two Years Police Service on the Yukon* (London: Sampson Low, Marsten, & Co. 1897), 87.

16 Adney, *Klondike Stampede*, 272-3; Josiah Edward Spurr, *Geology of the Yukon Gold District, Alaska* (Washington: Government Printing Office 1897), 147, 176-8.

17 William Ogilvie, *Information Respecting the Yukon District from the Reports of Wm. Ogilvie, Dominion Land Surveyor* (Ottawa: Government Printing Bureau 1897), 53; Walden, *Dog-Puncher on the Yukon*, 46.

18 Adney, *Klondike Stampede*, 272.

19 Haskell, *Two Years in the Klondike*, 197.

20 Walden, *Dog-Puncher*, 60-1.

21 Johns, 'Early Yukon,' 150.

22 Ibid., 151-2.

23 J.J. Healy, letter to Minister of the Interior, 7 March 1895, YRG 1, vol. 18, file 4636, National Archives of Canada.

24 Johns, 'Early Yukon,' 143.

25 Anna Fulcomer, 'The Three R's at Circle City,' *Century* 66, no. 2 (1898):223.

26 Ibid., 225.

27 Ibid., 229.

28 Johns stated about Bowen: 'He also circulated among the miners but his efforts were fruitless; the soil was too stony.' See 'Early Yukon,' 144.

29 Johns, 'Early Yukon,' 136-7.

30 Ibid., 134

31 Ibid.

32 Ibid., 135.

33 See Chapter 10 for a description.

34 *Victoria Colonist*, 20 March 1896, 3.

35 C.H. Hamlin, *Old Times in the Yukon* (Los Angeles: Wetzel Publishing 1928), 4.

36 Hamlin, *Old Times*, 4, 5.

37 *Alaska Searchlight*, 9 November 1895, 9.

38 Hamlin, *Old Times*, 26, 27.

39 Harry DeWindt, *Through the Gold Fields of Alaska to Bering Strait* (London: Chatto and Windus 1898), 161.

40 Josiah Edward Spurr, *Through the Yukon Gold Diggings* (Boston: Eastern Publishing 1900), 197-9. For another, similar account, see Anna DeGraf, *Pioneering on the Yukon 1892-1917* (Hamdon, CT: Archon Books 1992), 24-8.

41 Fulcomer, 'The Three R's,' 225.

42 Johns, 'Early Yukon,' 156.

43 Walden, *Dog-Puncher*, 77.

Chapter 12: The Discovery of Gold in the Klondike

1 See Pierre Berton, *Klondike: The Last Great Gold Rush, 1896-97* (Toronto: McClelland & Stewart 1972), Chapter 2; William Ogilvie, *Early Days on the Yukon and the Story of Its Gold Fields* (Toronto: Bell & Cockburn 1913), Chapter 8; Tappan Adney, *The Klondike Stampede* (New York: Harper Bros. 1900), Chapter 14.

2 All of the information regarding Carmack's first ten years in the Yukon comes from his account, which is found in the Snow Papers, Dartmouth College, Hanover, NH.

3 Ibid.

4 Adney, *Klondike Stampede*, 282.

5 Ogilvie, *Early Days on the Yukon*, 133.

6 M.H.E. Hayne, *The Pioneers of the Klondike: Being an Account of Two Years Police Service on the Yukon* (London: Sampson Low, Marsten, & Co. 1897), 134.

7 George W. Carmack, *My Experiences in the Yukon*, pamphlet (published privately by Marguerite P. Carmack 1933), 6.

8 *Whitehorse Star*, 6 October 1976, B, C, and E.

9 See T.A.K. Turner, 'The Gold Discovery of the Klondike,' 82/108, Yukon Archives, Whitehorse, n.d.

10 Ogilvie, *Early Days on the Yukon*, 121.

11 Turner, 'Gold Discovery,' 13.

12 Ibid.

13 Adney, *Klondike Stampede*, 279; Ogilvie, *Early Days on the Yukon*, 124, states he was getting two cents a pan.

14 The mining records (original staker #397) indicate that another miner, George Remillard, was on Gold Bottom Creek and staked a claim on 11 August.

15 Adney, *Klondike Stampede*, 279-80; Ogilvie, *Early Days on the Yukon*, 124, offers a slightly different version of these events on Gold Bottom Creek.

16 Adney, *Klondike Stampede*, 283.

17 Ogilvie, *Early Days on the Yukon*, 128. In Carmack's account, however, he claimed to have fully divulged his findings to Henderson, advising him to go and try his luck. Henderson declined (Carmack, *My Experiences in the Yukon*, 11). Adney, *Klondike Stampede*, 284, says that Carmack showed Henderson 'colours,' but since colours could be found just about everywhere, this did not convince Henderson to try this new creek.

18 Mining Records, Mining Recorder's Office, Dawson. Roll no. 3, p. 25, shows that this claim was staked by Carmack on 13 August and was filed on 14 December 1896.

19 Turner, 'Gold Discovery,' 18. Ogilvie, *Early Days on the Yukon*, 123, however, says that wolves were responsible.

20 Carmack, *My Experiences in the Yukon*, 11.

21 Ogilvie, *Early Days on the Yukon*, 129. Adney, *Klondike Stampede*, 284, makes the same claim, while Carmack, *My Experiences on the Yukon*, 12, claims to have found it himself. For a description of the discovery, as rendered in Native oral tradition, read Julie Cruikshank, *Reading Voices: Oral and Written Interpretations of the Yukon's Past* (Vancouver: Douglas & McIntyre 1991), 121-40.

22 Carmack, *My Experiences on the Yukon*, 13.

23 Mrs. Charles Constantine, letter, Yukon Archives, 1926. See also, Ogilvie, cited in Lewis Green, *The Boundary Hunters: Surveying the 141st Meridian and the Alaska Panhandle* (Vancouver: University of British Columbia Press 1982), 65, 66. Carmack had only $12 in gold. The filing fee was $15.

24 Ogilvie, *Early Days on the Yukon*, 131; William Douglas Johns, 'The Early Yukon, Alaska, and the Klondike Discovery as They Were Before the Great Klondike Stampede Swept Away the Old Conditions By One Who Was There,' typescript, Coutts Collection, 78/69, box F-89, folders 20 and 21, Yukon Archives, Whitehorse, n.d., 114, identifies the mining recorder as Dave McKay. Ogilvie, *Early Days on the Yukon*, 131, states that he was a Nova Scotian. Carmack, *My Experiences on the Yukon*, 14, claims that he named the creek himself.

25 Johns, 'The Early Yukon,' 114.

26 Patsy Henderson, *Lecture given by Patsy Henderson in Whitehorse, 1950*, oral history

tape series, no. 4-1, Yukon Archives, Whitehorse, 1950, claims that Carmack recovered $1440 in three weeks. Ogilvie, *Early Days on the Yukon*, 57, states that Carmack recovered $1200 in eight days but could have recovered more in less time if he had had better equipment to work with. Hayne, *Pioneers of the Klondike*, 140, says that Carmack was recovering about $70 per day. William B. Haskell, *Two Years in the Klondike and Alaskan Gold Fields* (Hartford, CT: Hartford Publishing 1898), 283, states that Carmack had recovered $1400 by 1 October.

27 Judge Collection, microfilm 36, frame 77, Oregon Province Archives, Society of Jesus, Gonzaga University, Spokane, WA, 1980. Judge reported that the steamer *Arctic* went to the Klondike with about 100 miners on board.

28 Take, for example, 'Famous Ground: First Strike in Camp is Recalled,' *Dawson Daily News*, 14 July 1928, or 18 September 1903.

29 Turner, 'Gold Discovery,' 1.

30 Arthur Walden, *A Dog-Puncher on the Yukon* (Boston: Houghton Mifflin 1931), 68. Jack McQuesten told Walden that he had been down Rabbit Creek many years before but had been looking for furs, not gold. Ladue (Carmack, *My Experiences on the Yukon*, 10) had camped on Eldorado Creek the winter of 1884-5 but was not aware that he was sleeping on a fortune.

31 Snow Papers, Pete Nelson manuscript; Carmack, *My Experiences on the Yukon*, 11.

32 *Dawson Daily News*, 21 May 1904, 4.

33 Johns, 'The Early Yukon,' 109; *Dawson Daily News*, 18 September 1903.

34 Snow Papers, George Carmack account, 13.

35 Henry Davis, 'Recollections,' in *Sourdough Sagas*, edited by Herbert L. Heller, 28-83 (Cleveland: World Publishing 1967), 76.

36 In 1904 Carmack explained that the reason he did not return to Gold Bottom Creek with word of the discovery was that he was short of supplies, and it was a long way to trek back. He said that no amount of coaxing could have convinced either Charlie or Jim to carry the news back, considering the treatment they had received from Henderson during their prior visit. See *Dawson Daily News*, 21 May 1904, 4.

Chapter 13: Epilogue

1 Government records, ser. 11, vols. 1444-5, files 2 and 11, Yukon Archives, Whitehorse, n.d.

2 Pierre Berton, *Klondike: The Last Great Gold Rush, 1896-97* (Toronto: McClelland & Stewart 1972), 414.

BIBLIOGRAPHY

Newspapers
Klondike News, 1 April 1898
Dawson Daily News (DDN)
Sitka Alaskan (SA)
Alaska Free Press
Klondike Nugget, 1 November 1899
Whitehorse Star
Mining and Scientific Press
Yukon Press

Archival Sources

ARCHEOLOGICAL SURVEY OF CANADA, OTTAWA
Clark, Donald W. 'Fort Reliance 1983: Preliminary Report of Investigations.'
Typescript 1984

BANCROFT LIBRARY, BERKELEY, CA
Schieffelin, Edward. 'Ed Schieffelin's Trip To Alaska [1882-1883].' Manuscript P-K 43,
1888

DARTMOUTH COLLEGE, HANOVER, NH
Snow Papers. (These papers include the personal accounts of Peter Roblin, George
Carmack, George T. Snow, George Matlock, G.H. McCloud, Chris Sonnickson,
L.N. McQuesten, Joseph A. Cooper, and others.)

DAWSON CITY MUSEUM, DAWSON, YK
Sims, Vincent. 'Journal of Trip on the Yukon, 1883.' Manuscript 1883
Turner, E. Letter dated 19 May 1895 published in unidentified newspaper article.
Research files on J. Ladue 1895

Energy, Mines, and Resources Canada, Whitehorse, yk

Ogilvie, William. Blueprints and field books of William Ogilvie, Dominion Land Surveyor, for the Fortymile area, Yukon Territory. Field books no. 4 (1896) and no. 5 (1897)

National Archives of Canada, Ottawa

Bowen, Richard John. 'Incidents in the Life of the Reverend Richard John Bowen among the Natives, Trappers, Traders, Prospectors, and Gold Miners in the Yukon Territory Before and After the Gold Rush of the Year 1898.' MG 29 C92, 1950

Brown, Staff Sgt. Charles. Letter to Inspector Charles Constantine dated 9 February 1895. RG 18, A1, Vol. 100, File 17-96, 1895

Constantine, Insp. Charles. Diary. RG 18, Vol. 1345, File 190 1895

Fletcher, E.H. Letter to postmaster-general. RG 18, A1, Vol. 133, File 140-97 (letter from comptroller to commissioner of NWMP also included in this record group)

Healy, J.J. Letter to minister of the Interior dated 7 March 1895. YRG 1, Vol. 18, File 4636

Various files pertaining to the North-West Mounted Police [NWMP] stationed at Fort Constantine, RG 18

National Archives, Washington, dc

McGrath, J.E. Letter to Mendenhall dated 16 February 1892. Coast and Geodetic Survey, RG 23, Ser. 22, Vol. 620, 1892

Oregon Province Archives, Spokane, wa

Judge Collection, Microfilm 36. Alaska Mission Collection. Society of Jesus, Gonzaga University 1980

University of Alaska Archives, Fairbanks

Buteau, Frank. 'A Short Story about the Yukon River and its Tributaries and a Yukon Pioneer.' Typescript. Buteau Collection 1935

Yukon Archives, Whitehorse, yk

Anglican Church Records. Register of Baptisms, Burials and Marriages, Buxton Mission 1888-1903. Box 54, File 2

Henderson, Patsy. *Lecture given by Patsy Henderson in Whitehorse, 1950.* Oral History Tape Series, No. 4-1

Johns, William Douglas. 'The Early Yukon, Alaska, and the Klondike Discovery as They Were Before the Great Klondike Stampede Swept Away the Old Conditions By One Who Was There.' Typescript. Coutts Collection, 78/69, Box F-89, Folders 20 and 21

Lind, John Grieve. Untitled Manuscript, 81/58

Records of Applications for Placer Mining, 1896-1924. YRG-1, Ser. 10, Vol. 288 (copy of original application books)

Records of the Yukon Order of Pioneers. Copy of Minutes: First Meeting of Yukon Order of Pioneers Organized at Forty Mile, Yukon Territories, 1 December 1894

Redmond, W.A. *Down the Yukon*. PAM-1891-7, 1891

Turner, T.A.K. 'The Gold Discovery of the Klondike.' Manuscript, 82/108

Wilson, Veazzie. *Guide to the Yukon Goldfields*. PAM-1895-3C, 1895

Published Sources

Adney, Tappan. *The Klondike Stampede*. New York: Harper Bros. 1900

Almstrom, Marjorie E. 'A Century of Schooling: Education in the Yukon, 1861-1961.' Whitehorse: Privately published manuscript 1990

Archer, S.A. *A Heroine of the North: The Memoirs of Charlotte Selina Bompas*. London: Society for Promoting Christian Knowledge 1929

Ball, Norman R. *The Development of Permafrost Thawing Techniques in the Placer Gold Fields of the Klondike*. National Historic Parks and Sites Research Bulletin 25. Ottawa: Department of Indian and Northern Affairs 1975

Begg, Alexander. 'Notes on the Yukon Country.' *Scottish Geographical Magazine*, November 1896, 553-9

Bender, Jim. 'Early Days in Alaska.' In *Sourdough Sagas*, edited by Herbert L. Heller, 85-92. Cleveland: World Publishing 1967

Bennett, Gordon. *Yukon Transportation: A History*. Canadian Historic Sites: Occasional Papers in Archeology and History, no. 19. Ottawa: Parks Canada, National Historic Parks and Sites 1967

Berton, Pierre. 'Fortymile: American Outpost in the Canadian North.' *University of Toronto Quarterly* 22, no. 4 (1958):413-23

—. *Klondike: The Last Great Gold Rush, 1896-97*. Toronto: McClelland & Stewart 1972

Bettles, Gordon. 'Some Early Yukon River History.' In *Sourdough Sagas*, edited by Herbert L. Heller, 119-22. Cleveland: World Publishing 1967

Bobillier, Fr. Marcel. *Une Pionnière du Yukon, Madam Emilie Tremblay*. Publications de la Société Historique de Saguenay, no. 13. Chicoutimi: La Société Historique de Saguenay 1948

Bompas, C.S. 'Mission Work on the Upper Yukon.' *Spirit of Missions* 60 (June 1895):231-2

Brooks, Alfred H. *Blazing Alaska's Trails*. Fairbanks: University of Alaska 1953

Buteau, Frank. 'My Experiences in the World.' In *Sourdough Sagas*, edited by Herbert L. Heller, 93-118. Cleveland: World Publishing 1967

Callahan, Erinia Pavaloff Cherosky. 'A Yukon Autobiography.' *Alaska Journal* 5 (Spring 1975):127-8

Calsanctius, Sister Mary. *The Voice of Alaska: Memoirs of a Missioner*. Lachine, PQ: St. Ann's Press 1947

Carmack, George W. *My Experiences in the Yukon*. Pamphlet published privately by Marguerite P. Carmack 1933

Chase, Will. *Reminiscences of Captain Billie Moore*. Kansas City: Burton Publishing 1947

Clifton, Violet. *The Book of Talbot*. New York: Harcourt, Brace & Co. 1933

Coates, Ken. *Land of the Midnight Sun: A History of the Yukon*. Edmonton: Hurtig Publishers 1988

Coates, Ken and Bill Morrison. *The Sinking of the Princess Sophia: Taking the North Down With Her.* Toronto: Oxford University Press 1990

Cody, H.A. *An Apostle of the North.* London: Seeley & Co. 1910

Constantine, Insp. Charles. 'Report of Inspector Charles Constantine, 10 October 1894.' In *Report of the Commissioner of the North-West Mounted Police Force, 1895,* 69-85. Ottawa: Queen's Printer 1895

—. 'Report of Inspector Charles Constantine, 20 January 1896.' In *Report of the Commissioner of the North-West Mounted Police Force, 1895,* 7-15. Ottawa: Queen's Printer 1896

—. 'Report of the Yukon Detachment, 20 November 1896.' In *Report of the Commissioner of the North-West Mounted Police Force, 1896,* 232-9. Ottawa: Queen's Printer 1896

Coutts, R.C. *Yukon Places and Names.* Sidney, BC: Gray's Publishing 1980

Cruikshank, Julie. *Reading Voices: Oral and Written Interpretations of the Yukon's Past.* Vancouver: Douglas & McIntyre 1991

Davis, Henry. 'Recollections.' In *Sourdough Sagas,* edited by Herbert L. Heller, 28-83. Cleveland: World Publishing 1967

Dawson, George M. *Report of an Exploration in the Yukon District, NWT, and Adjacent Northern Portion of British Columbia, 1887.* Reprint. Whitehorse: Yukon Historical and Museums Association 1988

DeArmond, R.N. *Klondike Newsman.* Skagway: Lynn Canal Publishing 1990

—. 'A Letter to Jack McQuesten: Gold on the Fortymile.' *Alaska Journal* 3 (Spring 1973):114-21

—. *'Stroller' White: Tales of a Klondike Newsman.* Vancouver: Mitchell Press 1969

DeGraf, Anna. *Pioneering on the Yukon 1892-1917.* Hamdon, CT: Archon Books 1992

DeWindt, Harry. *Through the Gold Fields of Alaska to Bering Strait.* London: Chatto and Windus 1898

Evans, Chad. *Frontier Theatre.* Victoria: Sono Nis 1983

Friesen, Richard J. *The Chilkoot Pass and the Great Gold Rush of 1898.* History and Archeology Series, no. 48. Ottawa: Parks Canada, National Historic Parks and Sites 1981

Fulcomer, Anna. 'The Three R's at Circle City.' *Century* 66, no. 2 (1898):223-9

Gartrell, George A. 'The Work of the Churches in the Yukon During the Era of the Klondike Gold Rush.' Master's thesis, University of Western Ontario 1970

Glave, E.J. 'Our Alaska Expedition.' *Frank Leslie's Illustrated Newspaper.* (1890): 6 September:86-7; 15 November:262; 22 November:175, 286-7; 29 November:310; 6 December:332; 13 December:352; 20 December:376; 27 December:396-7. (1891): 3 January:414; 10 January:438

—. 'Pioneer Pack Horses in Alaska.' *Century Illustrated Magazine* 22 (1891):671-82, 869-81

Goodrich, Harold B. 'History and Condition of the Yukon Gold District to 1897.' In Josiah Edward Spurr, *Geology of the Yukon Gold District, Alaska,* 103-33. Washington: Government Printing Office 1897

Gould, John and R. Stuart. *Permafrost Gold: A Treatise on Early Klondike Mining History*. Microfiche Report Series, no. 11. Ottawa: Parks Canada 1980

Green, Lewis. *The Boundary Hunters: Surveying the 141st Meridian and the Alaska Panhandle*. Vancouver: University of British Columbia Press 1982

Guest, Hal. *A Socioeconomic History of the Klondike Goldfields*. Microfiche Report Series, no. 181. Ottawa: Parks Canada 1985

Hamlin, C.H. *Old Times in the Yukon*. Los Angeles: Wetzel Publishing 1928

Haskell, William B. *Two Years in the Klondike and Alaskan Gold Fields*. Hartford, CT: Hartford Publishing 1898

Hayes, Charles Willard. 'An Expedition Through the Yukon District.' *National Geographic* 4 (May 1982):117-62

Hayes, Terry L. *They Didn't Come in Four-Wheel Drives: An Introduction to Fortymile History*. Tok, AL: Fortymile Resource Area, Bureau of Land Management 1976

Hayne, M.H.E. *The Pioneers of the Klondike: Being an Account of Two Years Police Service on the Yukon*. London: Sampson Low, Marsten, & Co. 1897

Henderson, Henry. *True Story of the Discovery of the Klondike by Bob Henderson*. Edmonton: H.H. Hull Printing, n.d.

Hunt, Williamm R. *Distant Justice: Policing the Alaska Frontier*. Norman: University of Oklahoma Press 1987

—. *Golden Places: The History of Alaska-Yukon Mining With Particular Reference to Alaska's National Parks*. Anchorage: National Park Service, Alaska Region n.d.

Johnson, James Albert. *Carmack of the Klondike*. Seattle, WA: Epicenter Press; Ganges, BC: Horsdal & Schubart 1990

Judge, Rev. Charles. *An American Missionary: A Record of the Work of the Rev. William A. Judge, S.J.* New York: Ossining 1907

Kirk, Robert C. *Twelve Months in the Klondike*. London: Wm. Heinemann 1899

Lyons, Esther, comp. *Esther Lyons' Glimpses of Alaska*. Chicago: Rand McNally & Co. 1897

McGrath, J.E. 'The Alaska Boundary Survey.' *National Geographic* 4 (1892):177-97

MacGregor, J.G. *The Klondike Rush Through Edmonton, 1897-1898*. Toronto: McClelland & Stewart 1970

McLain, John Scudder. *Alaska and the Klondike*. New York: McClure, Phillips & Co. 1907

McQuesten, Leroy N. *Life in the Yukon, 1871-1885*. Whitehorse: Yukon Order of Pioneers 1952

Mayer, Melanie J. *Klondike Women: True Tales of the 1897-1898 Gold Rush*. Athens, OH: Ohio University Press 1989

Mercier, Francois. 'Recollections of Monsieur Francois Mercier, 1868-1885, General Agent for the Alaska Commercial Company.' Trans. Linda Finn-Yarborough for the National Park Service Yukon-Charlie Proposed National Park Project 1977

—. *Recollections of the Yukon: Memoirs from the Years 1868-1885*. Alaska Historical Commission Studies in History, no. 88. Anchorage: Alaska Historical Society 1986

Mildred, Sister Mary. *The Apostle of Alaska: Life of the Most Reverend Charles Seghers*. Patterson, NJ: St. Anthony Guild Press 1943

Minter, Roy. *The White Pass: Gateway to the Klondike.* Toronto: McClelland & Stewart 1987

Moore, J. Bernard. *Skagway in Days Primeval.* New York: Vantage Press 1968

Morrison, Wm. R. *Showing the Flag: The Mounted Police and Canadian Sovereignty in the North 1894-1925.* Vancouver: University of British Columbia Press 1985

—. 'Policing the Boomtown: The Mounted Police as a Social Force on the Klondike.' *Northern Review* 6 (1990):83-97

Naske, Claus M. 'The Fortymile Country: A Historical Study of the Fortymile Mining District.' Report prepared under contract for Fairbanks District, Bureau of Land Management. Fairbanks: Department of the Interior 1973

Norcross, E. Blanche. *Pioneers Every One: Canadian Women of Achievement.* Toronto: Burns & MacEachern 1979

Ogilvie, William. *Early Days on the Yukon and the Story of Its Gold Fields.* Toronto: Bell & Cockburn 1913

—. *Information Respecting the Yukon District from the Reports of Wm. Ogilvie, Dominion Land Surveyor.* Ottawa: Government Printing Bureau 1897

—. *Lecture on the Yukon Gold Fields (Canada), Delivered at Victoria B.C.* Victoria: The Colonist Presses 1897

Oppel, Frank, comp. *Tales of the Canadian West.* Secaucus, NJ: Castle Books 1984

—. *Tales of Alaska and the Yukon.* Secaucus, NJ: Castle Books 1986

Palmer, Frederick. *In The Klondyke.* New York: Charles Scribner's & Sons 1899

Paxton, Wm. A. 'Men and Money.' *Alaska Sportsman* (July 1955): 16-21, 40-8

Pierce, W.H. *Thirteen Years of Travel and Exploration in Alaska, 1877-1889.* Anchorage: Alaska Northwest Publishing 1977

Pike, Warburton. *Through the Subarctic Forest.* London: Edward Arnold 1896

Russell, Israel C. 'A Journey up the Yukon.' *Bulletin of the American Geographical Society* 27, no. 2 (1895):143-60

Schwatka, Frederick. *A Summer in Alaska.* Philadelphia: John Y. Huber 1891

Sims, Vincent C. 'Exploration on the Upper Yukon River.' In Sheldon Jackson, *Report on Education in Alaska,* 52-5. 49th Cong., 1st Sess. Senate Executive Document No. 85, Appendix H. Washington: Government Printing Office 1886

Sola, A.E. Ironmonger. *Klondyke: Truth and Facts of the New Eldorado.* London: The Mining and Geographical Institute, Broad Street House 1897

Sourdough Stampede Association. *The Alaska-Yukon Gold Book.* Seattle: Sourdough Stampede Association 1930

Spurr, Josiah Edward. 'From the Coast to the Golden Klondike.' In *Tales of the Canadian West,* compiled by Frank Oppel (1986) 297-314. Originally published in *Outing* 30 (1897)

—. *Geology of the Yukon Gold District, Alaska.* 18th Annual Report, US Geological Survey, 316-79. Washington: Government Printing Office 1897

—. *Through the Yukon Gold Diggings.* Boston: Eastern Publishing 1900

Stanley, Wm. M. *A Mile of Gold.* Chicago: Laird and Lee 1898

Steckler, Gerard G. *Charles John Seghers, Priest and Bishop in the Pacific Northwest,*

1839-1886: A Biography. Fairfield, WA: Ye Galleon Press 1986

Steffens, J. Lincoln. 'Life in the Klondike Gold Fields.' *McClure's Magazine*, September 1897, 956-67

Stewart, Don. *Sourdough Ray*. Coos Bay, OR: Gorst Publications 1983

Stone, Thomas. 'Atomistic Order and Frontier Violence in the Nineteenth-Century Yukon.' *Ethnology* 22, no. 4 (1983):327-39

—. 'Flux and Authority in a Subarctic Society: The Yukon Miners in the Nineteenth Century.' *Ethnohistory* 30, no. 4 (1983):203-16

—. *Miners' Justice: Migration, Law, and Order on the Alaska-Yukon Frontier, 1873-1902*. American University Studies Series, no. 11, Anthropology and Sociology, vol. 34. New York: Peter Lang 1988

—. 'The Mounties as Vigilantes: Perceptions of Community and the Transformation of Law in the Yukon, 1885-1897.' *Law and Society Review* 14, no. 1 (1979):83-114

Stuck, Hudson. *Voyages on the Yukon and Its Tributaries*. New York: Charles Scribner's & Sons 1925

Walden, Arthur. *A Dog-Puncher on the Yukon*. Boston: Houghton Mifflin 1931

Webb, John Sidneys. *The River Trip to the Klondike*. Facsimile reproduction. Seattle: Shorey Book Store 1968. Originally published in *Century Magazine*, March 1898

Webb, Melody. *The Last Frontier: A History of the Yukon Basin of Canada and Alaska*. Albuquerque: University of New Mexico Press 1985

Wells, E. Hazard. 'Our Alaska Expedition.' *Frank Leslie's Illustrated Newspaper* (1891): 27 June, 354; 4 July, 370, 378; 11 July, 396; 18 July, 412, 415; 25 July, 422, 431; 8 August, 10; 29 August, 59; 5 September, 68, 75; 19 September, 106

—. *Magnificence and Misery*. Garden City, NY: Doubleday & Co. 1984

—. 'Up and Down the Yukon, 1897.' In *Compilation of Narratives of Exploration in Alaska*, 511-16. Washington: Government Printing Office 1900

Weppler, James. *Yukon Territory: A Community of Men*. Manuscript Report Series, no. 9. Ottawa: Parks Canada, National Historic Parks and Sites 1969

Wesbrook, Mary. 'A Venture into Ethnohistory: The Journals of Rev. V.C. Sim, Pioneer Missionary on the Yukon.' *Polar Notes* 9 (1969):34-45

Whymper, Frederick. *Travel and Adventure in the Territory of Alaska*. New York: Harper and Brothers 1869

Wickersham, James. *Old Yukon: Tales, Trails, and Trials*. Washington: Law Book 1938

Wills, A.E. 'Extract From Assistant Surgeon A.E. Wills' Report for 1895.' In *Information Respecting the Yukon District from the Report of William Ogilvie and Other Sources*, 64, 65. Ottawa: Government Printing Bureau 1897

Wilson, George F. 'Description of Indian Tribes.' In Frederick Schwatka, *Report on a Military Reconnaissance in Alaska Made in 1883*. Washington: Government Printing Office 1885

—. *Guide to the Yukon Goldfields*. Revised edition. Seattle: Calvert 1897

—. 'A Moose Hunt on the Yukon, Alaska.' In *Tales of Alaska and the Yukon*, compiled by Frank Oppel, 414. Secaucus, NJ: Castle Books 1896

Wright, Allen. *Prelude to Bonanza*. Sidney, BC: Gray's Publishing 1976

INDEX

Set in Scala
Printed and bound in Canada by D.W.
   Friesen & Sons Ltd.
Copy-editor: Joanne Richardson
Proofreader: Anne Webb
Designer: George Vaitkunas